YOU CALL THE SHOTS

Succeed *Your* Way—and Live the Life You Want—with the 19 Essential Secrets of Entrepreneurship

Cameron Johnson

with John David Mann

FREE PRESS

NEW YORK LONDON TORONTO SYDNEY

This book contains the opinions and ideas of its author. It is sold with the understanding that neither the author nor the publisher, through the publication of this book, is engaged in rendering investment, financial, accounting, legal, tax, or other professional advice or services. If the reader requires such advice or services, a competent professional should be consulted. The strategies outlined in this book may not be suitable for every individual, and are not guaranteed or warranted to produce any particular results. No warrant is made with respect to the accuracy or completeness of the information contained herein. Both the author and publisher specifically disclaim any responsibility for any liability, loss, or risk, personal or otherwise, which is incurred as a consequence, directly or indirectly, of the use and application of any of the contents of this book.

FREE PRESS
A Division of Simon & Schuster, Inc.
1230 Avenue of the Americas
New York, NY 10020

For information about special discounts for bulk purchases,
please contact Simon & Schuster Special Sales at
1-800-456-6798 or business@simonandschuster.com

Designed by Kyoko Watanabe

Manufactured in the United States of America

1   3   5   7   9   10   8   6   4   2

The Library of Congress Cataloging-in-Publication Data is available.

ISBN-13: 978-1-4165-3606-2
ISBN-10: 1-4165-3606-X

Contents

Foreword

In the fall of 2005 I was asked to be the keynote speaker at a seminar for entrepreneurs. As I waited backstage before my talk, the host of the event came over to me and introduced me to the young man next to him, who stuck out his hand and said, "Hi, I'm Cameron Johnson—I've read your books, and it's great to meet you!" It took a moment to dawn on me that this wasn't a young fan who'd made his way backstage: *He was one of the other speakers.*

We spoke for a few minutes about financial literacy among young people, which we agreed was a problem that needs addressing, so that young people begin saving sooner and avoid racking up daunting credit card debt. Then he told me a little about his career as an entrepreneur. I was truly impressed. He also mentioned then that he was writing a book, and quite a book it has turned out to be.

Cameron's story is compelling enough on its own, but he's taken it further: He's used it to introduce nineteen powerful success principles for young entrepreneurs. The principles he lays out aren't just good advice for those on the younger side, though, they're great resources for entrepreneurs of *any* age. That's because they're the product of many years of experience, even though Cameron is still so young.

Not only did Cameron start a dozen businesses while still in his teens, but he made every one of those businesses *successful.* It's one thing to create something that takes off; it's quite another to fly it around for a while after takeoff *and* bring it in for a safe landing. Ask anyone who was involved in starting Internet businesses during the late 1990s. There were a record number of business takeoffs in those days—and nearly as many crashes. Cameron cut his entrepreneurial teeth during those Internet "bubble" years, and it's a measure of his maturity, and of the strength and value of the insights he offers in these pages, that he kept his feet solidly on the ground and never lost track of common sense.

Cameron has as firm a grasp of the principles of successful entrepreneurship. What's more, he does a great job of articulating them so you can grasp them, too.

With the current boom in entrepreneurship, and so many easy-to-use and inexpensive business support services available on the Internet, there's never been a better time to start your own business. Just as with saving for your future, starting out young in entrepreneurship will give you a leg up. In my investment seminars I've been impressed by the interest so many young people have in taking charge of their lives. A third of my audiences are under the age of twenty-five. The other day I had a fifteen-year-old bring her twelve-year-old brother to a seminar. As Cameron's story shows, becoming an entrepreneur is a great way to make sure you're in the driver's seat of your life and you're never too young to start.

The purpose of my work is to help people become financially free so they can live a rich life, true to their values and purpose. Cameron's mission in *You Call the Shots* is to encourage people to take control of their work lives and find the work that will make them truly satisfied and happy. I believe every one of us was put on this Earth for a unique reason, to do something uniquely special. But most of us aren't doing that, because we're too busy living paycheck to paycheck. Starting your own business can be a great way to find your true calling, and to build a financially rewarding future. If that's your dream, then Cameron Johnson's story will be an inspiring source of a great deal of first-rate advice.

DAVID BACH
Founder and CEO, FinishRich.com
Author of the #1 *New York Times* bestsellers
The Automatic Millionaire and *Start Late, Finish Rich*
October 2006

YOU CALL
THE SHOTS

INTRODUCTION

The Entrepreneurial Life

I started my first business at age nine with $50 and a home computer, and ran it from my room at home as a one-kid operation. By the time I was nineteen I had started nearly a dozen profitable businesses, and for my latest venture I had received a very attractive offer of $10 million in venture capital. I turned that offer down and walked away because I didn't feel good about the conditions that would have been imposed on me if I'd taken the money. The venture capital firm would have called the shots, told me how to run my company, and paid me a salary that would've been less than I'd made on my own since I was twelve.

It was a lucrative offer, and who knows? Maybe with their backing and expertise I would have come out way ahead. But I didn't think it was the right deal for me. I made that decision without regret, and I've never looked back.

I knew this was not a now-or-never choice. There would be plenty of other opportunities to create even more successful businesses—because I'd learned the skills it takes to do so. Once you learn these skills, you never have to be tied to any one particular enterprise. I realized that while I could have taken someone else's $10 million investment, I'd rather invest in myself.

I've been fortunate enough to make my first million before graduating from high school and buy my own house at twenty. At twenty-one, I've now put away enough in savings and other investments that I could practically retire today . . . if I wanted to. But of course, that's the last thing on earth I'd want to do. I just enjoy it all too much. Not to say the money isn't important, but frankly, it's not why I do what I do. I do it because I love it.

I've always loved starting new businesses. I take pleasure in every aspect of it, from coming up with a new concept, or a unique twist on an existing concept, to finding a name that perfectly captures the nature of the business, to building the team, launching the enterprise, and watching it take off and grow. Of the more than dozen successful businesses I've launched over the past twelve years, every one of them has been a unique experience, and I've loved the process every time.

That's what I want to share with you in this book. How to build successful businesses, what it's like to do it, and why I love it so much—and hope you will, too.

Starting your own business is a great path for creating success on your own terms. It's an excellent way to build a financial base for yourself, but it's more than that. It's also about finding ways to exercise your creativity, to challenge yourself, and to rise to new levels of ability and experience. It's about the satisfaction of creating something that makes a contribution to other people's lives. And perhaps more than anything else, it's about freedom: the freedom to set your own hours, to do things your own way, to try out new ideas and put your talents to the test.

I wouldn't exchange the thrill of that freedom for anything in the world.

Entrepreneurship is more than a type of career; it's a way of life, and an exceptionally rewarding one. I was fortunate to learn this at a very early age, which is why I started my first business so young. I grew up in a family of self-made businesspeople, so I was exposed early on to the unique kind of satisfaction that comes with the entrepreneurial life.

In the South Roanoke neighborhood where I grew up, at the foot of southwestern Virginia's scenic Blue Ridge Mountains, most of my extended family lived within a four-block radius—my aunt and uncle, cousins, grandparents, and great-grandparents. And in one way or another, practically everyone in our family has been an entrepreneur.

In 1938 my dad's grandfather, Harry G. Johnson Sr., started his car dealership, Magic City Ford. Roanoke earned the nickname "Magic City" just before the dawn of the twentieth century, when the convergence of several major railways ushered in an explosion of jobs and the city's population boomed from six hundred to five thousand in just two years.

Harry Sr.'s son, Harry Jr. (my grandfather), eventually took over the business, and in 1972 *his* son, Bill (my dad), started out washing windows and worked his way up, eventually taking the reins when Harry Jr. retired.

My mom's dad, Hugh Jones, ran a wholesale food distribution business called Roanoke Restaurant Service. He died when my mom, Ann, was just thirteen; her mom, Dot, took over the business. After graduating from high school my mom started college, but soon dropped out to run the company. She did quite well, building the company to about $30 million in annual sales by the time she sold it to U.S. Food Service in the early 1980s.

It was always clear to me that my parents loved their work and relished building something of their own that they could be proud of. Talking about their businesses with each other was everyday conversation, and that made a huge impression on me. They weren't frustrated about their work, and they didn't come home full of stress. They were happy enough with their work that they wanted to share the doings of the day with each other, and with me, too.

Including me in the day-to-day flow of their businesses was normal for them, because that's what their parents had done. When my mom was little, her parents kept a cot for her at their office so she could nap whenever she needed to, and when she wasn't at school, chances were good she'd be at the office, doing her homework, reading, or napping on that cot. Sometimes I wonder how much business conversation soaked in while she slept.

My parents even took me with them sometimes on their business trips. My mom always considered travel a valuable education; in her view, learning how to adapt to different customs and cultures and styles of interaction was every bit as important as academic learning. They traveled a lot for my dad's business, and even as a very young boy, I was often allowed to accompany them to meetings. While I didn't understand everything they were talking about, I got to experience the life and shop talk of a business owner—and I loved it.

Maybe the most important thing I learned from them about being an entrepreneur was something my dad used to say: "If you love what you do, you'll never have to work a day in your life."

Some people never get around to starting their own business out of the fear that it's too difficult, or that the risks are too high and the chances of success are too daunting. Don't believe it. Starting your own business is hard work, but it's not rocket science. I started my first company with no real business training and almost no money, and although I had entrepreneurial parents, they never funded any of my businesses or helped me run them. The truth is, building a successful business is more about common sense and the right attitude than it is about any kind of special training or inherent talents.

And the risks? Part of being an entrepreneur is learning how to take only those risks you can afford. You don't have to take out loans or go into serious debt to build a successful business. I've never taken a single business loan—from a bank *or* from my parents. Risk is definitely part of the game, but you can take calculated risks without risking your shirt. You can make plenty of profit with a fairly small operation, then leverage those earnings by using them to build your next enterprise, growing your financial base step-by-step as you build your knowledge base. I've launched more than a dozen successful businesses and never lost a cent. This is not just luck. I've watched my expenses carefully, used common sense, and have never taken foolhardy risks.

During the "Internet bubble" years, a lot of entrepreneurs let their growth and projections get away from them. They lost touch with the core, everyday realities of business, and as a consequence, when the bubble burst, hundreds of thousands of people lost money—in some cases, *millions*—practically overnight. People then ran scared from the Internet because so many lost so much during those few years. And it wasn't just those involved in dot.coms who lost. Millions of people who worked at more traditional companies had invested their money in these new dot.com stocks, or had their 401(k)s invested aggressively in technology mutual funds—and they all lost money, too. The whole country lost money, and for the next few years everybody was afraid of Internet companies.

I was fortunate during that time: several of my businesses rode those same growth trends on the Internet, but were able to avoid getting blindsided or suffering dire consequences. In fact, one of my businesses, CertificateSwap.com, was singled out by *Entrepreneur* magazine as an example of the new generation of Web-based business successes.

While I've had lots of success with Web-based business, this isn't a book about how to start only Internet businesses. The success secrets I'll share with you in this book apply to starting, building, and managing *any* kind of business. The reason I didn't have the troubles so many others did during those days was that I had learned to follow faithfully these fundamental principles.

I credit a big part of my success to the experiences I've had in traditional storefront environments, from working summers in my aunt's furniture store to managing 140 employees as general sales manager at my dad's dealership, Magic City Ford. In fact, having the ability to combine the best of both worlds—the power and reach of the Web along with the tried-and-true lessons of traditional business—is one of the most important keys to successful entrepreneurship today.

The Internet boom isn't over. Far from it. In fact, I think it's just begun. Accessing the Internet is fast becoming easier, cheaper, and more convenient than ever, whether through cellular phones, PDAs, or laptops with wireless cards. (I used this same technology in Japan six years ago, when I was fifteen. We're still that far behind Japan in our consumer electronics—it's amazing to think of the great technology still on the way.)

Soon we'll all be connected to the Internet anytime we want, and anywhere we go.

In his 2005 book *The Next Millionaires,* bestselling economist and two-time presidential economic adviser Paul Zane Pilzer wrote:

> Many people now have a pessimistic or fatalistic view about the future of the Internet. "Oh, the Internet opportunities . . . they've come and gone, and it wasn't all it was cracked up to be." Nothing could be further from the truth! The fact is the Internet is a new and emerging growth super-industry that has barely gotten started. It is about to jump off our desktops and PC screens, onto our cell phones and into every aspect of our lives.

I agree completely. Technology is going to keep evolving, and it's only going to make business easier, better, and more efficient. There is as much opportunity today as there was ten years ago — no, strike that: there's *more* opportunity today.

The real subject of this book isn't me — it's you. The reason I'm sharing my story is so you can take whatever insights or ideas it may give you, and use them to create your own success. To create a life where *you* call the shots.

The truth is, you can start a successful business at any age; it doesn't matter if you're nine, nineteen, or ninety. You don't need big capital, expensive education, or specialized knowledge. You just have to have faith in yourself and in your ideas, be willing to take smart risks, and follow the basic principles that every successful entrepreneur learns sooner or later.

These secrets are simple, but that doesn't mean they're obvious. I've done the best I can to explain them by sharing my story of how I've learned them myself. At the end of the book I've added a brief section of specific tips and how-tos, along with references to some great resources on the Web that you can use for learning more of the nitty-gritty of how to plan, launch, and manage your own business.

I don't pretend to be a guru or a mogul. I'm just a seriously happy serial entrepreneur who's had some interesting and valuable experiences that I know can help you find your own success.

To me, true success is about being happy, living a full and rich life with great friendships, and about thoroughly enjoying what you do. It's about growing the economy in innovative, creative, and ethical ways, creating growth and jobs and opportunity for others. It's about leaving the world a better place than you found it—and having a seriously good time while you're doing it.

I want to show you a way you can achieve all that and more: the entrepreneurial life.

1

Put Yourself Out There

I have always believed in going after the things you want in life. So many people tend to hesitate, to overthink, or second-guess. Not entrepreneurs. One of the keys to being a successful entrepreneur is being willing to put yourself out there, to throw yourself headlong into the pursuit of your dreams.

It's natural to worry about how others will react to your ideas, about whether they'll try to shoot them down, say they're too risky, call them pie-in-the-sky, tell you they don't have a chance of working. But it's not their business, it's *your* business. And a big part of being an entrepreneur is having the courage to take chances, to embrace the fact that your success ultimately comes down to you, your vision, and your passion.

Becoming an entrepreneur requires learning how to take lots of noes to get to yes—learning to consider no as a challenge, not a defeat.

There's a lot to learn about being an entrepreneur, and most of it you can learn as you go. But there is one thing you have to know from the start: if you want it to work, you have to put yourself out there and ask for what you want.

In fact, the best business people will respect you all the more when you do.

This is a lesson I learned during the summer after third grade, and it's one I'll never forget.

＊　　＊　　＊

In late 1992, just after my eighth birthday, I saw the movie *Home Alone 2: Lost in New York*. Most of the film was shot at the famous Plaza Hotel in New York City, at Fifty-ninth Street and Fifth Avenue. Just a few years earlier, Donald Trump had purchased and renovated this landmark (at the cost of some $50 million—not counting the $400-million-plus purchase price). He even made a cameo appearance in the film.

I had never been to Manhattan, and when I saw the movie, I knew I had to go. My dad said he'd make a deal with me: "Tell you what: you get straight A's and I'll take you to New York."

So I did. For the second half of my third-grade year, I got straight A's. When the school year was over, I said to my dad, "Okay, I'm ready for New York! And by the way, can we stay at the Plaza?"

My dad agreed, and our travel plans were all set. What my parents didn't know was that once I knew for sure that we were going, I wrote a letter to Donald Trump:

Dear Mr. Trump,

Hi. You don't know me, but my name is Cameron Johnson, and I live in Roanoke, Virginia. My family and I are coming to New York next month, and I've never been to New York before, and we are staying at the Plaza. Could I possibly see the suite where they filmed the movie Home Alone 2? *I would really, really like to do that.*

—Cameron Johnson

I didn't hear back from him, but after all, he was a busy man.

Finally the day came: we flew to New York and took a cab straight to the Plaza. At the check-in desk, the lady registering us leaned over so she could see me and asked, "Are you Cameron Johnson?"

"Yes, that's me," I replied.

My parents were flabbergasted. Why was this woman talking to me instead of to them?!

"Well," the woman continued, "Mr. Trump has left some gifts here for you . . ." and she gave me an assortment of things that included a Talkboy tape recorder, just like the one Macaulay Culkin had used in the movie. I was impressed—but she wasn't finished yet.

"Mr. Trump has also arranged for a personal shopper to accompany you tomorrow morning to FAO Schwarz for a private shopping tour before the store opens" (I think my mom's mouth was hanging open at this point) "and, of course, you'll want to see the suite where they filmed *Home Alone 2*. Actually, Mr. Trump has arranged to upgrade your room—you'll be *staying* in that very same suite."

As if that weren't enough, when we got up to the suite, we found it filled with cookies, "I ♥ NY" T-shirts, and all sorts of New York–related gifts. And next to all the gifts, there was a note from Mr. Trump that said:

I hope you enjoy your stay here. Wishing you much success.
—Donald J. Trump

The next day, when we got back to the room after breakfast and our amazing visit to FAO Schwarz, the light was blinking on the phone in our room. We had a message: Donald Trump had called to make sure everything was okay. Had we met the man at FAO Schwarz? And had he taken care of me okay, and did I have everything I needed?

Trump had also left a signed business card for me. Of course, I didn't have any business cards at this point, but I'd gotten some little cards at FAO Schwarz, so I signed one of those and left that for Mr. Trump, along with a carefully handwritten message:

Dear Mr. Trump,
Thank you for the Talkboy, the suite, and for everything else. Keep watching, because I plan to be the next Donald Trump.
—Cameron Johnson

That whole experience at the Plaza taught me how important it is to go after what you want. There was no real reason why my parents and I should have been treated so well. We weren't VIPs, or connected to Trump or the Trump organization in any way. So why did we end up in that suite, and me with my own personal shopper and private tour of FAO Schwarz?

Because I wrote to him and asked.

Of course, Mr. Trump is also a generous, classy guy who knows how to treat people well. But that wouldn't have mattered if I hadn't taken a chance and written him that letter. I expect that he was also a little impressed that I'd done so.

There's an old expression in sales: *You can give the best presentation in the world, but you still have to ask for the sale.*

Are you always going to get a response like the one I got from Mr. Trump? No, but *sometimes* you will. And the more you put yourself out there, finding where your passion takes you and going after it, the more *often* you will. The truth is, success is not so much a matter of looking for opportunity; it's more that you actually *create* opportunities. And one way of doing that is not being afraid to ask.

Many people see "asking for the sale" as one of the most intimidating ways there is of putting yourself out there. But asking for the sale is the essence of what an entrepreneur does and even if you don't think of yourself as being "in sales," if you're in business for yourself, then no matter what your title is or how you see your role, *you're in the business of selling.* When you make yourself part of your brand, put yourself in your ads or speak with media contacts; reach out to your social network to look for contacts, resources, or customers; go looking for prospective partners or strategic alliances— as you go about building your business, you're selling *you* every step of the way.

I didn't launch my first actual business until I was nine years old, but I'd been having fun selling for years before that.

As I said in the introduction, my dad runs a Ford dealership in Roanoke, Virginia, that was started by his grandfather. When I was five years old, the May 1990 edition of *DealerWorld* featured an article on our family's business, which included a photo of my grandfather, my dad, and me. The piece was all about my dad and his father, but it mentioned me right at the end:

As Bill Johnson talks about his "family business," his sprightly five-year-old son Cameron runs around the offices selling employees his drawings of cars for a buck each.

The following year, I got a little more organized in my pursuit of the entrepreneurial life.

My great-grandparents owned a farm in Bedford, Virginia, about twenty miles from our home. In the summer, there would always be a surplus of tomatoes and corn, which we would bring home to Roanoke.

One day I asked my mom if I could take some of our tomatoes and sell them in the neighborhood, and she said she thought that'd be fine. So I loaded up my little red wagon and started down the street in our neighborhood. Halfway down our block, I came to a neighbor's house. I rolled my wagon up the walk to the front porch, reached up, and knocked on the door. A lady answered.

"Hello," I said. "Would you like to buy a tomato?"

"Well, I might," she said. "How much are they?"

"A dollar apiece."

She said, "That's a lot of money for one tomato!"

And I replied, "Well, ma'am, they're the best tomatoes you'll ever taste."

"Is that right?" she said.

I replied, "It is." And before she could think of the next thing to say, I added, "Does your husband like tomatoes?"

"He sure does," she answered.

"Well, then," I said, "you should buy two."

And she did. She gave me two dollars, I gave her two tomatoes, and I was off and running.

"Door-to-door" selling is supposed to be one of the hardest sales methods there is. The prospect of selling door-to-door strikes dread in the hearts of even some of the best salesmen in the world. But I didn't know that, and the truth is, I was having an absolute blast selling those tomatoes door-to-door to my neighbors.

Of course, not everyone I visited said yes. I got at least as many noes as yesses. But that didn't bother me—in fact, in a way I enjoyed the noes even more than the yesses. I saw the rejection as a challenge, part of the process—and part of the fun. When a customer said no, or no, thank you, I learned that this wasn't the end of the sale at all: it was when the actual selling really started.

I knew our tomatoes were delicious, so whenever someone said no, I was genuinely curious about why. Rather than simply take their no for an answer, I would ask them why they didn't want to buy. Sometimes, in the process of answering, they actually changed their minds. Sometimes they didn't. Either way, I was having a great time.

That summer, I watched some kids in my neighborhood open lemonade stands. I noticed that they often sat at their stands for hours, selling very little lemonade. I figured, there *had* to be a better way to get people to stop and buy. I thought about that for a while. When I set up *my* lemonade stand across the street, I sold not only lemonade but also cookies, brownies, and muffins. I also charged less for my lemonade—the lowest price in the neighborhood.

The first day my stand was open, I quickly sold out, and I continued selling out every day after that, too. The other kids eventually closed their stands and became my customers.

Of course, the lemonade stand was limited to the summer months, and I thought it would be great to have a way to make a little pocket money throughout the year, so when fall came, I decided to have a yard sale.

The day of my sale arrived—and it rained. But I wasn't willing to let that ruin my plans. I hauled all my items down to our basement and held my sale there instead. It not only worked, it worked so well that I made it a regular event, selling my old toys, stuffed animals, old records, whatever I could think of that we didn't want anymore. I called them "rainy-day sales" and continued running them for the next three years.

I soon branched out from selling my own old stuff to selling my friends' things for a commission, and this led to the idea of selling *new* toys that I won at fairs or game arcades. One arcade had those quarter-a-try crane machines that picks up toys, and I found one that was not all that hard to win. That summer, I won about a hundred stuffed animals from that machine, and sold them for three to five dollars apiece. Since I'd invested only a quarter a try, I thought that was a pretty good return.

I was making good money and having a lot of fun doing it. And while I never stopped to think about it in these terms at the time, I was also learning the basic principles of business.

Starting out so young gave me a certain courage that comes with blissful ignorance. I had the confidence that comes with not knowing any better. As I've grown older and seen more of the business world, there have been times when I've had to overcome doubts and work to maintain my confidence, just like anybody else. But the thrill of trying out new ideas and seeing them take root and grow has always made it worth the effort.

I was fortunate to learn very early on the key principle that all successful entrepreneurs need to know: *First, you have to believe in yourself.*

It's actually not that difficult to succeed. It's much more common sense than rocket science. But it starts with finding the courage to put yourself out there.

Believing in yourself is what gives you the confidence and resilience to deal with the rejections and doubts. It drives you to do the best job you can, no matter what you're doing.

Over time, I've learned to trust my instincts—and that's crucial. You can learn all kinds of things from other people, but ultimately it's your own instincts that you'll need to rely on. The bottom line of your business is *you.*

Whether you are selling door-to-door, on the phone, through an infomercial, or on a Web site, ultimately the venue doesn't matter. All of these methods work. First and foremost, you must be able to sell *yourself.* People don't buy your product or service only because they like it or want it; they also buy it because they like *you.* If they don't like you, then in many cases it doesn't matter how much they like the product you're selling, *they won't buy it.*

If you put yourself out there with confidence, you'll find that most people respect you and respond well to you, whether or not they want what you're selling.

Believing in yourself leads naturally to a second principle: *You have to believe in what you're selling.*

People sometimes think of selling as the art of being pushy, crafty, or even manipulative. In fact, it's exactly the opposite. The best salespeople focus on asking questions and listening, not pushing.

I don't believe in high-pressure selling. High pressure is what people use when they're selling something nobody wants, or charging far more than their product is worth. There's a difference between being persuasive and applying pressure. I'm persuasive when I'm selling, but that's because I truly believe in what I'm selling and the value it will create for my customer. My feeling is, I'd be doing my customers a disservice if I let them *not* buy my product.

The best salespeople are so dedicated to giving customers what they want that they are willing to be as rigorous, patient, and dedicated as it takes to make the sale. They don't give up easily because they believe in what they're doing.

I believe in everything I'm selling, and this makes it so much easier to give customers reasons to buy. I truly feel they're making a mistake if they don't buy my service or product. When I told that lady, "Well, ma'am, they're the best tomatoes you'll ever taste," I wasn't making that up. They *were* delicious.

I'm always genuinely fascinated to know why people *wouldn't* want what I'm selling. If you're not passionate about the product or service you're offering, how could you possibly approach people with genuine confidence? Make sure you're proud of what you sell and the value it creates in people's lives, and you'll instantly become a better entrepreneur.

Believing in yourself also leads to a third success principle: *When you respect yourself, treating other people with respect comes naturally.* The amazingly thoughtful response I got from Donald Trump at the Plaza is a great example of this.

Of course, Trump is a master of promotion, and never misses an opportunity to increase his public exposure. But what did he have to gain by impressing an eight-year-old kid or his parents? He had no idea I'd be writing this book thirteen years later. It was as clear to me then as it is today that he was simply being the gentleman that he is, and treating me with respect.

Trump is famous for his tough-talking, combative persona, but don't let that fool you. He knows what every truly successful businessperson knows: treating other people with great respect is one of the most powerful secrets of business success. Keep doing that over time with everyone you encounter, and you'll find that people are consistently receptive to you and to your products, services, and ideas. Any fears and doubts you have will start to melt away.

And then you won't hesitate to go ahead and ask for the sale.

2

Start Small

When people read in my bio, "His parents gave him a computer at age nine," I think they sometimes get the impression that my mom and dad were pushing me to become computer-savvy. Actually, the opposite's the case. By the time I got my first computer, most of my friends already had computers in their homes, and my parents were so intent on *not* spoiling me that they had held off getting me one. So when I got a brand-new Compaq computer and printer for Christmas in 1993, I felt like I had some serious catching up to do.

I got onto that Compaq as soon as I had it set up, and I didn't get off it again for the rest of the day, not even to eat lunch or dinner. It came bundled with Print Shop Deluxe (a popular desktop publishing package back then), and I spent the day teaching myself how to use it.

At eleven that night, my mom came up to my room and said, "Cameron, it's time to go to bed!"

I looked up at her and said, "Mom, look: I started a business."

She said, "You did what?!"

My room looked like a tornado had hit a paper factory. Sheets of different sizes and colors were strewn everywhere. I'd been designing all kinds of greeting cards and stationery, which was one of the basic options that came with the package, and had printed out samples that now covered the room. I'd also put together a complete business catalog, and as far as I was concerned, I was ready to start selling and move on with my life.

I had found a passion—and I was pursuing it.

My mom stood there in her nightgown, shook her head, and said, "Cameron, it's eleven o'clock. I think you need to go to bed. We'll talk about this in the morning."

The next day I showed her some of the work I had done, and she was impressed enough that she asked me to print her some greeting cards and invitations to her holiday party. I filled her order and printed her an invoice to go with it—and my first business was off and running.

I started selling greeting cards, business cards, stationery, signs, any kind of desktop printing I could think of, to our relatives, friends, and neighbors. Pretty soon I had more than two thousand cards to choose from, and I was having some *serious* fun.

One of the first business decisions I faced was coming up with a name for my company, and I knew this was not a lightweight decision. In fact, in all my businesses, finding just the right name has been something into which I've put considerable thought. Your company name says a lot about you, and prospective customers will often get their all-important first impression of your business from nothing more than the name.

I went to my dad and told him I needed to think of a good name. Could he help me? We thought about it together, trying out different words and phrases, trying to come up with something catchy, maybe something that would rhyme. He asked me to describe the business to him. I walked him through the different kinds of cards I had: happy cards and sad cards, birthday wishes and congratulations, condolences and get-well cards. Together, we came up with the perfect name: Cheers & Tears Printing Co.

I imagined myself in a big office, answering a phone that would ring off the hook and saying, "Cheers & Tears Printing Company. How may I help you?" Like this was a call center in the middle of some vast Hallmark-like organization.

Talk about starting small; it doesn't get much smaller. But I was already dreaming big. And though Cheers & Tears was a tiny operation, I learned a great deal from that little business that I've applied to all my businesses ever since.

*   *   *

To sell my products, I turned to my neighbors and relatives. I already had a relationship with them, and I knew they'd be more likely to buy. Of course, I didn't have the capital or the ability to buy advertising. I had to rely on personal selling and word-of-mouth advertising, and that worked out quite well. I'm sure that some of these people bought my cards at first because they felt they ought to. But the fact is, my products were genuinely popular, and they started catching on.

This experience taught me one of the most important lessons of entrepreneurship: never underestimate the value of tapping into your personal networks and your local community, whether it's for advice, for start-up cash, for building your customer base, or for publicity. Many people feel hesitant about that kind of networking, but this is one of the distinguishing characteristics of all good entrepreneurs: they are always growing their personal networks, always keeping in touch.

Networking is so important. As I would learn later, when I traveled to Japan, the Japanese value networking so highly that they have made a ritualized art form out of the act of exchanging business cards. As a kid, I had business cards for two reasons. One was that my company printed and sold them. (How would it look if I didn't use my own product?) The other reason was that I wanted to be professional. I soon learned to pass out my business cards and collect others' in return. Over the years I have faithfully kept up that practice, and it has allowed me to make quite a few key connections and create an incredibly valuable network.

I always write and thank people after I meet them. Since I normally do this via e-mail, it takes very little time, but I find that people remember it. Sometimes the simple act of a thank-you note establishes a dialogue that leads to a fruitful relationship. I add everyone I meet to my contact list, and since it syncs with my phone, I can always find the contact information I need, no matter where I am.

This is one of the basic lessons every entrepreneur grasps: you are not only building a company, you are also growing a *commu-*

nity of potential customers, whether that's your local community, a Web-based community, or a worldwide community.

You've got to identify your core community and grow from there.

One of the most important things I learned from my experience with Cheers & Tears was the advertising power of word of mouth. In fact, *all* my advertising was through word of mouth, and that good buzz was plenty to drum up quite a decent sales volume. Satisfied customers tell other customers.

Today, even though my businesses are much larger and more sophisticated, I still always start with as close to a zero-budget advertising plan as I can, because I've seen that nothing sells better than word of mouth. And one of the best ways to generate great word of mouth is free publicity. That was another lesson Cheers & Tears taught me.

In February 1995, when Cheers & Tears had been going for about a year, a monthly school newspaper called *Kids' World Journal* ran a front-page story about me with the headline, "Ten-Year-Old Entrepreneur Turns Fun into Cash." It was pretty exciting to realize that thousands of kids, including every fourth- and fifth-grader in Roanoke, were reading about me. But the real excitement came a year later, when I was contacted by a reporter from the *Roanoke Times*, who wanted to do a story on me.

A story in a real newspaper! To an eleven-year-old, this was the coolest thing imaginable.

When the article came out, it listed our phone number, and people started calling in from all around the city to order greeting cards and stationery. To handle all the calls, we set up a separate phone line in my bedroom. Soon I was picking up my phone—just as I had imagined it two years earlier—and saying, "Cheers & Tears Printing Company. How may I help you?"

The free publicity didn't stop there. Soon after the *Roanoke Times* piece appeared, we got a call from the local CBS affiliate, who wanted to do a segment on Cheers & Tears. On my Web site, www.cameronjohnson.com, you can see a video clip of that segment, with the camera crew following me up the stairs of our house and into my "office" as I talk about my business.

One exposure seemed to lead to another, which led to another. That early lesson about the power of word of mouth was one I would never forget. Of course, it was exciting to see a story about my business in a real newspaper. But it wasn't just exciting; *it also was effective.* Free publicity is the best way to advertise. Why would you want to pay ten or fifteen grand to take out a full-page ad in a metro newspaper if you could have a reporter write a story about you in that same paper at zero cost? And this publicity wasn't just free exposure, it also was exposure with *credibility.* People often won't believe an ad, but they'll trust a story.

Those lessons have been key to my promotional philosophy ever since. I *always* use free publicity to promote my businesses.

If you want to launch a $10 million or a $50 million company, you don't need to spend hundreds of thousands or even millions of dollars in an advertising campaign, or even a tenth of that. Instead, you can get that equal amount in free publicity. Free publicity serves as a validation of your product or service, and you can use it for any type of business. It doesn't have to be in a mainstream source such as the *New York Times* or *People* magazine. It can be in something as small as an online newsletter that goes out to a few hundred of the sort of customers your product is targeting.

When I was building Cheers & Tears, I didn't have any alternative. I couldn't have even considered spending any major money on advertising. Free publicity was the only thing I could afford—and I now realize I was so fortunate that this was true. If someone had given me a million dollars, I probably would have screwed it up. That happens to entrepreneurs all the time. They manage to get a major business loan or investment, and all at once they're saying, "Hey, let's get a $200,000 ad campaign, let's spend $200,000 on an office, let's do a $2 million Super Bowl ad. . . ."

Another key lesson I learned right away from Cheers & Tears was that while it's fun to generate some spending money, it's a lot more fun to use cash flow from a business to grow that business further.

When the business started growing rapidly after the *Roanoke Times* article, I reinvested some of the unexpected influx of revenue into upgrading my computer and printer. Before long, I upgraded my equipment again, and continued the practice of regularly reinvesting a substantial portion of profits into the growing business, especially in upgrading my equipment.

This is one of the strengths of the "start small" philosophy. If you're launching your business with the goal of building something solid, rather than with images of getting rich overnight, then you'll have the patience to reinvest your earnings into your own operation.

Being too hungry for rapid growth is one of the biggest and most common mistakes entrepreneurs make. A strong business can't be all about the profit you take out of it, especially not at first. I've always been able to come up with business concepts I could make work with very little start-up cash, and often I've been able to start turning a profit fairly quickly—but I've always been careful to turn a significant part of those profits back into building the business further. Growing up in a culture that constantly pushes us toward instant gratification, I know this takes some discipline. But believe me, in the end, it's well worth it.

When I started Cheers & Tears, I certainly didn't have any aggressive plans for expansion. But the best thing about the whole experience was not *how big it grew*, but *how small it started*. In every one of the dozen business I've started in the years since, starting off small has always been my biggest advantage. When you start small, you do things the right way. You have to.

From Cheers & Tears right up to the present, I've never taken any outside investors. Other than the $50 my mom gave me to open my first checking account, my parents have never given me anything to invest. I've also never taken any loans. And that's where so many people go wrong in starting a business: they think they need to start big right away and try to realize all their aspirations for it in a hurry—and this leads them to take on loans that become difficult to repay. This can put a crushing or even fatal burden on a struggling business.

When you don't have a lot of capital, you're forced to scrutinize everything you do, and there's nothing better for a business than ruthless self-examination. Starting small forces you to learn from early mistakes. You have to watch every single expense and justify it.

I've spent twelve years building what I've got, and even though it's been through a series of different companies, it's been one continuous process of building and rebuilding. As I write these words, I've just launched another new company, and even though it's brand-new, it has twelve years of continuous growth behind it, twelve years of successful businesses that have all grown from small starts. With each business I've started, I've taken the money I made through that business—whether in revenue saved, profits made by selling it, or both—and put that into a bigger company.

This is a whole different thing from saying, "Hey, I want to start a business. I'm going to quit my day job and take out a home equity loan for $100,000." It's good to take calculated risks, but don't risk the house you live in to finance your start-up. Then you've got so much at risk that you try to dive into everything right away, and it puts you under so much pressure that you lose your effectiveness and can't focus on the things you need to focus on. Too often that kind of pressure is lethal to a young business.

Make sure your business model is scalable, so that later you can grow it big, if that's what's meant to happen, or sell the business and move on to something else. But start off small; give yourself time to grow. That's how Dell got to be so big. Look at how Microsoft started out—and where it went from there.

And as both Michael Dell and Bill Gates showed, starting small certainly doesn't mean you can't end up making a good deal of money—which I was about to find with my next business.

I've always thought it was an interesting coincidence that I was born in 1984, the year Apple Macintosh introduced its "desktop" metaphor, a simple computer capable of using graphics, icons, and a mouse. The Macintosh was the platform that introduced the idea of "desktop publishing," without which there never would have been a Cheers & Tears Printing Company.

In 1994, when the Macintosh and I were both ten years old, the public was first starting to become aware of the Web through the introduction of the browsers Mosaic and Netscape Navigator. A decade after technology had brought publishing and professional-quality graphics into our homes, computers were bringing a whole new dimension of commerce and enterprise to our desktops, too.

As my printing business grew, so did the Internet, and soon I was selling my wares through a Web site. The home computer had been my means of production. Now it became my avenue for conducting every phase of business, from purchasing to promotion to selling to distribution.

By the way, this doesn't mean I was especially computer-savvy or had any exceptional skills in programming or Web design. Far from it. I had taught myself basic HTML and knew a little bit about computers, but my technical computer skills have never been anything beyond the ordinary.

The thing about technology is that it's always advancing and improving, and if you don't keep up, your skills will quickly become antiquated. Early on, I knew that I could be far more productive hiring other people who were experts at these tasks than if I tried to master these skills myself. Relying on the special skills of others allowed me to focus on the business itself, which was where my own abilities were.

In September 1995, just before my eleventh birthday, a computer programmer named Pierre Omidyar launched a little online auction Web site as a hobby so that collectors of knickknacks and oddities could sell their wares to other collectors. When Omidyar tried to register the name "EchoBay.com" (after his consulting company, Echo Bay Technology Group), he found that URL was already taken, so he shortened it to "eBay.com," never imagining what a household word that name would become.

A year later, eBay opened up to let people sell just about anything—and I sold my sister Claire's Beanie Baby collection.

I was eleven; Claire was five. I bought her Beanie Baby collection from her for $100 and sold it on eBay for $1,000. She couldn't have been happier, and neither could I. What's more, I was intrigued: there was huge potential here. These inexpensive little stuffed animals were becoming a genuine craze, like the Cabbage Patch kids of the early 1980s: everybody wanted them. Demand was constantly running way ahead of supply, and people were paying huge premiums for the most desirable ones.

I had stumbled onto a terrific business opportunity, and I wanted in. But I had a problem: we were sold out. Claire didn't have any more Beanie Babies.

I did a little research, looking into the Beanie Baby suppliers available on the Internet, and soon learned that there were several wholesale sources of Beanie Babies. I wondered if I could apply to these manufacturers to become a retailer myself.

Amazingly enough, when I requested some retailer applications, I found that the manufacturers didn't ask for the applicant's age. All they wanted was a name and a credit card number. As it happened, this was about the time when Visa check cards first came out, and I was able to get a Visa card to go with the checking account my parents had set up for me (more about this in chapter 3). I never had to talk with anyone on the phone, so nobody ever heard my voice. Because they never heard my voice, they never realized they were doing business with a twelve-year-old.

I vividly remember filling out my first order. This was in the very early days of the Web, and most of these companies didn't have Web sites yet, so I had to fill out their order forms on paper and mail them in.

That first order was for two thousand Beanie Babies, to be delivered to my home by UPS. As I dropped the order in the mailbox, all I could think about was that on the day of delivery, I'd better make sure I got home before UPS showed up. My mom didn't yet know I'd gone into the Beanie Baby business big-time, and if the order arrived while I was still at school, I didn't know what she'd think.

Sure enough, a few days later, I came home from school to find the house absolutely filled with boxes. I hadn't even come close to imagining how much space two thousand Beanie Babies would take up. There were boxes everywhere. My mom was home wondering what on earth was going on. At first I really didn't know what to say. So I just casually commented, as though it were the most normal thing in the world. "Oh, great, they came."

She looked at me and said. "*What* came?!"

"The Beanie Babies," I replied. She just stared at me. She actually thought I'd ordered them all for my own personal collection.

I quickly moved all the boxes to our basement, which was my hub of operations for the whole next year. Soon I was representing five different Beanie Baby manufacturers and had become a major player in the online Beanie Baby retail business. Some I sold on eBay, but mostly I sold them through my own Web site, using both the site I'd created for my printing business and the name Cheers & Tears for the new Beanie Baby business. I considered creating a new name and a new site—but again, this was in the early days of the Web, and I already had an established and trusted online presence. Why not build on what I already had?

Before long I was shipping forty orders a day. I had sold those first two thousand Beanie Babies within the first month, and continued ordering more by the thousands. The wholesale price was about $2.50 per Beanie Baby, and they'd retail at $5.00 to $20, even $50 and more. By the time I was up to forty orders a day, I was carrying an inventory of about five thousand Beanie Babies in my parents' basement.

I had entered a whole new world of business. To do business locally, I would have to use my DMV-issued ID for people to accept my Visa check card. Over the Internet, it was a different story.

If any of my customers or suppliers had done business with me on the phone, they would have known I hadn't even hit puberty yet. But nobody knew this. I could write properly and compose intelligent e-mails, and I knew about good customer service. I'd found a truly level playing field that would let me compete in the world of business on any scale I cared to dream. My computer had become my window to the world.

*   *   *

At night, after doing my homework, I would go online and take all the orders that had come in during the day. Before going to bed, I'd have everything boxed up and ready to go for the next day. I wanted to make sure all my shipments would be in the mail before the close of business the day after they were ordered. My packaging was quite professional-looking, too, with beautiful customized labels printed from my computer.

I'd wake in the morning and go to school for a normal school day. When I'd get home, my mom would drive me and my black trash bag full of USPS Priority mail packages to the post office, where I'd stand in line surrounded by this little black plastic mountain of merchandise, inching my way toward the window.

One day, my parents were out of town attending a Ford dealer meeting. I had three very special orders going out that day. While I was at school, it suddenly hit me that there was nobody around to drive me to the post office—and it was Friday, which meant that if my orders didn't go out that day, they wouldn't go out until Monday.

No way—that was unacceptable.

I got home from school at about three-thirty in the afternoon, gathered up my packages, loaded them up in my backpack, grabbed my bike, and was off to the post office, pedaling as fast as I could. When I reached the big white building, I heaved my bike into the bushes and rushed in, slapped my backpack up on the counter, and breathlessly asked, "Did I make it?" like I was putting in their hands the most important packages of their career.

And the man behind the counter said, "Yes, you made it . . . you still have a good hour yet." It was barely four o'clock.

I also started selling Beanie Babies in bulk. The more I could buy at once, the bigger discount I could get. I liked to buy as many as possible, because I never like paying more than someone else. (As much as I like to charge my customers the lowest prices, I also like to *pay* the lowest prices.) They came bundled two dozen in a big plastic bag, so I started selling them in cases of two dozen as well. People would buy them for school fund-raisers, party gifts at birthday parties, those kinds of things. For this wholesale business, I secured the domain name www.beaniewholesale.com.

Then, to grow the business even more, I started shopping around on the Internet and buying select Beanies from individuals, sometimes paying a real premium for them—and often selling them at an even greater premium. There were collectors who would pay $1,000 and up for some of the rarer ones. Back in 1997, if you visited www.cheersandtears.com, you could find the rarest Beanie Babies anywhere.

By the middle of '97, Cheers & Tears had grown to become the second-largest Beanie Baby retailer on the Internet. At the height of the business, I was doing as much as $15,000 a month in sales, outselling toy companies with as many as fifteen or twenty employees. And it was completely a one-man business—unless you count the fact that I usually relied on my mom to drive me to the post office to ship my orders.

That year, I netted about $50,000 from Beanie Baby sales.

Not bad for starting small.

One of the most important pieces of advice I can give is to think of ideas that will require the least cash investment up front and the least in advertising money, especially for your first venture.

Find a business that will be low-cost to run and will generate strong word of mouth, and you'll be way ahead of the game.

3

Make Your Money
Work for You

You may be wondering what I did with the $50,000 I cleared from my Beanie Baby business in 1997. After all, that's quite a bit of cash for a twelve-year-old to bring in. So what did I do with it?

Most of it went into savings. I suppose it could have been tempting to blow large amounts of it on things I didn't need. But my parents had always done a pretty good job of helping me keep money in perspective.

One of the most important qualities of the most successful entrepreneurs is that they appreciate the true value of money and pay close attention to how they manage it. Good money management isn't a minor detail; it's often the difference between lasting success and the kind of success that quickly crumbles into failure.

New entrepreneurs often make the mistake of thinking that the purpose of building a business is to make money. But money isn't an end in itself; it's only a tool. At first it's a tool to help you build and grow your business further. Later, once your business is off and running, it becomes a tool for building financial security and retirement. It also can become a tool for starting additional new businesses. The key point is that your money is a tool for accomplishing what you want to accomplish—and that only happens when you control it. If you take care of your money, your money will take care of you. If you don't, it can enslave you.

For me, the purpose of building a business is to create more freedom in my life, to exercise my creativity, and to contribute to the world around me. Money just helps me do those things.

People often ask me why I've been so consistently successful in business, and the single biggest reason I can give them is this: I was fortunate enough to learn about money from my parents at an early age. I've never carried any debt; I pay off my cards every month. I've never spent more than I had—not personally, and not in any of my businesses.

If you want to successfully start and grow your own business, you need to have a firm grasp on basic money management skills. This is something you cannot delegate to people you hire, and even later, if your business grows large enough to warrant an accounting staff, all the really important financial decisions have to come from you—and you can't make those decisions clearly unless you have a solid grasp of how your cash flow is running.

So many people I know don't think about how they're managing their money or their credit. As soon as they get a paycheck, they spend it. They find themselves with credit cards with a $5,000 limit, and next thing you know, they're paying the minimum payment— "Hey, it's only $30 a month"—and they're $8,000 in debt. What they don't realize is that by not being in control of their money, they're letting their money control them—and that can have long-range consequences.

That kind of debt is the entrepreneur's worst nightmare.

The biggest problem I see in American business today is that people spend more than they have; they let expenses grow more than income; and they try to become too big too fast. This is no different from the way so many people overextend their credit cards, just on a much larger scale.

And here's the thing: the basics of cash flow are simple. You don't need a business course to learn this. You just need to be determined to stay on top of your finances and make your money work for you.

For me, my real education about the value of money started when my parents taught me how to manage my own checking account at age ten. This meant that by the time I was a teenager, I'd mastered the basic, everyday financial skills that every adult—and certainly every entrepreneur—needs.

When I started earning income in my first business, my invoices said, "Pay to the Order of Cameron Johnson." When people would pay me, I would just turn the checks over to my mom. She would countersign them, the bank would cash them for her, and she would turn the cash back over to me. But as my business continued to grow, I could see that this wasn't going to work forever.

Besides, I didn't really *want* the checks made out to "Cameron Johnson." I wanted them made out to "Cheers & Tears Printing Co."

When I turned ten, my mom said, "Cameron, if you're going to have a business, you need a checking account." She gave me $50 as a birthday present and took me downtown to the bank, where she and my dad did business, to make that $50 opening deposit.

We ran into a problem, though: they said I needed to be eighteen to open an account.

My mom told them that she'd also be listed on the account—but they wouldn't budge. She said she'd be willing to countersign checks, if necessary; she'd do whatever we had to do to make this work. No dice. They just couldn't open a regular checking account for a minor. Sorry. Rules were rules.

My mom is someone who does not take no for an answer. (In fact, this may be the most important thing I've learned from her.) When she was young, she'd had her own checking account, and she was not about to take this bank's refusal lying down. She marched us over to the bank across the street and told them what we were after, and the people at that bank said "No problem!"

I still have that account today. In fact, from that day on, I've never done business at that first bank—and I've brought all my business to the second bank. I will always remember that they were the ones who gave me the chance.

I learned another valuable lesson that day: I would rather be the business across the street—the one who says "No problem!"—and treat my customers better than the competition.

Now I had my own account, but I still needed some sort of ID if I wanted to use any of my checks. Here we ran into another logistical problem: I was only ten, and it would be years before I'd have a driver's license.

Once again, my mom refused to be stopped by a mere technicality. She took me right over to the DMV and explained our situation. They issued me an ID card.

Finally, thanks to my mom's support and persistence, I was all set: I could go shopping for my own business and computer supplies with my new checks. Some of the clerks at those stores must have been a little surprised to see a ten-year-old come into their store, walk up to the counter with $300 in software, pull out a checkbook, and write a check for it. All I knew was that having the freedom to make my own purchases with my own money was one of the most satisfying rewards I got from my business dealings, and that remains true today.

The day my mom and I went to open that checking account was one of the most important days in my life. More than anything else, I credit this as the event that put me squarely on the entrepreneurial path. There was more at stake here than the convenience of my being able to cash checks; my parents knew that I'd learn the true value of money, and learn it so well I'd never forget it, if I learned to manage it myself.

In addition to staying on top of your cash flow, it's also essential to know how to make your cash *grow*. Investing your profits back into your business is probably the single best investment you can make. But there also comes a time when your business provides extra cash flow that you can afford to invest elsewhere, and that's when you need to know how to invest in stock markets wisely.

At the end of 1995, when my first business was not quite two years old and I was still months away from selling Claire's Beanie Baby collection, my parents gave me two shares each of stock in three companies: Disney, Marriott, and CSX Railroad. (Years later, one writer joked, "Instead of getting a toy train set for Christmas like most kids, Cameron got railroad *stock*.")

I learned how to follow the stocks' progress on AOL and in the newspapers, and started watching them every day. After a few months of seeing my stocks fluctuate only very slightly, I decided that this was pretty boring. Nothing was happening. I knew that the stock market itself couldn't be this dull—but I needed more exciting stocks. I wanted to invest in something that would really grow. So I asked my mom, "Can I sell the stocks you guys gave me?"

She said, "Sure, but you'll have to pay a stockbroker to sell it for you," and she explained how we would call her broker, and he'd make the sale for me and take his commission from my earnings. Later I discovered that I preferred doing my own trades online, using a service such as E*Trade. The cost per trade was far cheaper (about $19.95), which allowed me to trade more frequently. Today, after handling my own trading for nearly a decade, I work with a broker at UBS, where I also have a financial adviser. But these developments all came later. At first I was only too happy to use my parents' broker as I started trying my own hand at picking the stocks I wanted to invest in.

I sold all the stocks I had, took the proceeds, and added money I'd saved from birthdays and Christmas gifts, along with some profits from the business, for a grand total of $680. Now the question was: What should I do with it?

By this time I had become a pretty voracious reader of books on business and marketing. I especially liked reading biographies of successful entrepreneurs, people I looked up to, such as Donald Trump, Bill Gates, and Michael Dell. I also regularly read *Business-Week*, *Forbes*, and other business magazines.

I had read about Warren Buffett, the famed billionaire investor. Dubbed the "Oracle of Omaha" because of the uncanny accuracy of his investment strategies, Buffett was the second-richest man in the country (after Bill Gates) and widely considered to be the greatest investor of our time. One thing he is famous for is the strategy of investing in those businesses which you know well from your own experience, and he often invested in companies whose products he personally liked and used regularly.

"Buy what you know," said Buffett—so I did.

I was becoming a huge fan of Michael Dell's. He had built an empire on the brilliantly simple concept of cutting out the middle-man, and thus could offer his customers better computers at lower prices. I also admired the risk he took, basing his business model on the belief that consumers would be happy to put money down and order their computers without actually seeing them in a show-room first. Nobody believed that would work—but it did, and the concept "direct from Dell" was a huge success.

I was confident that Dell would continue growing, so I put my entire $680 investment nest egg into Dell stock.

When I first bought that stock, Dell was doing about $10 mil-lion a day in sales. Soon that climbed to $15 million a day, then $20 million, and I watched my Dell stock climb right along with the company's earnings. This was definitely more exciting than watching my CSX Railroad stock sit still.

Six months after I bought it, the Dell stock split, meaning that the company doubled the number of shares each stockholder held—something that usually happens only when the stock's value is rapidly increasing. Before long it split again, and then again.

Within a few years, my $680 investment had grown to about $6,000—a return on my investment of nearly 1,000 percent.

That's what I mean by "making your money work for you."

When Dell's stock finally started to level out, I sold it and looked for something else to invest in. Still following Buffett's dictum "Buy what you know," I decided to buy some Toys "R" Us stock. After all, I was a kid: I knew the place, I used it, and I liked its products. It made sense.

By the time I turned fifteen, I had learned to trade online using my own E*Trade account. I continued building my portfolio and watching it closely, often several times a day.

I also experimented with some high-risk stocks, typically newer, smaller companies. I invested about $1,000 in one such stock at $1.20 per share, and watched it grow to $6 or $7 per share before selling it. I was very pleased with my almost six-times return on investment. After I sold my shares, the stock continue to climb, tripling to $20 per share, and then soon plummeted to the $2.00 range. This was a small pharmaceutical company that had appreciated mainly on hype and rumor, rather than on any solid financial performance of the company itself.

Still, while it was exciting to play with these sorts of stocks, I never allowed myself to put too much cash into them. There's sometimes a fine line between investment and gambling, and I care too much about smart investment for the long term to let myself get too crazy with my money. From the start, I always carefully weighed risk against return, and as a rule invested in companies with solid track records I could count on.

I've come to realize that gaining a basic understanding of the stock market is as much a part of money management as balancing your checkbook. To me, knowing how to make your own trades and knowing how to intelligently pick those companies you're willing to invest in are essential skills for any entrepreneur.

The stock market still fascinates me today. It amazes me that even after the debacles in late 2000 and 2001, people are still investing in companies whose stocks are highly valued but that aren't really making any money. In fact, people are doing it now more than ever. It's starting to look like we're about to go through another cycle like that all over again—and when the real investors bail out, it will all catch up to everyone else.

Now I'm going to recommend something that may sound a little crazy coming from a twenty-one-year-old: there is probably no single better way to have your money work for you than to put it into retirement savings. Of course, for most people around my age, retirement is the furthest thing from our minds. But that's the whole key to savings: the earlier you start, the more time your money has to work for you, and the better off you'll be. When you start the saving habit early, not only are you *not* spending that money, but you're also giving it the opportunity to compound and appreciate for years and even decades.

Americans are among the most cash-strapped people in the developed world. One out of four adults in the United States goes through the weekly or monthly paycheck without putting a single penny into savings.

Not long ago I had the privilege of getting to know David Bach, the financial expert and bestselling author of the *Finish Rich* series (*Smart Women Finish Rich, Smart Couples Finish Rich,* et al.). In his book *The Automatic Millionaire,* David cites some shocking figures: "Nearly half of all American workers have less than $25,000 in savings—and nearly sixty million Americans (that's one out of five) have nothing in the bank. That's right: zero, nada, zilch." At the same time, says David, "the average American currently owes more than $8,400 in credit card debt."

In the summer of '98, at about the time I shut down Cheers & Tears, I decided to use some of my profits from the business to start a Roth IRA, a new type of retirement account that had become available at the beginning of that year. The main benefit of a Roth IRA is that all the earnings are tax-exempt when you withdraw them (which you can't do until you are at least age 59½).

My parents' financial planner was surprised, because he didn't know it was possible to open an IRA at age thirteen—but you can. The catch is that you can't start a Roth IRA with money you've inherited or been given: you have to use money you have earned yourself. I certainly qualified for that. At thirteen I was one of the youngest people in the country with a Roth IRA.

I'll keep putting cash into my retirement accounts over the years ahead, but because I started so early, I already know I have financial security down the road. For an entrepreneur, building that kind of personal financial security is crucial. Starting out your career with the thrill of risk and adventure is great, but as the years go by, you also need to build a foundation for long-term peace of mind. So no matter what your age or financial level, if you haven't already started building your retirement, *start doing it now.*

The most important thing I've learned about money is not to chase it. If you chase money, it will ruin your life. If instead you put your energies into pursuing skills, knowledge, and understanding, the money will follow you.

Don't put money on a pedestal, but treat it with the respect it deserves. Manage it wisely, grow it intelligently. Make it work for you—not the other way around.

In other words, don't put money first. Keep your focus on building your business and delivering value to your customers. When you do, you will be successful—and the financial rewards will come.

4

Look Close to Home for Great Ideas

In the 1985 film *Back to the Future*, there's a moment when Doc (the Christopher Lloyd character) slips in his bathroom, hits his head, and suddenly has his inspired brainstorm for the "Flux Capacitor," the gizmo that allows his DeLorean to travel through time.

I wish I could say I'd had an amazing "Eureka!" moment like that. But the truth is, great ideas for successful new businesses don't need a miraculous moment of inspiration. Good business ideas are all around us—and they start coming to you a whole lot more naturally if you just keep your brain working on them and your mind open to them.

People often ask me, "Where do you get your ideas?" There's no single answer, because they can come from anywhere. When I was a teenager, I loved to play basketball. Sometimes an idea would hit me while I was shooting baskets or just talking with my friends. I have never sat down at a desk and applied any sort of fixed process or "method." But I'm always thinking about it, mulling ideas over in the back of my mind.

Sometimes I keep a Word document on my computer with a running list of random business ideas—or even just seeds of an idea—that I've had but haven't yet pursued.

How do you judge whether an idea is a good one? To some extent it's like the question "How do you know who will become your best friends?" There's a chemistry to it, an intuitive sense that goes beyond calculation. It clicks or it doesn't.

It helps to apply Warren Buffett's investment advice here: start with *what you know*. You don't need to stray far from your own home to find great ideas. If your passion is antique cars, video games, or first-edition mystery books, any of those could be a good place to start hunting for business ideas. Maybe you have a skill you love, like carpentry or knitting. For me as a kid, Beanie Babies was home turf.

It's not just that this approach is easier; there are also major benefits to starting with what you know. For one thing, it will be something that has value to you, and ideally *you* should be the perfect customer for your service or product. What's more, starting with what you know means that you'll have a solid grasp of what your customers really want and how much they'll be willing to pay for it. Starting with what you know means you've already done a ton of market research.

Kevin Plank had the idea for Under Armour Performance Apparel, a line of microfiber clothing that keeps athletes cool and dry, when he was playing college football and grew tired of constantly swapping sweat-soaked T-shirts for dry ones. Yvon Chouinard, the founder of Patagonia, started out by making the ice-climbing equipment he wanted for his own climbs but couldn't find anywhere.

One of the best ways to come up with a strong idea is to start with a problem—especially one you've experienced yourself—and see if you can spin it. Ask yourself, "How could I change this problem? How could I solve it?" A good example of this is my first completely Internet-based business, which I started when I was thirteen.

By 1998, my Beanie Baby business was winding to a close. The craze couldn't go on forever, and besides, I had entered seventh grade the previous fall—and when you're in junior high school, spending a bunch of time in your basement with stuffed animals is just not cool.

As it turned out, my timing was good: the Beanie Baby craze was about to run its course. I more or less stopped selling Beanie Babies in the fall of 1997 and shut down the Cheers & Tears Web site in the middle of 1998. Finally, in May 1999, I sold the domain name I had for my bulk Beanie business (www.beaniewholesale.com) to a buyer who had contacted me through the Internet. That same month proved to be the peak of Beanie Baby sales nationwide, and it wasn't long before the "Beanie bubble" burst, leaving those companies that were still trying to make the business work, with thousands of Beanie Babies that were worth next to nothing.

Now in the spring of '98, I was actively hunting for something new to do.

This was in the early days of the Internet and a heady time for online enterprise. E-mail was really starting to take off. In fact, the press was reporting that it was starting to rival regular postal mail in volume and soon might even overtake it. I was on e-mail a lot myself, and thought it was amazing, except for one thing: spam.

With the e-mail explosion, junk e-mail was becoming a serious issue and a major pain for dedicated e-mail users. Today, of course, all the major e-mail providers offer powerful junk-mail-filtering features, but back in the frontier days of the Web, no such thing existed. I hated getting junk e-mail and knew others must feel the same way.

And that planted the seed of an idea.

I thought, what if I could provide people with a way to protect themselves from junk e-mail, and at the same time protect their privacy—especially young people? That idea became the basis for my next company, MyEZMail.

MyEZMail would be an e-mail-forwarding service that would allow subscribers to keep their real e-mail addresses confidential. As a subscriber to MyEZMail, you could set up your own e-mail address—for example, cameron@myezmail.com—and we would forward all the e-mail sent to that address to, say, your AOL address. At the same time, we would prevent the sender from knowing or being able to find out that "real" address. This also would prevent people from knowing your AOL screen name, so they couldn't IM (instant message) you, and provide complete privacy for your online profile. Nobody would know your "real" e-mail address, age, gender, physical address, or any other information unless you wanted them to. And it would filter out junk mail.

I knew that if I could find a way to make this work, it would catch on. I definitely wanted a service like this, and I knew all my friends would, too. But how much would we be willing to *pay* for it? That I wasn't so sure about—and that is where *method* comes into play.

While I have no set method or formula for finding an idea, I *do* have a process I take it through once I've got one. No matter how cool, fascinating, or exciting it seems, I know I need to test any idea carefully before acting on it. I've learned to take ideas and chase them, follow them, play with them, explore them to see if they might work.

Sometimes I'll come up with a very simple idea and file it away in my head for later. Then, when I have total peace and quiet (such as in an airplane or hotel room), I'll start to push on it, see how I might expand it, maybe come up with new ways to pursue that idea or new ones that spin off from the original concept.

I'll go online and search to see if there are any other companies like it, and if there are, are they making money or losing money? How many customers do they have? If they sold their business today, what could they sell it for? You can figure that a company will typically sell for about five times its annual earnings, plus the market value of whatever assets it has (which might include such things as inventory, buildings, real estate, or even a recognizable brand). If you dig a little—press releases, articles on the company, financial news, etc.—you can usually find out roughly how successful a company is and extrapolate from there.

I ask myself as many hard questions as I can think of about the financial realities of my hypothetical business. Do I have all the expertise I need to do this well? And if not, what will it cost to pay someone who does have that expertise? How much will it cost just to get operational? And after that, what will it cost to generate enough business to start breaking even, and how quickly will that happen?

I'm looking for those ideas that will give me the best return for the least amount of start-up money and effort. These questions are crucial to ask *now*, before I've invested major time, money, and effort. Once I've chosen an idea to run with, I focus all my efforts on that idea and let the others go.

Typically I don't compile a formal business plan at this stage of the game, but will create more of a preplan, a simple outline of the business with whatever key notes, market research, and financial estimates I've put together. I'll want to have basic projections of start-up costs and recurring monthly expenses, along with a summary of how the company will make money and how quickly I expect to grow our customer base. I project these figures as much as possible based on similar companies or companies with similar markets.

I've gone through this process dozens of times. Sometimes, in the course of research, I've decided that the idea wasn't one I wanted to pursue. And of course, sometimes it turned out to be one I did.

As I tested out the idea for MyEZMail, the question of how much people would be willing to pay for such a service was a critical unknown, and not an easy one to resolve. But I knew that the idea would work, and that I was going to run with it, once I found the key ingredient: *I would offer it free.*

How was that possible? Because of a revolutionary new business model: making money from online advertising.

In 1998 this was a brand-new concept, and it was catching on like wildfire. Even two or three years earlier, most people had barely known what the Internet was, let alone what it looked like or how to access it—or why anyone would want to. Now thousands of businesses were rushing to put up their own online presence and stake their claims on the Internet frontier. It was very much like the history of settling the western half of the United States—only compressed into a time frame of months instead of decades.

The more businesses started to populate the "real estate" of the Web, the more the value of online advertising skyrocketed. Suddenly everyone was talking about "eyeballs" and "stickiness" and "hits per day." The "stickier" your site, the more you could get advertisers to pay you to post their ads.

I wanted to capture some of this boom in online advertising revenue, and I could see that MyEZMail would be perfect. Users
would flock to our site for the free services it offered, and companies would flock to our site for all the eyeballs we had—and pay us
for the privilege.

In addition to creating my site, I also would need to populate it
with advertisers. Finding them was not difficult; it just took legwork.
I looked at other Web sites to see which online ad agencies were
handling their advertising, then went to the agencies' Web sites and
filled out their applications to become what's called a "publisher."
They would then review my site and decide if my "potential ad
inventory"—my community of visitors—was worth their placing
advertising with me.

At this point I was convinced that I had a solid business model. But
I knew I couldn't do this on my own. Taking MyEZMail from idea
to reality would take some fairly sophisticated Web design—far
more complex than anything I could put together on my own. I was
going to need help.

When they first hear about the businesses I've started, people
often get the impression that I am some kind of computer geek. In
fact, nothing could be further from the truth. I'm not especially
skilled at the mechanics of computer programming and Web
design. I can get around the computer just fine in a basic way, but
it's never really been my area of expertise. My rudimentary Web
design skills had been sufficient to serve my needs in the days of
the Cheers & Tears Printing Co. and the Beanie Baby business, but
not anymore. If I wanted to make this new business viable, I would
need to hire someone to help me build the software machinery.

So at age thirteen, I went through a rite of passage: I hired my
first computer programmer.

In later years, I would find genuine partners I would work with
closely and even share ownership with. But for this first Internet
business, I found a programmer I would use just for this project and
hired him to develop the whole e-mail-forwarding package I
needed to make the business concept work. We never met or even

spoke. To this day, I can't remember his name. I think he lived in Missouri.

Hiring a programmer presented a challenge in itself. I didn't know anything about programming or the different languages, so I didn't have a firm grasp of what questions I should ask. I also had no clear idea of how much a job like this ought to cost, although I figured it had to be at least a few thousand dollars. In those days it wasn't easy to find inexpensive programmers, as it is today.

I went online and started looking for a programmer who had already done something similar to what I wanted, so I could see examples of his work. I found someone fairly quickly, looked over some of the things he'd done, and was pretty impressed. I contacted him, described my project, and asked for an estimate. He explained everything he was going to do, how long it would take, and how much it would cost: the package I wanted would come with a price tag of $2,500. I think the arrangement we worked out was that I would pay 25 percent of this up front, 50 percent halfway through the project, and the final 25 percent upon completion. I knew that it was a good idea to always get these agreements in writing, so we wrote out our agreed-upon terms, and he was hired.

Thus a second rite of passage came on the heels of the first: I would need to make a serious capital investment in my idea.

This wasn't like buying wholesale lots of Beanie Babies. Those were merchandise I knew I could turn around and sell immediately. This was different: this was capital investment in infrastructure. Now, $2,500 may not sound like all that much money, but for a thirteen-year-old, it's plenty. In fact, because I'd put most of what I'd earned from previous enterprises into investments and my IRA, that $2,500 was just about all the available cash I had.

In other words, I was betting everything I had on this idea.

One of the biggest barriers that keep people from starting their own businesses is fear of risk. But risk isn't something to be afraid of; it's the entrepreneur's best friend, the source of the best opportunities. The key is to understand what kind of risks are worth taking, and which are not.

There's a difference between taking risks and taking *calculated* risks. I'll take a calculated risk any day of the week—but I evaluate each risk very carefully to make sure the return is worth the risk. I think this is one of the biggest mistakes people make in business: they misjudge the return on their investment, in both time and money, and jump in without an accurate sense of the risk they're taking.

Calculated risk-taking is not the same thing as gambling. In gambling, the odds are always in favor of the house. The gambler is counting on being able to beat those odds, either by skill or sheer luck, and most times, of course, it won't happen. I *never* take a risk when I think the odds are against me—and I never depend on luck. I depend on practiced, good instinct and thorough, careful research.

Investing that $2,500 in the programming for MyEZMail was a benchmark for me, and based on what my research had told me, it was a risk I was prepared to take, and it worked out beautifully, as well as I'd hoped or even better. A few weeks into operation, I had more than six hundred customers on the service and dozens of paying advertisers.

Keeping pace with its growth was too much for me alone, so I hired a media company to sell advertising in exchange for 35 percent of ad revenue. This was great: it was a 65 percent commission to us with zero up-front investment and zero ongoing expense. If they didn't sell anything, it cost us nothing; and if they did—which, of course, they did—we got paid.

It kept growing. Soon I was being flooded with e-mails from hundreds of people a day asking questions and wanting to register for the service. I was still doing this by hand, and it was becoming a huge task. It was time to make yet another steep investment: I went back to my programmer and paid him another $2,000 to develop a software system that would automate registration. Once we'd installed that new software, the site practically ran itself.

By the middle of 1999, about a year after it had begun, MyEZ-Mail was a huge success, with about ten thousand users. I had invested $4,500 in software design, but my operational costs were virtually nil: my only real recurring expense was a monthly hosting fee of probably $15 a month, and even that I could piggyback off another server I already had. Since the media company sold advertising on a strict commission basis, I had no out-of-pocket cost there, either. It hadn't taken long to make back my initial investment, and from that point on I was operating in pure profit.

I'd taken a risk, but I'd calculated it carefully—and I was more than happy with the results. On the scale of blockbuster Internet businesses, this was still a small company. But it was a milestone for me. I kept it running for another two years, during which time I never really had to do much with it, because it was by now wholly automated.

If I were thinking about starting a business today in a brand-new niche, a market I'd never thought about before, I would start by asking myself, "What do people in this industry need? What's bothering them, hassling them, costing them money, keeping them from getting what they want?"

You can do this for any size market, large or small. What kind of service do homeowners need? What kind of service do renters in your city need? What do people need who use telephones? Whoever came up with the caller ID box probably started out with that question, and I wonder how well *they* have made out. What do airplane travelers need? The answers to that question created Southwest Airlines and JetBlue.

Think about your own life: Is there some service or product that you don't have now, but if you did, would help you save money, save time, or make your life easier and thus more productive? If it's something you could use, there are probably others who could use it, too.

Think about small businesses in your area: What do they need? Maybe your local dry cleaner or clothing boutique needs a delivery service, or your coffee shop or ice cream shop needs local promotion. What if you created a Web-based community for your town where all these small businesses would pay to advertise? A lot of communities have sites like this—and even more do not. You could promote your Web site with billboards, flyers, word of mouth. You could do a partnership with your local TV station and highlight their top stories in exchange for free ads mentioned during the news. This idea just occurred to me now, as I'm writing, and I haven't tested it out, but I'll bet it would be profitable.

From early on, I started asking these questions, and whatever answers I got, I would then try to come up with products that met those needs.

Here's what's so solid about this approach: *customers with needs* come along every single day. There are *always* people and niches with unfulfilled needs. With this approach to business, you don't need to rely on luck, timing, or the fickleness of fads and crazes— just on your own ability to observe and create. Choose a niche, find a need, and then see what could help those people do their job better.

In fact, here's what I suggest: before reading any further, take a pad of paper and for the next ten or fifteen minutes jot down any and all everyday customer needs you can think of—things small businesses need, things your family and friends need, things you need yourself. Don't think too much about it; just let it flow, have fun with it.

Then go back over your list and consider each one in turn: What sort of business might serve this need?

Once you've come up with a business idea that works, it's tempting to keep coming up with more ideas and finding ways to expand your new business. That's only natural, and building on the base of a business you've already started can be a smart thing to do. But this is also where entrepreneurs often go wrong. It's easy to make the mistake of going into too many different areas, to overextend the business and end up losing all kinds of money because you diversified way too much. You don't want to lose your focus and direction, or let your resources (time, people, money) become spread too thin. Focus on what you do best and don't take your eye off your goal.

MyEZMail is a case in point. Once I had it up, running, and profitable, I started thinking: How could I build on this?

One option would have been to spend some money on advertising to bring in more users. But since we were offering a free service, that would actually cause us to *lose* money.

This may sound obvious, but I'm often amazed at how business owners will throw money into expanding an existing business with the idea that "bigger is better"—but without a solid plan for how the additional investment will actually pay off. Just as "Start small" is sound advice, it's often equally wise to "*Stay* small." At the very least, it's wise to be careful about how you grow. Even if your business is starting to generate solid profits, the best strategy is to pretend for a moment that those profits aren't available, and approach any expansion plans with the same question you had when you started the business in the first place: What is the best return I can generate with the least expenditure?

As I looked at ways to expand MyEZMail, instead of looking for ways to bring in more users or to spend more money, I began asking how we could generate more income with the users we already had.

This was 1999, and along with the online advertising boom, the concept of multipurpose, one-stop-shopping "portals" was a very hot topic of discussion, speculation, invention, and investment. Individual online shopping sites were popping up all over the place, and consumers began hungering for online "malls" to sort through the chaos. Internet entrepreneurs were going crazy exploring the huge new world of opportunity this need represented.

At the same time, companies such as Amazon.com were putting on the map the concept of affiliate programs—online businesses that let you offer their products as an "affiliate" and pay you a small sales commission for all purchases made through your site. Utilizing this model meant that an online "mall" landlord could offer spots to individual vendors rent-free, and make his own revenue stream through the small sales commissions generated by the click-through affiliate programs associated with all those vendors.

I already had substantial traffic coming to my e-mail-forwarding business site. I thought, why not direct all my customers "next door" to do their online shopping—and in the process, generate a whole new revenue stream? This idea turned into my next business, MyEZShop.

*   *   *

MyEZShop was essentially a suite of affiliate programs I promoted to my customers as "your central source for online shopping."

Unlike MyEZMail, building MyEZShop took next to nothing in dollar investment. The actual Web site was a fairly straightforward thing to build, because it really consisted of nothing more than a battery of affiliate links—1-800-Flowers, Amazon.com, Barnes & Noble, Omaha Steaks, Fogdog Sports, et al.—and this was something I could design myself using out-of-the-box software (FrontPage or something similar). Beyond the site design, all I really had to do was sign myself up as an affiliate for these other sites and coordinate the whole thing into one coherent package. I put my category links on the left, some vertical banner ads on the right, and featured "stores of the week" in the center. By the time it was ready to launch, MyEZShop was a full-scale one-stop shopping portal with sixty-five online merchants in one location, offering everything from books to electronics, toys to travel packages.

To drive traffic to my online "mall," I added a link to MyEZMail so that all ten thousand customers of my e-mail service would be directed to our new portal. One day in May 1999, a new button appeared on the home page of MyEZMail: *Our new Web site, MyEZShop!*

And the business was off and running.

Of course, it would take a lot of sales to make any real money through the site, because I was getting only 2 or 3 percent per clickthrough in commissions. When someone went through my site to buy a $100 CD player from Best Buy, I would make $2.00 or $3.00. With a total sales volume of $20,000 or $30,000, I was making $600 to $1,000 a month. Along with some additional revenue from the banner ads on this site, my business was suddenly generating an additional $15,000 a year. Not a huge revenue stream—but still, this was essentially free extra income.

The lesson I learned from MyEZShop is that a business is never "finished" or "done." It pays to look for creative ways to build on what you already have, to stay alert to new opportunities to evolve or grow the business. If you find a way to have it earn even just a little additional revenue, it's worth it: you never know what extra service or feature you provide might really take off. Look at what Google has done. When you search for a book title, you'll see a list of sponsored links on the right, representing a substantial additional revenue stream for Google.

Soon after I launched MyEZShop, dozens of similar sites started popping up, and the marketplace for portals started heating up. It would have taken a lot of investment in development to stay competitive, and I wasn't interested in going that route. Since I had essentially no operational costs, I was under no pressure to sell or shut down my operation, so I let it coast and continue generating its modest revenue stream. I sold it in 2000 to a buyer I met through a message board, and it has since been turned into a vendor of e-commerce shopping cart solutions for Web sites. You can buy a complete shopping cart setup to add to your own Web site for approximately $450.

MyEZMail.com still exists, too, though not in the same form. I kept it running as well, eventually converted it to a Web-based system, and in 2001 sold it to a private buyer. You can still go to MyEZMail.com today, but it's no longer an e-mail service; instead, it's a simple search portal consisting of a series of search keywords.

To go into business for yourself, you don't necessarily have to come up with a brand-new idea. Another great strategy is to spot a trend that's just starting to pick up steam and ride that wave. For example, I rode the Beanie Baby wave, and would later cash in on the dot.com advertising boom with a business called SurfingPrizes. Just a few years ago I hit the gift card trend just at the right moment with a company called CertificateSwap.

How do you find the right trend? You don't have to be a genius: you just need to stay on top of current events and keep percolating those ideas. Ever since my early teens, I've been in the habit of reading business magazines, in part to keep my thumb on the pulse of what are the hot topics of the day. If you put the kind of energy into this that others put into keeping up with celebrity gossip, you'll be way ahead. (I'm always amazed at the amount of time people put into reading celebrity gossip magazines. I've been in tabloids a few times, once because I was supposedly dating Mandy Moore — whom I've never met.)

During the dizzying days of the late nineties' Internet boom, I was always looking for every revenue stream I could find. One of these was the hot new, wild, and crazy business of buying and selling domain names. Today, domain name registration is a multibillion-dollar business and is highly structured and regulated. Back in 1999 it was a rough-and-tumble frontier world of virtual real-estate claims.

Most businesses were slow to realize how valuable and even essential it would become to "own" their own Internet addresses. (No one really *owns* a domain name except for the central domain name registry, the Network Information Centre or NIC. Instead, people and businesses pay a fee for exclusive control for a period of time, essentially a "lease" on the real estate.) And in this, as in most aspects of business, the bigger the company, the slower they tended to act or react.

The late nineties was like a golden era of virtual real-estate speculation. It didn't last that long, because the entire business community quickly realized how important the Internet had become. Today, a new business wouldn't even think of launching without registering its domain name (and as many possible variants as it can, too). Back then, most businesses hadn't caught on yet.

I started buying domain names and selling them, often for a significant profit. A July 4, 1999, story about me in the *Roanoke Times* said, "A site [*sic*] he bought for $70 sold the other day for $450." That was not an unusual transaction for those days, although I don't remember which particular URL (not "site") they were talking about. However, there was one domain name purchase I made that I remember very well, because a year and a half later it would land me in a major lawsuit . . . but more about that in a later chapter.

Another growth industry in those days was the basic bread-and-butter business of designing Web sites, and I wanted a piece of this business, too. Remember, this was in the day when your average small business did not yet have its own Web site, but chances were good that it knew it needed one. So I started a Web site design company called EmazingSites, complete with the cheesy slogan "We make your site *emazing!*"

At first I did these site design projects myself. My target market consisted of small businesses who had no Web sites at all or very simple ones that needed improvement. In either case, the design requirements were modest—nothing I couldn't do myself.

But sheer volume was another story. Pretty soon I had more customers than I could handle. I started hiring other Web designers I knew, mostly friends of mine right in Roanoke. I would deal with the customer and work out the parameters of the site design, then pay the designers on my team to build the actual Web site.

Web site design was nowhere as sophisticated back in 1999 as it is today. Today, with components such as Shockwave and Flash and the widespread availability of broadband, site design has become incredibly complex, and the level of expertise has leapfrogged. In the six years since I was doing hands-on Web design myself, the people I worked with in EmazingSites have grown better and better. Today they could design circles around me, because six years in this business is like six decades in any other business. I've learned to leave all site design to the people who have the skills.

For me, this was also another rite of passage. In setting up MyEZMail, I had hired a single programmer to perform a single task (albeit a complex one). I had hired a media company on commission to sell advertising. But now, for the first time, I was putting together a team.

I quickly learned how important it was to make sure I clearly and thoroughly communicated to my team. If I didn't tell my designer specifically what the customer wanted, he might have a totally different picture in his mind than I did. I also learned that it's far easier to have complete control of your schedule when you're the only person involved, and that once you're working with a team, it takes meticulous management to avoid missing deadlines.

This was also when I began learning about the dynamics of partnership and shared ownership. There have been times since then when I have brought partners into a business by giving them stock in exchange for their work. However, I've found that partnerships generally work out better when there's a cash buy-in involved—in other words, when the partner is contributing some of his or her own funds to the business—because then each person is clearly invested in the outcome. In one instance, I hired a guy who had real talent but no cash, so I brought him in and gave him a smaller amount of stock. I ended up having to buy him out because he would miss deadlines and slack on the project while he was trying to make money elsewhere. When I hired him, I thought that he saw the potential in our company—but I had misjudged him. Perhaps if he had sunk his own cash into the business he would have treated the job differently. It was a costly lesson, but a valuable one.

Another concern people sometimes have, when considering bringing in partners or hiring people to help launch a business, is that other people might steal their ideas. People often ask me, "How do you protect your ideas when you work with other people?" It's a question I love answering, because it gets to the real heart of business, which is working with people.

Of course, in today's litigious society, you have to protect yourself, and this means using carefully worded contracts (as I did with my programmer for MyEZMail), nondisclosure agreements, and noncompete clauses, so that people would be legally liable if they did violate their confidentiality. Sometimes it's wise to trademark, which costs only a few hundred dollars. (A patent is a much bigger deal, and can easily cost $10,000 and up.) But I always try to find the most straightforward ways to protect my business interests and to avoid complexity. More than anything, the real answer to the question is this: take care to choose people you can trust.

The real challenge of building a team is also the real joy of it. It's all about bringing smart people together, getting to know them and their skills and abilities. I love meeting new people and asking myself, "Can we work together and do something great?"

Assembling and managing the team for EmazingSites was a great experience, and it helped to prepare me for situations I would face in the future, when I would work with dozens and even hundreds of employees. The risk always seemed minimal, and the teamwork paid off beautifully.

EmazingSites continued to operate for many years as a highly profitable business, because all we were selling was our time and expertise. As time went on, we stopped doing Web site design, and EmazingSites evolved into being a brand, an umbrella site that housed a number of other Internet businesses; eventually we sold it.

Sometimes I'll develop an idea and end up deciding that for whatever reason, it's just not going to work right now. Maybe some new development would have to happen to make it feasible, such as a substantial increase in the number of Web users or a dramatic decrease in the cost of Web design.

I recommend that you keep a file of such "not right now" ideas and revisit them periodically. Just because an idea may not seem quite right at the moment doesn't mean it won't make great sense at some point down the road.

In the summer of 1999 I was playing with the concept of paying the Web site user a fixed percentage of revenue. As I turned this concept over in my mind, I came up with an idea for a company that would pay users to fill out surveys.

How valuable would it be, I wondered, for companies that do surveys to get honest responses? To have a way to get potential customers to actually take the time to fill out a survey with their real views?

This is not what typically happens. When people are called at home at seven in the evening and asked if the caller can "ask you a few questions," the one out of five who agrees to do so is just shooting from the hip with yes-or-no answers to get the caller off the line, and not really putting any serious thought into the answers. I've done that; most of us have. These results are all skewed, and companies know it.

But what if people were rewarded for filling out the surveys, say, with a point system, or with cash?

From small businesses to Fortune 500 companies, all kinds of companies are constantly coming up with ideas for new ad campaigns, new product features, even new product lines—really, *any-thing*—and they need consumers' genuine opinions before they spend $100 million to act on it. And this isn't like a test market, where you feel obligated to say, "Yes, that's a good idea." We're talking about getting people involved and rewarding them equally no matter what their real opinion is.

What would that data be worth to the company giving the survey? Probably a dollar or two per survey, I thought, maybe even four or five.

I liked the idea, and got as far as giving it a name—Paid Thoughts.com—because you would be paid for your thoughts. But I never developed that idea any further. For one thing, it would have been pretty complex and time-consuming. I would have had to do all the legwork involved in contacting these companies, asking them what kinds of questions they'd want to ask and to what groups of customers, designing the surveys, etc. As I started researching the idea, I saw that I'd need to have a number of people involved and a good amount of capital backing it—more than I was willing to put up. Unless I went looking for venture capital (which I had never done and wasn't interested in doing at this point), I couldn't really see myself developing it the way it would need to be developed.

I was pretty sure the idea would work. And in fact, it did: a few years later, a company came out with the exact same idea as PaidThoughts, and today there are a number of such sites that have been quite successful. But it wasn't the right idea for me, at that time and in those circumstances.

So I let it go—but I didn't throw it away. That fall I took that starting idea (paying the Web user a fixed percentage of revenue), gave it a twist, and started a company called SurfingPrizes, which went on to become the most successful company I'd ever started.

There is no shortage of great ideas for amazing businesses, and never will be. The trick is to stay open to them and keep looking for them—and to take the time and care to figure out which ones will pay off.

5

Balance Work with Life

From the start, I'd always loved the process of starting and running each of my businesses. But now it was more than love—I was absolutely hooked.

By May 1999, my businesses were booming at a level I'd never experienced before. MyEZMail was a year old and growing like crazy. I had just started MyEZShop, which was already going strong out of the gate, and I was working on the plan for Emazing-Sites, which launched a month later. I'd had more than enough opportunity to experience the thrill of building a business out of nothing, starting with only an idea, and watching it take off and soar.

This may be the single most satisfying thing about being an entrepreneur: seeing an idea of yours take shape and become a fully functioning real-world phenomenon. By the spring of '99 I was experiencing this thrill at full throttle—which was why I also came face-to-face with one of the biggest challenges an entrepreneur faces: striking a balance between working and living.

Running your own business can really take over your life. That may be fine for some people, but I've never wanted that to happen to me. I've always taken care to keep a clear distinction between my business life and the rest of my life.

For example, I've never felt the need to brag or boast about my businesses to my friends. In fact, for most of my career, my friends never even knew I *had* any businesses. It just wasn't something I ever talked about. Once, when I was fifteen, one of my best friends told me, "Hey, my parents said you were in *Newsweek*?!"

I said, "Um, yeah, last week . . . it was about a business I started."

He didn't think it was a big deal, and I'm not even sure he believed me—until his parents showed him the article.

People have asked me whether I ever felt weird or different from other kids my age. My answer has always been no, because the truth is, everything I've done has always *seemed* normal to me. I've never let my businesses control me or interfere with my personal life. I played soccer for thirteen years, all the way through high school.

Keeping a clear sense of boundaries can help keep things in proportion. Success can be fleeting, but friends last forever. It's good not to lose track of what's real.

But in the spring of '99, this is exactly what my parents were afraid was happening.

My relationship with my parents has always been good—but it hasn't always been smooth, and when I turned fourteen and started working really crazy hours to build this series of online businesses, we went through a rough patch. Like any other teenager, I was in the process of figuring out who I was and what I wanted for myself in life, rather than just always doing what my parents wanted.

I've always admired and appreciated my parents. They've been role models and mentors, and by and large have supported me in my choices, even when doing so was hard for them. But right now I was a teenager, and as far as I was concerned, everything they said was wrong. My mom and I, especially, started butting heads more and more often; as she puts it, "Cameron and I were at loggerheads."

The crux of their worry was that I was spending too much time online and growing too fixated on my businesses. As my mom still says today, "We don't see Cameron as some business superstar, we see him as our son, period—one-quarter of our family unit, no more and no less." And while Cameron the teenage entrepreneur was doing great, they weren't so sure about Cameron the son.

My position was that I had a completely normal life—at least in most respects. I had great friends, I played sports, I always had a girl-friend. Their position was, how could anyone call this "normal"? I was up into the wee hours of every morning on my computer, running my growing business empire. And about that, of course, they were absolutely right.

It wasn't that I was necessarily all that driven. I didn't feel I was compulsive or obsessed about it. I was just in love with business. I loved everything about it. It was fascinating, and it was fun. I was my own boss, making my own decisions and my own money, and I was learning valuable skills that I knew I could always use later in life.

But they were worried that I was becoming addicted to my computer—and maybe a little addicted to the bottom line, too.

My mom used to set her alarm for about 3:00 A.M. She would wake up, trudge over to my bedroom door, poke her head in, and say, "Cameron, go to bed! You have school in the morning!" Sometimes she and I were really at each other. She would find me at my computer and say, "Cameron, get off that computer! Go *do* something!" This was probably the toughest time our relationship ever had.

She now says she thinks that I was just trying to become a teen and she wasn't letting me. But however you describe it, my parents were both worried about me; they wanted to get me off my computer and see me put more focus on school. They thought my education was a whole lot more important than any of the business stuff I was doing, and they wanted me to apply myself more to my studies. As far as they were concerned, doing well in school would give me more of a leg up later in life than my fixation on my businesses.

Looking back, I can see why they were concerned. But honestly, I wasn't worried about my grades or my school performance. Granted, I hadn't gotten straight A's since third grade, when I made all A's so I could stay at the Plaza in Manhattan. The one time I aced a writing test was in eighth grade, when we were given this assignment: "Write a sales pitch to your principal to convince him to cancel school." In my written pitch, I pointed out all the advantages that would come with giving us a day off: the students would come back more relaxed and ready to work; our attitudes would all improve because we'd appreciate this surprise gift of a free day, and the same would be true of the teachers; and because it was winter, the school would also save on heating costs, as well as bus expenses and janitorial services for the day. I got the only perfect score on the state-wide writing test.

These were the highlights of my academic career so far—that, plus the fact that I outsold everyone in my school in raffle tickets and wrapping paper. But in general, my schoolwork was average. I was doing okay in school—not great, but okay. In fact, everything about me was average, really: I was having a good time living the normal life of a normal teenager. It's just that I was throwing myself into my businesses in my spare time and not getting much sleep.

My parents finally decided that they had to take some action to get me more focused on my schoolwork, and in the spring of 1999 they decided it would be best if I went to boarding school.

To put it mildly, I was not crazy about this idea. I didn't want to leave my friends; I liked things just fine the way they were. I argued that I didn't need to go to a prep school because I didn't plan to go to college anyway.

"Michael Dell doesn't have a college degree," I told them. "Bill Gates doesn't have a college degree."

They pointed out that I was not Bill Gates and I was not Michael Dell. I was their son, and they wanted me to get a good education! My dad went to an all-male boarding school when he was a teenager, and he knew what the experience was like. He thought it would be great for me, and my mom agreed.

We argued, and finally struck a compromise: if I would go to boarding school for the summer and improve my academics, they wouldn't force me to go in the fall if I didn't want to. So that summer I packed my stuff and headed up to Orange, Virginia, to attend the summer session of the Woodberry Forest School for Boys.

I liked the people there and quickly made friends. In fact, I had such a good time that I decided this was not such a bad idea after all, and decided to return to Woodberry that fall for my freshman year of high school.

My parents were thrilled. Not only would I be in a focused, high-performance academic environment, but I would also be away from all my businesses. And even better—from their point of view—was that there was no Internet access in the dorm rooms. In fact, the only place where I could find Internet access was in the library.

At Woodberry, I pretty quickly changed my routine: instead of staying up until two or three in the morning, I would go to sleep early and get up at five so I could spend a little time in the library until the breakfast hall opened. That was the only time I could find to do my e-mail, and I could barely manage that.

From my point of view, this was a serious problem. I loved being at Woodberry. I loved the freedom of living on my own, waking up on my own. And I was making great friends. But I was really wrestling with this whole issue of balance.

I've always valued education. It wasn't only my parents; I wanted to do well in school, too. But I also wanted to keep working on my businesses. I had seen enough to know that whatever I needed to learn about business—and, for that matter, about life—I was more likely to learn from my own hands-on experience than from classes. But now the pendulum had swung too far the other way. How could I even think about running an Internet business, let alone starting another one, if I could hardly even get on the Internet?

It looked like my career as a teenage entrepreneur might grind to a standstill—which, truthfully, was probably just what my parents were hoping. But then things took a twist.

That summer, while I was attending the Woodberry summer session, my dad got a letter from a friend of his who lived out of state. The man had sent along a clipping he'd seen in USA *Today*:

Junior Achievement is in search of a teenage Michael Dell. If you know of a teenager who has started their own business and would like to share their story, we are accepting applications for a Young IT Entrepreneur of the Year Award.

Along with the clipping was a note from my dad's friend saying, "This is Cameron!"

When my dad showed me the clipping, I got online immediately. I learned that Junior Achievement (a nationwide educational organization) was cosponsoring the national contest along with an Internet business guide called BrightLane.com (since defunct). The contest was called the "Young IT Entrepreneur of the Year Award," and it was open to anyone twelve to eighteen who owned his or her own successful information technology business.

Perfect. But there was one problem: the deadline for submitting applications was just three days away—and since the completed application form with all the required information had to be mailed to the contest headquarters in Colorado, I really had only two days. It was a good thing I had looked up the contest right away, instead of putting it off for a few days.

They say that "luck is preparedness meeting opportunity." I've certainly had my share of events that were blessed with very lucky timing, but I agree with the aphorism that *being prepared* and *taking action* are the sparks that set off the dynamite of opportunity. And I absolutely believe that opportunity is around us all the time.

By this time I had been in the local papers probably half a dozen times, and in a few other regional publications, too. I was used to reporters asking all about my businesses, and because of that, answering all the questions on the application came quickly. And I didn't have to scramble to pull together the specific information they wanted—I make a habit of always keeping facts and figures and summaries compiled and up-to-date. It's important, when you're running a business, to know where you stand.

I quickly filled out the application and sent it off by FedEx.

As it turned out, overnighting that application was one of the most fortunate things I ever did, because it started in motion a chain of events that would profoundly affect my future.

A little over a week after I arrived at Woodberry Forest for my fall semester, as I was struggling to figure out how I was going to keep my businesses going while I pursued the academic life, my parents called and said, "You're one of the three finalists for that

Young Entrepreneur of the Year Award—they're flying you to Atlanta next week!"

Within a few days I was on a plane to Georgia to attend a gala celebration honoring the finalists of the Young IT Entrepreneur of the Year Award. My adviser from Woodberry, Anthony Sgro, went with me; my dad met up with us when we reached Atlanta—and so did a long black limousine. Our all-expenses-paid trip included limo service and a two-night stay at the Ritz-Carlton.

There was a big ceremony right there at the Ritz-Carlton. The place was packed, and included among the crowd were some amazing figures from the business world, along with a substantial media contingent to record it all.

As the ceremony got under way, they announced that of about a hundred thousand applicants, they had narrowed the field to three: Jeremy McGee, from North Augusta, South Carolina, whose company built and sold computers; Aaron Greenspan, of Shaker Heights, Ohio, who offered computer consulting, training, and troubleshooting; and me, with MyEZMail. Jeremy and Aaron were both sixteen; I was fourteen.

They called the three of us up to the stage. The place got quiet. This was not exactly the Academy Awards, but you could definitely feel the suspense hanging in the air. Then they announced the first runner-up:

"Jeremy McGee!"

Everyone applauded as Jeremy shook the announcer's hand and was presented with a $2,500 check. (All three prizes included checks intended for college scholarships: $2,500 each for the runners-up and $5,000 for first place. I never did put my prize money toward college, though: I used it to buy a new computer.)

Meanwhile, I was thinking, "Okay—my chances of winning just went to fifty percent!" At this point I was pretty sure I was going to win. After all, I was two years younger than either of the other two. And since we'd all seen each other's numbers, I knew that my business made more money than either Jeremy's or Aaron's.

Then they called out the name of the second runner-up:

"Cameron Johnson!"

And suddenly I was the one shaking hands, being congratulated, and handed a check for $2,500—and first prize went to Aaron Greenspan.

I was sorely disappointed, because I love to win. Don't ever let anyone convince you that winning doesn't really matter: it does and it should. When I play sports, I always try like crazy to win; that's what elevates the level of play to something great. And the same is true in business.

But the really critical point about winning is this: when you *don't* win, you can't let that get in your way. Winning gives you the confidence and the courage you deserve—but it's important to know how to appreciate the opportunities for growth that often come with just having been in the race.

The way I saw it, Aaron was two years older than I (in fact, a few of the judges later hinted that this may have been a strong factor in his winning: since I was only fourteen, I still had a few years to come back and try again). I had placed in the top three out of some one hundred thousand applicants, which was a major achievement— one that would attract lots of attention to my career.

Most important of all, I made some great contacts. I was impressed with Aaron and what he'd done, and thought he was someone to watch. I got his contact information—and sure enough, only a few weeks later I got in touch with him about a business idea that turned out to be more exciting and successful than anything I'd done before.

Making finalist in the Young IT Entrepreneur of the Year Award competition paid off in another way: it helped resolve the looming conflict between school and business.

Back at Woodberry, I talked to my adviser and hinted that I might not be able to stay long at Woodberry. I liked being there, I told him, but I really couldn't run my business effectively. Staying current with my e-mail correspondence was one thing; that I could manage in the library in the quiet hours before breakfast. But this wasn't enough to keep up with my business activities. No, I just didn't see how this was going to work.

Within a few days, the administration called me in to talk with me.

By this time, a number of stories had circulated in the national press about the Young Entrepreneur contest and gala event at the Atlanta Ritz-Carlton. Because I was the youngest of the three finalists being honored at the event, the stories tended to focus on me. No doubt the school administration was aware of these stories—and no doubt this had some influence on where they were coming from.

I went to the administration building and was ushered into an inner office, where I was greeted by some of the school's directors. I was really curious to hear what they were going to say.

At the time, as part of the school's standard requirements, I was enrolled in three sports: soccer in the fall, track in the winter, and lacrosse in the spring. Soccer I absolutely loved. Track was okay. But my feelings for lacrosse could best be described as "antipathy" (actually, that's putting it politely; I hated the game), and the directors were aware of this. I guess I had been pretty vocal about my feelings.

They told me that they were considering letting me drop lacrosse and pursue business as, um, "a third athletic." And they had decided they wanted to offer me my own private office. Right there in the administration building.

With my own phone line.

What could I say? I stayed.

I was really relieved that we were able to work this out, because I loved being at Woodberry and didn't want to have to choose between my school and my businesses. This experience also taught me a big lesson about balancing your work and life needs: if you work at it, you can find a way to get the balance right. In future years I'd have to make tough choices again, more than once, but for now I'd carved out an ideal situation for myself, and it was about to pay off in a big way.

I genuinely appreciated the education I got at Woodberry. But the biggest education I would have over the following year would come not in the classroom, but through the hands-on experience of the business that Aaron and I started together.

6

Surround Yourself with Great People

Even before I'd gotten settled into my new office at Woodberry, I was working on a new business idea, one that would be more challenging than anything I'd done before.

I started with the idea I'd played with the previous summer when I dreamed up PaidThoughts: the idea of making money by paying people to spend time online. Our users would download a software program that would sit on the top of their screens and rotate banner advertisements while they were connected to the Internet. The money to pay them would come from advertising fees paid to us by the advertisers.

This was the fall of 1999, and the online advertising boom I'd cashed in on the year before with MyEZMail was building more momentum every day. Advertising on the Internet was already a multibillion-dollar industry. People were hailing it as the industry of the future.

Since I'd be paying people to surf the Web, I decided to call the new business SurfingPrizes.com.

SurfingPrizes was an example of how you can start a successful business by modeling off an existing business model and improving on it. Some ideas come from stumbling on a great product (Beanie Babies); others come from identifying a clear need in the marketplace (MyEZMail). Here was yet a third way to find a great idea: notice someone else doing a poor job.

The idea for SurfingPrizes first hit me when I read about another company, called AllAdvantage. They hadn't actually launched yet, but all the prelaunch publicity included a pretty complete description of their model. As soon as I saw what they were planning, I thought it was flawed.

AllAdvantage claimed they were going to pay their members $0.50 an hour to surf the Web, in exchange for letting the AllAdvantage software display ads on their computer screens. Their income would come from the advertisers, who would pay big bucks to have their ads displayed on all these users' computer screens.

It was a great idea—but, in my opinion, their numbers didn't add up. Given what banner ads (called "impressions") could bring in the current Internet climate, there was no way they could pay users $0.50 an hour. Here's how the numbers crunched:

Normal ad rates at the time were about $3.00 per thousand impressions, or $3.00 CPM (cost per thousand). The more ads you displayed in your rotation the better, because you're being paid on a per-impression basis—but if you rotated them too fast, users wouldn't have enough time to see a specific ad and react to it. I calculated that the optimum rate would be to display three ads per minute, which would mean changing the banner ad every twenty seconds.

Three ads a minute translates to 180 ads per hour. Let's say you could garner a $3.00 CPM from advertisers; that would work out to $0.54 in advertising revenue per hour per user.

How could they pay $0.50 on a gross revenue of $0.54?! They couldn't—unless maybe they thought they would be able to get two or three times these ad rates. Did they really think they could command a $10 CPM?

I thought, "There's no way they're going to be able to make that work. They could go broke."

This was a perfect example of the kind of unrealistic, "sky's the limit" thinking that often happened during these few years of the first Internet boom. Dot.coms were going crazy, stocks were going through the roof, and the magical three letters "IPO" were on everyone's lips.

It was exactly the kind of business climate where you want to step back, take a careful look at what everyone else is doing, and think hard about how you can be sure not to make the same mistakes.

No doubt, the people who created AllAdvantage did indeed think they would be able to command these high ad rates. But I didn't think so.

Still, that didn't mean the concept itself wasn't sound. In fact, I loved the concept. Was there a way to make it practical?

I made some further calculations, and when I'd factored in costs and worked out all the numbers, it looked like a realistic projection of net income for an operation like this would be something under $0.30 an hour per user. So instead of paying $0.50 an hour, I worked up a model based on paying out less than half that amount—just $0.20 an hour.

I was confident this would work. Now I just needed to put the working pieces together—and I knew that doing this would take more expertise and more manpower than anything I'd done before.

For the first time, I decided to create a partnership.

Partnership brought with it a whole host of issues I'd never dealt with before. Working out the division of ownership and distribution of responsibilities and decision making is not something you can leave "for later"—and the details matter.

Of course, the most important decision of all is choosing who you want to work with. I had often heard my dad say, "Good people are key. Surround yourself with the best—it's better to have the best working with you than working for your competition." So I decided to do just that. I called Aaron Greenspan, the sixteen-year-old who'd taken first place in Atlanta, and said, "Hey Aaron, you want to come work with me!"

Aaron laughed and said, "Why would I want to do that? I already have my own business."

And I said, "Let me pitch you on my idea—and if you like it, you can come in on it with me. You'll be involved in something with huge potential—and you won't have to let go of what you're already doing."

He laughed again and said, "Okay, pitch me, and I'll tell you if I like it."

I did—and he did.

But the partnership wasn't finished yet. Aaron and I knew that our first step had to be hiring a top-notch programmer, because the site we envisioned was going to require programming skills well beyond what either of us could manage. And this wasn't even something I could just pay someone to build as a one-shot deal, as I had done with MyEZMail. Paying an outside company to do all this work would be expensive, because it was so complex. What's more, we knew that to stay competitive, we would need to have the capacity to keep improving the program.

This would be too central a part of the operation to give to a contractor. We really needed to find someone who could join us as a third partner and take an integral role in developing the project.

We started looking, posting messages on message boards and asking around, looking for talented people with the right skills and experience—and soon I learned about a programmer in California named Tommy Kho.

As I looked through Tommy's work, I realized that he had already built something strikingly similar to what we needed. His work was superb. I contacted him, told him a little about what we were up to, and asked if he thought he could create a version of his technology, only adapted to a pay-to-surf company, and he said, "Yeah, no problem."

For some reason, I assumed that Tommy was in his forties or maybe even his fifties. One day, after we'd been writing back and forth for quite a while, I asked him, *By the way, how old are you?* And he e-mailed back, *I'm a junior in high school.*

I was stunned: he was exactly Aaron's age—just two years older than I. I had to laugh. I thought about all those manufacturers and customers who'd done business with Cheers & Tears without dreaming they were transacting business with a teenager—and now I'd just done the same thing.

I introduced Tommy to Aaron—of course, this was all online: Aaron in Ohio, Tommy in California, and me in Virginia—and we brought Tommy into the company as a partner.

Bringing in Tommy Kho as a partner was one of the best business moves I ever made. He was the best in the country at what he did. What's more, it cemented for me a business lesson that every entrepreneur needs to learn sooner or later—and the sooner the better: *you can't do it all.*

When you create a business, you are the idea person and the bottom line: not only does the initial concept come from you, but also all decisions ultimately come down to you. Whether you are a business of one or have ten thousand employees, you are the one responsible for the success of the business.

But at the same time, it's not reasonable to think you can expect to master all aspects of your business. Part of building a business is knowing how to find and work with people who have more expertise than you do. The bigger it grows, the more you'll need to bring in others with more expertise than you have—and they need to be people you can trust and on whom you can rely.

This holds equally true for advisers. If you want to be the best, you have to have the best people, whether they are attorneys, accountants, tax advisers, investment advisers, or any other type of adviser.

How do you know if they're the best? Ask questions. I always ask my advisers tons of questions—about both things I know and things I don't. If it's something I don't know, I ask so I can learn. And if it's something I already know, I ask so I can see what answer I'll get from them. If I'm looking into potential advisers, I'll look at their past work and past client experiences. Of all the ways of assessing someone's skills, talents, and possible value to your business, nothing beats a great referral from someone you trust.

To take on partners, I needed to draw up partnership agreements—so I turned to a trusted adviser I had learned about through the best possible referral: my dad's lawyer, Neal Keesee.

Neal is not only a friend of my dad's, he is also one of the top business attorneys in the area. A few years earlier, when the need first arose for me to sign a contract, I had hired Neal to help me figure out how I could do this. As a minor, I couldn't legally sign a business contract. Neal came up with the solution: while I was unable to enter into a legally binding contract myself, I could legally do so *on behalf of a corporation*.

I now contacted Neal and asked him to draft the necessary paperwork and buy-sell agreements, which would prevent either party from selling stock without the other parties' approval. We reviewed and signed everything, Neal filed the papers—and we were an official corporation with two stockholders—who were soon *three*.

This was another rite of passage for me. I had never shared ownership of a company with anyone, let alone with two other people. But by the time we launched SurfingPrizes in March 2000, we were three partners with a clear division of shared labor and responsibilities along with our shared ownership. I was president, Aaron was vice president, and Tommy was chief technology officer and secretary; we split the stock up roughly 40/30/30, so that I had the largest share but nobody had a clear majority—in other words, it would take at least two of us to make any major decision.

On a practical level, Aaron was in charge of designing the Web site, Tommy was in charge of software development, and I oversaw the project overall, including advertising, financing, and accounting, as well as design of the whole concept and making sure all the pieces fit together and made sense.

We started working on the new business in January 2000. It felt a little daunting, even a little intimidating—but very exciting.

No doubt about it: developing SurfingPrizes would be the most complex project I'd done to date. It would require sophisticated software development and extremely thorough, careful work in accounting, logistics, and interface with the membership (for reasons you'll see as this chapter unfolds). It also would take a huge investment of time and energy as well as significant cash.

Having all that pay off would depend on the booming trend of online advertising, which was something we knew we couldn't necessarily count on in the long run, and couldn't even predict very accurately in the short run. In other words, it was a somewhat risky undertaking—but it was a risk we were willing to take. With MyEZ-Mail and MyEZShop, I'd already developed an online membership community, and we were explicitly building on that experience.

Besides, as I said before, while I never gamble, I'm always happy to take a risk, as long as I've assessed it carefully and believe the ratio of risk to payoff is solid.

We called the software Tommy designed the "PrizeBox" and even went to the trouble of trademarking it to protect ourselves from knockoffs and rip-offs. (As it turned out, we were not being paranoid. As soon as they saw our success, other entrepreneurs immediately sought to emulate our model.) Tommy spent countless hours while the project was in development, often working through the night on this little masterpiece of online machinery.

PrizeBox was a little ad bar that would sit on the upper left of the user's screen and rotate ads every twenty seconds. When you moved your mouse over it, it would highlight whatever ad was displaying at that moment; for example, "Click for Dell Computer Corporation."

This sounds simple, but it was incredibly complicated to work out. It had to be programmed so that when your cursor rolled over the ad, it would freeze and stop rotating; otherwise, by the time you actually clicked your mouse, the rotation might have already moved on to the next ad. It had to be set up so that the moment your mouse was sitting on it, it would know to halt its cycle of changing ads. But since the advertisers were paying for specific amounts of exposure time, the exact number of seconds the ad was displayed had to be kept track of accurately and reflected instantly in their online SurfingPrizes.com accounts. If this information wasn't 100 percent accurate 100 percent of the time, we'd have 100 percent problems.

We also had to develop technology so that people couldn't just leave the thing sitting on their screen and get paid to surf the Web. We designed it so that every five minutes—every three hundred seconds exactly—you had to move your mouse at least once, or else it would quit rotating ads and quit paying you.

The ad companies could track exactly how many ads we were showing, because every time an ad was viewed it was downloading off that advertiser's server. That meant they knew how many people were clicking on each ad, which meant we had to keep our CTR (click-through rate) as high as possible, so we could reasonably charge decent ad rates. That was another reason why we wanted to make sure people were actually sitting at their computers, which in turn was another reason why we needed to build it so the mouse would be required to move over the screen every three hundred seconds to reactivate it.

And all of this had to communicate in real time with our database and all the individual accounts, because we were talking about real dollars here. Every time an ad was shown, we were paying real money into a user's account. We would receive checks from our ad companies for $60,000 or $70,000 and have to know precisely what our payout was to each member on that particular day.

We not only had to have very accurate and stable software for the PrizeBox and Web site, we also had to teach ourselves a lot about accounting—a case where having a solid academic background was actually quite helpful. I've never minded hitting the books and learning whatever subject I needed to know, as long as I could see exactly how it would be useful to my business.

After two and a half months of intensive development, we launched SurfingPrizes in March 2000—and the concept worked perfectly. Before long we attracted such major advertisers as Amazon, Warner Brothers, and Discover Card. In less than six months we had more than 140,000 users, and we were displaying *fifteen million* advertisements per day. That translated into roughly $15,000 in daily revenue. And a significant portion of that revenue was being paid to our members—some of whom were making serious money. Some users posted their referral links on their Web sites or sent them out in their e-mail newsletters and garnered hundreds and even thousands of referrals, earning them as much as several thousand dollars a month.

This was an integral part of the business model from the start. We knew that in addition to paying our members to surf, we would build our user base both larger and faster if we gave our users cash incentives to refer other users. As I'd learned back in the days of my very first business, there's no more powerful channel of promotion than word of mouth.

So we worked out a model for paying our users flat-percentage commissions on the surfing fees that we paid to anyone *they referred* to the site. In fact, we paid these commissions down through *five levels* of referrals.

Here's how this worked: we would pay you a flat rate of $0.20 per hour to surf the Web with our PrizeBox on your screen. If you referred, say, your friend Tom, we would pay Tom $0.20 per hour for his surfing time *and* pay you a 10 percent commission on that, or $0.02 per hour. When Tom then referred his friend Rachel, we would pay Rachel $0.20 per hour for her time, Tom $0.02 per hour for Rachel's time (in addition to $0.20 per hour for his own surfing time), and you an additional 5 percent—or $0.01—per hour for Rachel's time, along with your $0.02 per hour for Tom's time and $0.20 per hour for your own time.

Whew! Do you follow that?

Counting Rachel as your second level, we also paid an additional 2 percent on third-level referrals, another 2 percent for fourth-level referrals, and 1 percent (two-tenths of a cent) on the fifth level.

Of course, these are very small numbers when you look at individual hours. But the number of referrals can easily grow geometrically with each successively deeper layer. One person could potentially end up with a referral group of tens, hundreds, or even thousands of people—which in fact did happen. This meant that there was a very real income opportunity here—and we had to make sure we had an absolutely impeccable mechanism for accounting for every fraction of every cent.

Users could be paid by check (which we paid monthly), or could request payment through a type of online currency then in vogue called Flooz. Each month, for those who requested checks, we would export our database to a fulfillment company, including name, address, Social Security number for 1099s, and the check amount, and they would print and mail the checks.

By the way, in case you're thinking this sounds like a "pyramid scheme," it wasn't. In true pyramid schemes, you have to pay just to participate (which is illegal), and there is often no real product. This was a free service, with a legitimate affiliate program paying out real commissions. Companies paid real dollars to advertise to our members, and we shared that ad revenue with those members—because they were in essence what gave the ads value.

From the accounting standpoint, this cascading series of referral commissions also meant that instead of paying only a flat $0.20 per user hour, we could potentially be paying out as much as $0.24 per hour with all the commissions that hour might generate ($0.20 plus $0.02 plus $0.01 plus four-tenths plus four-tenths plus two-tenths). From a budgeting standpoint, we had to assume the worst-case scenario—in other words, that we would pay out the full commission on every dollar of income.

Of course, not everyone developed referrals groups that went five levels deep, and not everyone came onto the site through a referral themselves. If someone just went to our Web site and signed up on their own, rather than through a friend, then there would be no referral percentages to pay and we would pay out less than that full potential $0.24 on their surfing time. But to guarantee the integrity of the system, we had to build the program based on the assumption that everyone would come in through a referrer and build five levels deep. You can imagine how complex the back-end functionality was—and how tight we had to ensure its security was.

Even before they launched, AllAdvantage had provided the concept that inspired our company. Now that we were operational, they were our major competitor. They were the market leaders, the ones to beat, and going head-to-head with them was a fascinating and engaging process.

You might have thought it would be no contest. How could we even dream of competing? After all, AllAdvantage started out with

$100 million in venture capital. We started with the comparatively tiny budget that Aaron, Tommy, and I invested. They had thousands of employees; we had three.

Still, we grew to become their number one competitor, and we were pretty proud of that accomplishment. But it got better than that. In one crucial way, we even ended up outperforming them. How? By surviving.

During its brief career, AllAdvantage blew through $100 million in cash—and went broke by the end of 2000 according to news sources. Not only did we keep going, we also became quite profitable and went on to become one of the largest online advertising firms around. Annualized, our network was serving 5.5 billion ads per year.

This taught me yet another valuable lesson: biggest is not always best. Most highly capitalized is not always best. And even being the first to market with a new concept is not always best. Apple was not the first to bring an icon-driven computer system and mouse to market; Xerox was. (The Alto, in 1973, more than a decade before the first Mac.)

Never underestimate the potential of a good idea. And never underestimate the *better execution* of a good idea that someone else is executing poorly.

Of course, there was a flip side to the ingenuity of our plan. Where there is great opportunity, there will be potential for fraud, and sure enough, some people tried to defraud our service. One guy actually wrote a program that would move his mouse for him. He would leave his computer on for days at a time, racking up surfing points while he slept.

To fight the perpetrators, we developed scripts that allowed us to track individual members' click-through rates. We could detect that something funny was going on if a user was looking at ads for, say, twenty-four hours straight, or even twelve hours straight, without a single break in the period. This was a pretty clear clue that someone was trying to do an end run around the system. When we discovered any suspicious usage, we would suspend that account;

once we froze an account, that user would no longer be able to log in.

Some people even began selling the hacking software they developed as work-arounds to cheat not only our program but AllAdvantage's as well. AllAdvantage, with their major capitalization underneath them, created an entire fraud department with dozens of employees to combat these efforts, and we followed suit by developing our own fraud department—which consisted of me, Aaron, and Tommy. We would go into the search engines, type in a search string like "fraud SurfingPrizes," and ferret around to see if we could turn up people who were selling the system-defrauding software. We even found message boards where people described their defrauding experience with SurfingPrizes. In those cases we simply copied the person's e-mail address, looked up the account, and suspended it.

AllAdvantage pursued people a lot harder than we did, because they were operating on a much larger scale and had the resources to throw at it. Eventually we communicated with AllAdvantage's fraud department and gave them information about where to find the people we'd picked up on—after all, if they were doing it to us, they were probably doing it to AllAdvantage, too. (And we knew where they lived, because we mailed them checks.)

We also reported the worst of these cases to the FBI, which got involved once the level of fraud got pretty serious. Some of these folks ended up being prosecuted.

It might sound like we were being pretty tough on people who were doing nothing worse than the usual hacking shenanigans— but fraud is fraud, and it's unacceptable no matter what the level.

When you build your own business, it's your reputation that's on the line, and there's no asset you own more precious than your reputation. Fraud is not only a legal issue but also a moral and an ethical one. It may seem like cheating a Web-surfing program that pays pennies per hour is no big deal—but it can be a slippery slope.

Honesty isn't simply the best policy. If you want to be truly successful, it's the *only* policy.

*   *   *

Of all the businesses I've been involved with, SurfingPrizes was the one that taught me the most. This was the first time I used attorneys extensively and got deeply involved in learning about all sorts of legal aspects of business. It was by far the most complex business from an accounting standpoint. It was the first time I worked with partners, the first business I'd built that operated at such a huge scale, and the first time a business of mine attracted a wave of national media attention.

The value of that last point was not lost on the administration at Woodberry. After all, publicity is publicity, and for a private institution such as Woodberry, there's no such thing as too much positive public exposure. (Which was quite an ironic twist, considering that my parents had sent me to Woodberry to take my attention *off* my businesses.)

The media flocked to interview me. First came a reporter from *Yahoo!* magazine; then *Newsweek*, where my picture was displayed on the same page as the pope's. Then came a story in the *Nikkei* (Tokyo's version of the *Wall Street Journal*), followed by a two-column *BusinessWeek* picture of me (in braces) for a cover story titled "Teen Moguls."

What made SurfingPrizes such a good story, more than anything, was that I was so young, and I was CEO of a company doing business with well-known, publicly traded ad agencies staffed by people in their thirties and forties.

These agencies were promoting us, too, because they were selling so much advertising for us ($15,000 a day's worth), and they were taking their 20 to 30 percent cut, so they were making huge money off our effort. But it was the media that really promoted us, with lines that played up the fact that I was only fifteen:

Fifteen million ads a day; $15,000 in daily revenue; fifteen years old.

I certainly understand why people have always seen my youth as an intriguing part of the story, why that makes the headlines and always frames the interviewer's questions. But for me, the real story of SurfingPrizes had nothing to do with my age. The real story was about the core principles of solid entrepreneurship.

If you know how to generate solid, inventive, well-researched ideas, how to calculate risks and take measured steps, and how to find the best people to work with, you can leap over virtually any barriers and obstacles. You can even beat the competition — even if they are a thousand times larger and more heavily capitalized than you are.

People often introduce me by saying how many companies I've started. To me, how I've *ended* those businesses is even more significant than how I started them.

The significant thing is not just that I've started a series of companies, but that I've *made money* with them. With some, I've made quite a bit, while with others I've just done slightly better than breaking even. But I've never *lost* money on a single one, and one reason for this is that I pay as much attention to a company's end as to its beginning. I never have any kind of preplanned timeline for how long I intend to run it or keep a company, or when I plan to sell it or close it. However, I've always had a pretty good sense of when it was time to get out.

There can be all sorts of legitimate reasons to close a company. It may no longer be feasible, because market conditions have changed, or the field has grown more competitive. There may be investments in further development you're not willing or able to make. Or you may simply have come up with another idea that you're aching to pursue.

I think your ideal goal should be to build a business that is working *for* you and that can run itself one day, not one that keeps you more and more involved. Starting your own business is about earning the freedom to live your life and make your own decisions, not becoming a slave to your creation.

With SurfingPrizes, this distinction soon became a very real issue.

We had started SurfingPrizes that March, while I was in my freshman year at Woodberry, and it grew quickly — in a way, too quickly. Within six months we had 180,000 registered members from 60 different countries, and we were supplying 15 million ads a day.

By late August we knew we had a problem.

As more and more users signed up, providing more and more surfing time, they created more and more available ad space to sell—in fact, ad space that we *needed* to sell. But this was mid-2000; the tech boom had already peaked, and the gigantic online advertising bubble was already showing signs of deflating. While we had more and more online advertising to sell, advertisers were buying less and less of it. Demand was shrinking, and our supply was still mushrooming. The marketplace was changing rapidly, and the model we had put in place couldn't continue long without significant changes.

We had a few different ways we could go. We could place limits on how much surfing time our members could be paid for, and thereby keep our inventory down so we wouldn't need to sell so much advertising. We could close off membership where it stood and quit taking new sign-ups. We could cut off some members who were flirting on the edge of abusing the system.

But no matter what course of action we might take to solve the financial and logistic issues, there was another and more intractable problem: the business was growing to a point where it was taking way more time and attention than the three of us combined could provide.

After all, we were in high school and had tons of homework.

We had to make a choice. One possibility would be to try to raise venture capital to fund the next chapter in the company's growth. In those days, that's exactly what a lot of Internet entrepreneurs were doing, and in fact we were approached by a few VC companies that wanted to fund our growth. But I was wary. I had read quite a bit about venture capital and understood the concept pretty well, but I didn't know the ins and outs of it from my own experience. If we went that route, I figured there was a pretty good chance we would be taken advantage of.

And of course, there was another alternative: sell the company—

and we soon realized that this idea presented a major problem in itself, because here we ran into some really sticky privacy issues.

The real value in the company was our database of 180,000 registered users. This was a very high quality, real-value database. We had everyone's real information: their real addresses, real phone numbers, even their Social Security numbers, which we had to have because we were paying out real money. It was the same information a credit card company would have.

Our attorney Neal said, "You can sell it if you want, but I'd advise against it."

At the time, companies were typically paying $4.00 or $5.00 per customer, so we were looking at the likelihood of pocketing at least $700,000 or $875,000 in a single transaction. And this was before factoring in brand recognition, trademarks, software, and all the other assets involved in our operation. Taking all of that into account, along with our daily revenue and current growth rate of 2,500 new users *per day*, many would have valued our company at several million dollars, if not more. It was conceivable that the three of us could walk away from this pocketing a cool million in cash *each*.

But there also was the possibility that we would be smacked with a class action lawsuit over privacy of personal information, which could cost us two or three times those profits. We might have made all that money but then never seen a penny of it, because we'd have to spend it all on legal bills.

We had venture capital offers, all of which we declined. We even declined potential mergers and buyouts. While our terms of service allowed us to be acquired, and thus we would have had legal grounds for going that route, it could have been messy and risky. And it just didn't feel right.

After weighing all this, we finally said, "Let's just do the right thing. Let's close it down."

On September 10, 2000, we closed SurfingPrizes, and my first truly major enterprise as an entrepreneur ended after just over six full months of operation. Hundreds of thousands of dollars had moved through the company while it was open, based on an idea designed and developed by three high school kids with hardly any capital and a zero-dollar advertising budget. Not too shabby.

When we shut the company down, we sold off its "hard" assets — but not the customer information. Rather than sell a database that might have netted us a million dollars or more, we destroyed all the customer information and moved on with our lives.

This was my last active association with Aaron, who has gone on to create a very successful career. He graduated from Harvard in 2005 and now runs ThinkComputer (the same company for which he won the Young IT Entrepreneur of the Year Award), which offers consulting and Web-based applications.

Tommy and I stayed in touch and later went on to do more creative business-building together.

From initial idea to closing its doors, SurfingPrizes had lasted not quite ten months. Now it was gone. Did I regret its passing? Not for a moment.

I'd formed new partnerships and learned years' worth of experience in all sorts of areas. I'd garnered national press attention and built a business worth several million dollars. I was proud of what we'd done together. Even better, I knew I'd be able to take all that experience and learning — along with my share of the profits — and pour it into the next good idea. And that's exactly what I did.

7

Make Yourself Your Brand

I pointed out before that no matter what product or service your business sells, you first and foremost must be able to sell yourself. This principle operates at every level of your business, no matter how small it starts or how large it grows.

In the past few years a lot has been written about "branding," and some businesses pay top dollar for consultations with branding experts. But there's one basic law of branding that I think supersedes anything else that can be said about the subject, and I can give it to you in four words:

You are your brand.

Bottom line, what you have to offer your customers is your own commitment to quality and integrity, your own devotion to customer service and an excellent customer experience, your own passion for doing it right and then finding a way to do it even better. No matter how big your business grows, it will always be an extension of you.

There was a time when CEOs worked in the anonymity of their offices and let the Madison Avenue people take care of what the public saw and heard. But then entrepreneurs such as Lee Iacocca (Chrysler), Dave Thomas (Wendy's), and Frank Perdue (Perdue Farms) started bringing their companies' messages straight to consumers themselves, and demonstrated how effective it is when the person in charge forges a bond directly with the customer base.

I learned this principle early on from the mentors I admired, especially Donald Trump and Michael Dell. Trump is possibly the most famous master of personal branding, with his name emblazoned over everything he builds. But many others, such as Dell, Steve Jobs, and Richard Branson, have embraced the art of becoming their own brand just as effectively as Trump.

This was a lesson that sank in for me in the unlikeliest place I would have expected: the heart of downtown Tokyo.

When I described sending in my application for the Young IT Entrepreneur of the Year Award in mid-'99, I mentioned that it "started in motion a chain of events that would profoundly affect my future." Actually, entering that contest was something like lighting a fuse, and in early 2000 that chain of events exploded like a stick of dynamite.

Back in the fall of '99, months before SurfingPrizes started generating its wave of national publicity, there had been quite a bit of national press about me and the Youth Entrepreneur of the Year Award. One such story was picked up in Japan, translated, and run in the *Nikkei*, where it was read with great interest by a Japanese entrepreneur named Takechika Tsurutani.

Takechika Tsurutani, who likes to be called simply "Taka," was CEO of a Tokyo-based company called Future Institute Corp., whose mission was to teach teenagers and middle-school students how to use the Internet. The Future Institute is also the parent company of FutureKids, a school where Japanese children can go to take computer lessons. Taka had founded FutureKids just the previous fall and was brainstorming for ways to promote the company and its message.

As technologically advanced as Japan is, and as much as we tend to think of Japan as being the leader in all things electronic, this was at least one way in which they were then lagging far behind the United States. Back in 1999, the Japanese had virtually no computers or Internet access in their schools or homes. There was no way for most teenagers to learn about computers or to use the Internet— at least not without going to one of Taka's FutureKids programs.

When it came to video games and other electronics, such as cell phones, the Japanese kids were light-years ahead of American kids. But amazingly, when it came to the Internet and computers in general, it was the exact reverse.

There were two main reasons for the lack of technology in the Japanese schools. First were the prohibitively expensive phone charges. In Japan, residents and businesses alike were being charged $0.10 per minute, even for local phone calls. The cost of maintaining dial-up Internet access in the school systems would have been exorbitant.

The second reason is Japan's tight family culture. Family structure lies at the core of Japanese life. Children often don't leave home before their twenty-ninth birthday. Japanese parents support their children for all those years, and in return, their children respect, honor, and obey them. It would be unheard of for a child to pursue an interest in computers or the Internet if a parent did not approve of this choice.

Taka was one person who clearly saw how far behind Japan was in this critical area, and he had a big vision: he wanted to see every Japanese child become computer-literate and Internet-savvy by 2005.

When Taka read the *Nikkei* story about me and the Young IT Entrepreneur of the Year Award, he instantly knew he wanted to hire this young American kid to be a board member and spokesperson for his company. Essentially he wanted me to be an ambassador of the Internet to the youth of his country.

He e-mailed me and said:

> We would like to invite you to become an advisory board member to our company, to come to Japan and help us grow in our mission to teach teenagers here how to use computers and the Internet. We'd like to fly you to Japan to spend a week with us, and because you're a minor, we're going to pay to fly someone with you.

I thought this was extremely cool, and I forwarded the e-mail to my dad, who was just starting to learn how to use e-mail. Basically, he knew how to hit "Reply" or "Forward," so he hit "Reply" and wrote:

Right. I'll believe it when I see two plane tickets to Japan.

When I read his e-mail, I thought he had a pretty good point. After all, the guy lived halfway around the world. There was a good possibility that this thing would never materialize.

But sure enough, two weeks later, what showed up at my parents' house but two first-class tickets to Japan, along with a ten-day itinerary putting us up in a top hotel. We were set to go.

My dad and I had no idea what to expect, but whatever we could have possibly imagined, it would never have come close to the reality of that first trip to Japan. Of course, I didn't speak a word of Japanese, and knew very little about the country or its culture. I had no clear sense of exactly why Taka wanted me to come, or what would be expected of me once I arrived. In fact, I really didn't know much about FutureKids.

But I did know one thing: this was an opportunity I wouldn't dream of passing up. My mother had always said that travel was the best kind of education there is, and I believed it was important to be open to new experiences. And especially in today's business world, it's important to have a good sense of what's happening in the rest of the world. Business is globalizing at lightning speed — these days, it's often just as easy to extend even a small business overseas as it is to go across the state.

We left Roanoke at seven or eight in the morning, flew to Atlanta, and from there took a nonstop fourteen-hour flight to Tokyo. Because of the time difference, we arrived at about noon the following day, feeling like we'd been flying for days. We were both exhausted and looking forward to getting to our hotel right away. We desperately needed to get some rest, and figured we'd probably have at least a few hours before going to meet with Taka.

We couldn't have been more wrong.

As we stepped off the plane, we saw media everywhere — a

crowd of probably twenty or thirty reporters with a bristling phalanx of microphones, camera flashes going off, TV cameras whirring, and people speaking Japanese at a mile a minute. It was bedlam. With a start, my dad and I realized there must have been a celebrity traveling with us on the plane. We turned around and craned our necks, looking back to see who was the center of all this attention. We hadn't seen anyone famous on the plane, at least no one we recognized, and since we'd been sitting in first class, we ought to have seen any famous faces there.

I turned back to the throng of reporters, and one of them had enough command of English to ask me, "Are you from Virginia?" I said that yeah, I was. And suddenly everyone starting yelling, "Kamelon! Kamelon! Kamelon!"

The celebrity was *me*.

The person they were looking for, the reason for all the microphones and flashes and TV cameras, was *me*. What we didn't realize was that Mr. Tsurutani had spent a huge amount of money promoting this visit to every media outlet in Japan. And much to the astonishment of both of us, there was no bigger news going on in Japan at that moment than *Kamelon! Kamelon! Kamelon!*

Suddenly a sharp-looking young man appeared at my side and snapped in excellent English, "Mr. Johnson! Come with me, please — just walk with me!" It was Taka.

He took off at a clip and we followed in a daze, cutting right through the mass of reporters and TV cameras. We found ourselves on a moving walkway, with the crowd of reporters flanking us on the carpets on either side, running backward with their bulky video equipment so they could keep pace with us as they shot footage and fired questions at me. I don't know how it was humanly possible to run backward with all that equipment and not come crashing down, but they managed it.

Someone shouted at me, "Kamelon! What are you going to share with the Japanese teenagers?"

As my dad and I kept running after Taka, I replied, "Well, I'm here to share my own experiences and hope that they might start their own businesses, too." To hear the buzz this set off, you would have thought I'd said I was here to announce a solo mission to Mars in a hot-air balloon.

As I said before, things are very different in Japan than they are in the United States. When kids grow up, after they graduate from school, they generally come back home and live with their parents until they're nearly thirty years old. A Japanese teenager would never start his own business without his parents' approval. These people had never heard of such a thing as a young entrepreneur starting his own business. It wasn't just Taka's clever promotional skills; this was genuinely newsworthy to them.

Taka and a contingent of Japanese airport security escorted us through the airport, bypassing all customs and security and leading us straight to a curbside limousine. We piled into the long car and slammed the doors, and my dad said, "Whoooh! Finally! Let's go to the hotel."

From the front seat, Taka leaned back and said, "Okay, but we have one press conference to do first."

And we were off to our "one press conference," which would be followed by another, and another, and another. We didn't know it yet, but we wouldn't make it to our hotel room until eleven-thirty *that night*.

At the first press conference, I was to announce that I was going to be their spokesperson. I still knew very little about what their company even did. Plus, I was exhausted from our trip. (Although it was noon for them, it was late at night for us.) And I'd never been part of a media event like this before, let alone being the center of it.

In the United States, I'd been in the newspapers and had a handful of taped interviews. Here I was all over TV and radio—often live. It was an absolute media frenzy. They told me I was bigger than Mariah Carey, who had been on this same show the day before. In fact, they said, I was bigger news than *anyone* from the United States. It was ridiculous. Suddenly I was being treated like a rock star.

When we got to the press conference, we found there were as many cameras there as had been at the airport. In fact, we were actually being broadcast on live television as a feature on all the local lunchtime newscasts. Here I was, fifteen-year-old Cameron Johnson from the United States, on live television throughout Japan.

I didn't have time to be nervous. I didn't even have time for culture shock; I was in media shock—and having a blast.

Fortunately, Taka was translating, and whenever they asked a question about FutureKids, he would answer them in Japanese and then tell me (in English) what he'd just said. I had read a bio sheet on Taka and had the chance to look at an English version of their Web site, but my knowledge of their enterprise was pretty sketchy, and I was getting an education along with the reporters.

As soon as it ended, we did three more press conferences in different places around Tokyo. And that wasn't all; they had me scheduled to deliver a speech that evening!

Giving that speech was pretty rough. I felt as if I'd been up for a week. Fortunately, I had to pause every thirty seconds for the translator to translate, then someone would ask a question and we'd wait some more while the question was translated, so I had a few minutes to think about each question. Besides, since nobody but the translator knew what I was saying, I told myself I couldn't really mess up too badly, could I?

As he left us at our room, Taka said good night and added, "I'll be here at eight-thirty in the morning to get you." We were completely wiped out. All the next day I yawned my way through the interviews. It was intense.

I started holding media events from the moment we landed in Japan, and it never let up the whole time we were there. We did ten to fifteen interviews a day, with media coming in and out, again and again. It was pretty grueling, but a lot of fun, too.

I spoke at Internet symposia, some of them with audiences of five hundred or more. I spoke to the graduating class at Tokyo Digital Hollywood, which was fascinating. It was such a whirlwind. When we were out in traffic, every time the streetlight would change I'd say, "Dad, there are more people crossing the street here than there are people at Woodberry!" There'd be six hundred, seven hundred people—and they'd all recognize me from the media coverage.

The traffic was so bad that sometimes the car ride from one interview to the next would take an hour. Taka would sit in the front seat, with my dad and me in the back. Taka had a tiny laptop with a cellular modem card. This was back in 2000, remember, and I'd never seen anything like it. I would say, "Hey, could I check my e-mail?" and he'd reach back and just hand me his laptop. I was blown away; I thought it was the most amazing thing I'd ever seen. He also had a cell phone that was twice as tiny and twice as cool as anything we had in the States: paper-thin and incredibly light-weight. I could see that Japan was indeed at the cutting edge of con-sumer technology—this was where all the hottest new gadgets started out. They're always way ahead of us.

Taka actually bought me my own cell phone so that he and I could communicate whenever we were separated and so his staff could find me if they needed me for an interview. It works only in Japan (they have a unique cell phone protocol there that doesn't work in any other country), so I brought it back with me on our sec-ond trip to Japan. I still have it today.

I soon noticed that the prices in Japan were outrageous. Our hotel was $795 a night. Breakfast: $100 for toast and orange juice. I remember orange juice being $12 a glass. (Although, I have to add, just the other day I noticed it was $5.00 a glass at the Westin here in D.C., so maybe we're catching up.)

I started thinking about Taka's costs. Our first-class plane tick-ets ran something like $10,000 apiece for my dad and me, and we ended up going over there twice. With breakfast and amenities, accommodations were running at well over a grand a day, for a total of nearly thirty days. We went out to very nice restaurants; I remem-ber one meal noticing a bill of $1,500, just for Taka plus me and my dad. And Taka must have spent a huge amount on promotion, both before we arrived and while we were there.

But you know what? I'll bet he got a return of at least ten times whatever he spent. Nothing gives you credibility like the press—and the press my visit generated gave him the kind of mileage no amount of money can buy.

Taka had the rights to FutureKids for the whole country of

Japan. At the time I think he had some twenty-seven franchises where kids came and paid to take computer classes. His goal was to bring his program into the school system there—and having me there was a great way to build the value of his learning technology. He could say, "Look at this kid—look at what's happening in America. We're behind—we have to catch up and then stay ahead of the United States!" That was the whole strategy behind his bringing me over there, and it was brilliant.

When the ten days ended and we were at last leaving Japan, we headed to Tokyo Nanita International Airport. After we said our good-byes to Taka, it was finally just the two of us, my dad and me, sitting at the airport waiting to board. We looked at each other and said, "Whew! Back to normal!"

Suddenly I looked up and noticed a girl, just a few years older than I, standing next to us, politely waiting to speak. She held out a Magic Marker and said what sounded like, "Sine, priest?"

After ten days, I'd gotten pretty good at understanding their English, but it still took me that split second of puzzlement before I understood what she was saying:

"Sign, please?"

I didn't know what she was talking about—and then I did. Of course, one last autograph seeker. I looked for something to sign. Her dad was standing there beaming, so proud that his daughter was meeting me. I looked at him and then back at her. Along with the Magic Marker, she was holding out her pocketbook.

She wanted me to *sign* her pocketbook.

It was a Prada.

So I signed it with a Magic Marker, "Cameron Johnson," right across her $600 Prada pocketbook. Welcome to the weird world of celebrity.

Even six months later, when we returned for a second Japan trip, while I wasn't hounded this time by the same kind of media attention, people still recognized me everywhere. We would walk down the street and hear a voice shout, "Oh, there's Mr. Kamelon!," and suddenly I was signing autographs again.

In fact, the second trip ultimately created even broader public exposure for me than the first—because I was there to promote a book about me and my businesses.

During the first trip, a Japanese author approached me and proposed writing my biography—in Japanese. "I'll do the writing," he explained, "and we'll publish it under your name." They had all the contracts drawn up, and it sounded exciting to me. He was a bestselling business author; I figured we couldn't go wrong.

We spent two days with the man in nonstop interviews, for twelve straight hours a day. A few months later they came out with a 185-page book—in Japanese only—titled *15-Year-Old CEO*. Before long, there were two more first-class tickets in the mail from Taka: we were on our way back to the Land of the Rising Sun. That August, six months after our first visit, my dad and I returned to Japan to promote the book on a six-city book tour.

Our first trip to Japan had lasted about ten days; this time we stayed nearly twice as long. Although we were not mobbed by the press when we arrived, the second trip introduced me to yet another aspect of celebrity, as I sat in Japanese bookstores with two hundred to three hundred people lined up for me to sign their copies of *15-Year-Old CEO*.

It got great reviews, was all over the Japanese media, and went to number four on the Japanese business bestseller list.

Growing up, I'd learned a lot about how to run a business by spending time at my dad's dealership and going on business trips with my parents. My experiences in Japan opened my eyes to a whole new level of huge, cutting-edge business. They also introduced me to a completely different culture, which included a very different set of business values.

One of the most intriguing of these experiences was meeting an especially shrewd and accomplished friend of Taka's who ran Tokyo Digital Hollywood, where I'd given a talk. This guy was so wealthy he drove a Range Rover, which in Japan is like driving a Ferrari over here, because *nobody* there had SUVs.

One night he took us out to dinner at a seriously expensive restaurant, after which he brought us to see his offices. I was surprised to find that some of his employees were still there, working away. If they didn't get their work done during the day, Taka's friend told us, they'd stay easily till ten or eleven at night. One guy was spending the night there sleeping on a couch so he'd be ready to pick up where he'd left off early the next morning. This wasn't explained to us as something amazing or outrageous; this was *normal.*

I thought of my mother, catching naps on her cot tucked off to the side of her parents' office. My mom and the Japanese.

It was a vivid demonstration of what tremendous work dedication the Japanese have. They may take it to an extreme, but still it was amazing to see the breadth and the depth of their commitment to excellence.

Don't get me wrong: I'm not saying there's anything heroic or laudable about being a fanatic about work or focusing on business to the exclusion of everything else. Even though my parents went through a period when they worried about whether I was developing a "normal" life, they eventually realized they had nothing to worry about. (As I like to put it, "they were just going through a phase.") I've always made time for my friends, for soccer, and for family, and always will—and I hope you do, too. There's nothing noble or admirable about becoming enslaved by your work.

What I admired so much about what I saw in Japan wasn't so much the long hours they put in, but the passion and dedication they bring to their business. They said they had a lot to learn from us, and I'm sure that's true, but I think I learned some valuable things from them as well.

That dedication extended to market research. The Japanese have a passion for learning everything they can about their customers. One of the principal strategies that Nintendo used to create some of the most popular video games of all time was constant, painstaking research into their customers' interests and preferences. And that same passion for attention to customers is shared by one of Nintendo's principal competitors, Sega Enterprises Ltd.

Another businessman Mr. Tsurutani introduced me to was Isao Okawa, the CEO of Sega, which had just come out with its Dreamcast console. Dreamcast was the first game console to combine video game play with online connectivity, allowing gamers to communicate online and even play games with each other, real-time, from anywhere in the world.

I went to their headquarters and met Mr. Okawa. He asked me, "If I give you some samples of our new Dreamcast consoles, do you think you could report back to me and tell me what your friends like and dislike?" Of course I agreed, and sure enough, shortly after I returned to the States, a tractor-trailer showed up at the Woodberry campus carting a hundred brand-new Dreamcasts along with hundreds of games. It blew my mind. At $200 a pop (retail price), this was $20,000 worth of brand-new Dreamcasts, along with a good $30,000 or $40,000 worth of software and peripherals.

Mr. Okawa asked me if I would divide the hundred units into two groups, give fifty to kids and the other fifty to parents, so they could keep in touch through the devices. He wanted to know not only what kind of feedback the kids gave, but also whether the parents found the consoles useful. I was pretty sure the parents would not participate that well, and convinced him we should just give them to kids, who would put far more time and energy into our product sampling.

For months afterward, I consulted with Sega and gave them all sorts of feedback, critiques, and suggestions, many of which they took. At the time, Dreamcast was losing money, and their strategy was to let the console be a loss leader and count on making their money back as the consumer bought games and accessories. But their break-even point was roughly three games. I suggested that they drop the console altogether and concentrate on making games for other manufacturers' systems. In the end, that's exactly what they did; Dreamcast was their last game system.

Of all the lessons I learned in Japan, I think the most important was that in this modern, media-driven world, becoming a public figure is to some extent part and parcel of being a successful entrepreneur, which goes back to the issue of personal branding.

Of course, this will vary from person to person. Some people are naturally more comfortable being in the spotlight, while others are shy or simply more private people. And obviously, not every successful businessman is going to become nationally known or go through the kind of media frenzy I experienced in Japan. But even if only on a smaller scale at the local level, if you want to build a successful business, it's going to be important to embrace the notion of being a public figure in your community.

To a great extent, you are your brand. You may think people are buying your product or service, but ultimately what they are buying is *you*.

What this also means is that sooner or later, if you want to build a successful business, you'll want to become comfortable speaking in public.

I've heard a statistic that Americans rank public speaking as their number one fear, with fear of death ranking a distant fifth. If that's true, I have some advice for Americans: go overseas and give your first speech in a country where nobody can understand you.

My experience in Japan was probably the best way to learn public speaking, because I was talking to people who had no idea what I was saying. What's more, they were all people I didn't even know; I didn't have to worry about them talking about me afterward.

But in September 2000, just after returning from my Japanese book tour, I had my first opportunity to give a major speech — and to an English-speaking audience right in my hometown of Roanoke, Virginia.

Junior Achievement sponsored an annual event where they would induct a major business leader into their Southwest Virginia Business Hall of Fame. That year, they were inducting two community icons: entrepreneur Elizabeth Bowles (the organization's first woman inductee) and Dr. Paul Torgerson, president of Virginia Tech. And guess who they wanted to be the keynote speaker for their eleventh annual Hall of Fame event?

The fifteen-year-old CEO.

To tell the truth, I was pretty nervous about giving this speech. Appearing at the awards ceremony at the Atlanta Ritz-Carlton was one thing — it was an exciting event, and the three of us who were being honored as finalists were certainly at center stage—but we weren't called on to speak.

And giving all those press conferences and appearances in Japan . . . well, that was a surreal experience, and I was certainly in the limelight, probably more so than at any other time in my life. But as I said, I was always speaking to an audience who didn't speak English, so I could rely on my translator (who was often Taka). What's more, in Japan I was treated as such a celebrity that everyone was all primed to be impressed with whatever I had to say anyway. It would have been hard to mess that up.

But here? Giving a keynote to an audience of businesspeople in Roanoke? I could imagine messing *that* up. I could imagine it very easily.

I was a Cub Scout for years, and now the famous Scout motto came back to me: "Be prepared." Probably the single most important thing I have learned about public speaking is to be prepared—*very* prepared. You really can't practice too much for a speech or a media appearance.

For my Hall of Fame speech, I typed out a script—double-spaced, because that's easier to read, especially when you're nervous—and practiced reading it over and over. I read it out loud dozens of times.

My parents also gave me coaching. My dad had never really given speeches per se, but he'd certainly been in front of large groups many times, and he had some great pointers to share. At one point in my speech, I was planning to say that there were three major differences in something or other (I forget what exact point I was making), and my dad said, "Cameron, when you get to this part, use your hands. Actually count off those three points with your fingers." It was good advice, and I followed it. I knew it would put me at ease, because I naturally use my hands when I talk anyway.

The most helpful piece of advice I remember from my parents was, "Just look up—look at the audience." My dad said, "Just connect with one person at each table; no one will know which one you're looking at, and everyone will feel like they're involved."

He was exactly right, and now I love that feeling of connecting with different people in the room. Even if you're delivering the same message you've given before, even if you're reading from the exact same set of notes, every speech is a unique experience—because each time, you're interacting with a different group. You're going to receive different reactions and responses, different questions.

Over the years since then, I've learned lots of specifics about how to address audiences effectively. For example, when you first arrive at the podium, adjust the mike before you start speaking. Once you begin, stand flat on both feet and don't lean on the podium or shift your stance. This changes the tone of your voice, and the audience will notice it and feel uneasy. It's important not to start your speech with small talk, like you're "warming up," even though that's what a lot of amateur speakers do. Start your talk off with a clear, firm point—let your audience know you're in command of your topic. It will make them relax, because they know they're in good hands.

But the most important thing I've learned about public speaking is this: be yourself. It's okay to be nervous, and if you are, there's no point in trying to hide it. For one thing, it never works—it only makes your nervousness more obvious. And for another thing, your audience knows that if they were in your shoes, they'd be nervous, too. If you have something valuable to tell them, they'll cut you the slack you need. Focus on your message and the value you want to bring to your audience, and don't think about how you look or what impression you're making—if you're genuine about your message, all that will take care of itself. Authenticity goes a long way; people sense it and respond to it.

When I arrived at the event, I was definitely nervous, but I knew that I was as prepared as I could be. I'd done all that I could; there was nothing else to do now but give the speech. It's like anything you do: you do your best, and rest content with that. I approached the podium, feeling more exposed than I ever had before. It was nerve-racking—and at the same time, it was exhilarating.

I gave the speech. When I was finished, I got a standing ovation.

Of course, the crowd may have been easy on me because I was only fifteen years old. But I think the applause was genuine, and that all the preparation had paid off. It felt like I'd hit my stride and delivered the address I wanted to deliver.

Now I give speeches all the time, and the more I give, the more I love it. It's not that I revel in the attention — it's that I love having the platform to share what I have to share. This more public part of being an entrepreneur is closely related to what got me into business in the first place: I love selling. Sharing what I've experienced and learned in life and business with an audience is very much like telling my next-door neighbors about our delicious tomatoes.

8

Don't Be Afraid to Negotiate

People sometimes ask me if I've ever been taken for a ride by anyone in my business dealings, given that I was so young and considering how tough the business world can be. They have a point. Chances are good that somewhere along the line, someone will try to force unfavorable terms on you or even bully you, especially if they're with a company that's much bigger than yours, and you need to be prepared to watch out for your interests. You can't let yourself be pushed around or taken advantage of, even by the "big guys." If you're going into business for yourself, it's essential that you become comfortable with the process of negotiating.

Effective negotiation means coming from a place of total confidence. It's just like effective selling: you need to know, with rock-solid conviction, the value of what you're offering, and have a clear sense of what you want from the other party. To know where you are willing to give, and where you are not.

The ideal negotiation is always a genuine win for both parties. However, sometimes it works to compromise—and sometimes it doesn't. There are times when you need to be able to take a position and stick to your guns, no matter how formidable the odds may seem. During my sophomore year at Woodberry, when I had just turned sixteen, I had an experience that drove this lesson home for me.

One day in December 2000, our doorbell at home rang. We weren't expecting company, but we know practically everyone in our neighborhood and have tons of friends and relatives all living within the few blocks around us, and people drop by all the time. As it turned out, this visit was from neither a friend nor a relative.

My mom went to answer the door—and came back with an odd look on her face and some papers in her hand. "It was a process server," she said. She looked at me. "You've been served."

A deputy from the local sheriff's office had come by with a set of legal papers to serve on me. We opened the papers and read through them with disbelief.

I was being sued by the Ford Motor Company for trademark infringement.

Back in early '99, when I was growing MyEZMail and getting ready to launch MyEZShop, I was in the habit of buying and selling domain names. It was an interesting trade, occasionally lucrative, but more of a hobby than a business, and I didn't keep it up for very long. However, as I mentioned in chapter 4, there was one domain name purchase I made that would eventually make me the target of a major lawsuit.

This was it.

In March 1999, my dad had called me up from work one day. Ford had just announced that they were going to create a new corporate subsidiary, consisting of Volvo (which they had just bought), Jaguar, Lincoln Mercury, and Land Rover; this new company would be called the "Premier Automotive Group." As he told me about this, I hopped online and quickly checked to see if anyone had yet registered the domain name, www.premierautomotivegroup.com. Nobody had. I also checked the two other most logical choices, premierautomotivegroup.net and .org. Nope, not those, either.

Then I looked up the U.S. Patent and Trademark Office online (www.uspto.gov), where you can search for a trademark. They hadn't even secured the *trademark* yet. I couldn't believe it: here they were announcing the name of their new division, and they hadn't gotten the trademark.

This was in the covered-wagon days of the Web, and people were just beginning to realize what significant value lay in domain name registration. It was also before any laws were passed disallowing the purchase of domain names for names that were already trade-marked. Even so, I always carefully checked to make sure the domains I was registering were *not* trademarked—and these weren't. In fact, Ford didn't get around to registering their trademark for "Premier Automotive Group" until that October—seven months *after* I had snapped up the URLs.

Before my dad and I finished our conversation, I had put down my Visa card and registered all three domain names for $9.95 apiece. That $29.85 purchase would eventually prove to be quite costly. The question was, costly to whom: Ford Motor Company, or me?

That July, four months after I registered the URLs, the *Roanoke Times* ran an article on me in their "Business" section. During the interview, I was talking with the reporter about the domain name trade and mentioned the Ford group names. I knew that Ford had paid an eighteen-year-old kid in Canada something like $150,000 for the domain name "FordVehicles.com." I figured this had to be at least as important.

What was I looking to get out of this transaction? Well, I thought it would be cool to have a Jaguar XK8. Of course, I didn't have a driver's license yet, but I still thought it would be cool.

So I quipped to the reporter, "I'm going to get a Jag out of this."

One of the hazards of media exposure is that you can say one thing, just one little sentence, something that slips out casually without any forethought—and it can come back years later to haunt you.

Six months later, in January 2000, as I began to experience my first wave of national publicity, that nine-word line was picked up from the *Roanoke Times* article and prominently featured in a short piece on me in *Yahoo! Internet Life*—and presto! My comment had been transformed from local to national.

I'm going to get a Jag out of this.

It showed up again in other articles, too. It was the quote that wouldn't go away. To this day, I don't know for sure if executives at Ford ever saw any of the press that featured this line. Chances are good that they didn't. But if they did, I'm sure it didn't help their mood.

Now here we were, in our living room, a week before Christmas 2000, with the legal papers in front of us. My parents couldn't believe it.

I said, "Don't worry. This is not a big deal."

They looked at me and didn't say anything. But I was pretty sure I knew what they were both thinking: *Just exactly how is this "not a big deal"?!*

I had just turned sixteen, and I was being sued by one of the largest corporations in America.

What's more, I was being sued by the company my father's dealership represented. My dad was a third-generation president of a dealership his grandfather had founded sixty-two years earlier. And his son, who potentially stood in line to become the first fourth-generation Ford dealer in history, was the target of a Ford lawsuit.

"Really. This is no big deal," I repeated. "They're not going to press this. How would it look for them if it got out that they were suing a teenager? And for something they should have been on top of in the first place? It would hurt them a lot more than it would ever help them."

The way I saw it, it had been really careless of Ford to publicly announce this new group without even bothering first to trademark the name, let alone secure the domain names. And if their oversight turned into a lawsuit with a Fortune 100 company pitted against a teenager, the media would eat it up as a modern-day David and Goliath story. If worse came to worst, I could just turn over the domain names and be out my $29.85. But I didn't see any need to give in so easily. I just couldn't see them following through with it.

I started looking on the Internet for "Ford Motor Company trademark infringement" and found that in just the past thirty days, Ford had filed a number of other lawsuits similar to mine against people who had registered domain names that related to the Ford business. For example, one guy had snapped up FordExplorer.com. But these names were trademarked Ford brand names, and Ford was suing these individuals for up to $100,000. I'd been careful never to register any trademarked names. I knew I was in a solid position.

I gave the papers to my company's attorney, Neal Keesee, and explained what had happened. Neal got on it right away and contacted Ford.

They were demanding that I turn over the domain names to them—plus $3,000 in damages. How they came up with that amount I have no idea. (A thousand per URL, I guess, or maybe that's how much their lawyers charged to draft the letter.) They said, "If you'll pay us three grand and give us the names, then we won't move forward with this lawsuit."

Neal replied, "Hey, you have no grounds for this. You didn't even have the trademark when he registered the names! We're not giving you these domain names. If you want to go to court, that's fine—but we're going to countersue."

He also pointed out that taking a teenager to court would probably not be great publicity. This was a shock to them: they had no idea that the guy who'd bought the domain names they wanted was sixteen years old. (They also had no idea I was the son of a Ford dealer, and we never brought that fact to their attention.)

After Neal contacted them and let them know we weren't going to budge, we held our breaths and waited to see what would happen next. And what happened next was . . . nothing. We sat tight and waited. And waited. I was truly not worried about it, but it's safe to say that the unresolved specter of the Ford lawsuit cast something of a pall over that Christmas season.

Weeks turned into months, and the entire next year passed without hearing a word from Ford's lawyers.

Finally, in April 2002, nearly a year and a half after I was served with the original papers, they responded. We agreed on a settlement and I turned over the domain names. I had been afraid that they might drag it out and bleed me dry with attorney's fees, so I was ready to expedite things in any way I could.

It worked out well. Since I promised, I can't reveal the terms, but the *Roanoke Times* reported the event with a bit of a swagger:

He's been sued by the Ford Motor Company and lived (and rather well) to tell about it.

That doesn't happen very often when you mess with the big guys. Still, I didn't see it as any big victory. I'd never intended to go to battle with the company; trading in domain names was an interesting sideline, not my main pursuit.

At the same time, I was glad about the way it worked out. I'd certainly done my part in helping give the corporate world a quick education in some Internet facts of life. I think the fact that so many companies had to spend substantial amounts to get domain names they could have had for under ten bucks, if they'd been on their toes, was a valuable lesson. Sometimes larger corporations learn important truths only when it hits them in their pocketbooks. The corporate world learned pretty fast that they had to take the Internet seriously.

I have absolutely no hard feelings about the lawsuit. I've always loved Ford Motor Company, not only because they've been in my family for four generations, but also as a result of all the good experiences I've had working with them, as we'll see in later chapters of this book. I often say, "If I'm cut, I bleed Ford blue." I have always looked up to Ford Motor Company as one of the greatest American companies, and certainly one with one of the best histories and one of the largest impacts on developing this country in the early years of the twentieth century (Ford was started in 1903).

But you want to know the really amazing thing about the whole saga? To this day, they have *never* used those domain names. Of course, it could be that they just wanted to be sure that nobody else could ever use them. Only here's the thing: I just took a look at the Patent Office Web site before writing this paragraph—and note that they released the trademark last year and reported that they are no longer using the name.

As I said, the best outcome of any negotiation is a mutually beneficial one, where both parties are genuinely happy with the deal they've struck. And when you go into it with win-win as your ideal goal, you may be surprised how often you can achieve it. The archetype of the "wheeling and dealing" business tycoon who's always looking for ways to cut corners and outsmart the other guy is just that: an archetype, not reality. Smart entrepreneurs know that it pays to be generous.

But never confuse generosity with weakness. This is your business: don't be afraid to fight for it if you have to.

When you're faced with a tough negotiation, go into it with complete confidence. Take it as an opportunity to create a defining moment, both for your business and for yourself. Trust that you have the knowledge, skills, and know-how to make the deal happen in a way that works for you.

9

Make Your Own Tough Decisions

One of the biggest mistakes I see people make is thinking that if they become successful, they'll be happy. For me, it's always been the opposite: being truly happy with my life and with the work I do is what *leads* to success, not the other way around.

When you're considering a new business, it's important to consider how financially profitable it will be, what its prospects are in the marketplace, and other business factors. But before any of that, there's an even more important consideration: *Is this something you would love doing?*

If you want genuine success, it's crucial that you listen to your true interests and gain a clear sense of what you really want to be doing, even if it doesn't happen to be what other people think you should be doing. I'm not saying your friends' and family's opinions aren't important or that you shouldn't ever listen to them. But they aren't going to live your life, you are.

Respect is a powerful motivator. People often pursue a line of work because they think that by doing so, they will gain others' respect. But the most powerful type of respect by far is the respect you hold for yourself.

Money is another motivator. But if you go into a certain line of work purely because you think it will bring you a good income, you're asking the cart to push the horse. To me, money is evidence that I'm pursuing what makes me happy. It's not the goal, it's a type of feedback that tells me I'm on track in pursuit of my goals.

I've known people who felt they were stuck in jobs that weren't bringing them any joy. I'm fortunate to be able to say that I have never felt that way. I have always loved and been fascinated with every business I've started. If I hadn't felt that way about them, I wouldn't have started them.

There's no doubt about it: successful people know how to work hard. But people often don't realize that most truly successful entrepreneurs also know how to play. I certainly put a lot of time into my businesses, and I have done so ever since I was nine. But I have never let my businesses, control my life. My friends and family and sports and other aspects of my life have always been just as important to me as running a successful business and making money. You can always lose your money and lose your business, but good friends are forever.

Still, it is your path you're looking for, and nobody else can find it for you. Sometimes finding and following it means you will disappoint people who are important to you. As with business negotiation, there are times when you can compromise—and times when you can't. Sometimes these can be very difficult decisions, and only you can call those shots.

During my Christmas vacation in 2000—right at the same time I was being served with papers from Ford Motor Company—I faced one of those decisions, and it was one of the most difficult ones I've ever had to make.

By this time, a lot had changed about my life at Woodberry. Even in my first few months there, any chance I'd had at keeping a low profile or living a "normal" freshman life were utterly blown. The national wave of publicity from SurfingPrizes had penetrated every corner of my life, and most people who knew me had by now heard something about "Cameron and his businesses."

At one point in 2000, a team from *BusinessWeek* came down from New York to do a photo shoot and spent the day there, eventually settling on the Woodberry library as the venue for the session.

When a team of New York photographers spends a day shooting you in the campus library, word gets around.

The administration at Woodberry loved it. They were already one of the top ten college prep schools in the country, and they had a great name—but all this media attention wasn't hurting them at all. And even though they happened halfway around the world, my trips to Japan had plenty of impact at Woodberry, too, and not just when a truckload of Dreamcasts showed up.

Soon after my sophomore school year began, I got word that the Japanese media were flying over to do a story on me for the Japanese equivalent of NBC's *Today* show. In fact, they were sending over their version of Matt Lauer to come to Woodberry and conduct an interview with me for live broadcast back in Japan.

One day, I got a call on my cell phone from the Japanese crew: they'd just arrived at the airport in D.C. and were on their way down. Since this was going to be broadcast live as part of a morning show in Japan, we would have to do the production here at about six in the evening. They decided on the school's alumni lounge for our staging area and impromptu TV studio.

Woodberry is a small school, with a total population of about four hundred students. As the crew spent the day preparing for the live broadcast, a constant stream of students walked by the lounge on their way to and from classes, watching this knot of TV technicians bustling around. It was a bit of a spectacle. Whenever anyone who didn't know me asked what was going on, they got a shrug and a simple answer: "Oh, that's for Cameron's interview." By this time my friends had gotten pretty used to this sort of thing.

We shot the interview that evening, with the tech crew pausing every minute or so to insert translation. It was a weird experience standing at dinnertime in the alumni lounge of Woodberry Forest School in Orange, Virginia—and knowing that as I spoke, millions of people were watching and listening to me over breakfast on the other side of the world.

The Japanese crew was there for two days. It was all quite exciting, but it passed quickly, and soon I was back to dealing with my everyday life on campus . . . except that my "everyday life" as a Woodberry sophomore was growing more and more complicated.

I had good friends there, and there was still a lot about the place that I loved. But I was a year older now, and in a way my concerns were the opposite of what they had been when I first arrived at Woodberry. I wasn't worried about whether I could run a business at Woodberry. I *knew* I could do that—over the previous year I'd built my most successful company yet. At this point, though, I was growing less concerned about my businesses and more concerned about my *life*.

I missed my old friends at Patrick Henry High. I was tired of being at an all-male boarding school, where the only girls I saw were at an occasional mixer. I wanted to have a car. I wanted to have a real job.

I wanted to come home.

That December, when I came home for Christmas break, I went out with all my good friends with whom I'd gone to elementary and middle school. We went to a basketball game together.

I'd just turned sixteen. I was spending time with the friends I'd grown up with, and they were driving their own cars. (We couldn't keep cars at Woodberry.) The girls were looking a lot better to me in high school than they had in middle school. Everything was hitting at once.

There I was, telling my friends how great Woodberry was and how much I loved it there—and the truth was, Woodberry was just about the exact *opposite* of what I'd pictured as the typical high school life. My friends were living the life *I* wanted.

I wanted the freedom of being able to travel when I wanted to travel and not be hassled by how I was missing school. Even though the education at Woodberry was probably of a higher caliber than what I would have in the Roanoke public school system, I felt like I was being held back.

And there was one more thing: I met a girl.

The summer before, between my freshman and sophomore years, I had taken a driver's ed course in Roanoke. Of course, I wouldn't be doing any driving at Woodberry, but I would be turning sixteen in November, and I certainly wasn't going to pass up getting my license.

The class lasted only a few weeks, but that was long enough for me to be attracted to a classmate. Stephanie Harvey was my age, but I'd never met her before because she went to Cave Spring, a rival high school. I liked her, and we became friends. (Stephanie and I are still good friends, and we manage to see each other often.)

Now that I was back in town for a few weeks at Christmas break, Stephanie was on my mind. While I was out with friends one day I mentioned her, and someone said, "Stephanie Harvey? Well, her sister's right over there."

Her sister? I didn't know she had a sister. We were introduced, and we talked. Her name was Emily. I'd never met anyone quite like her.

Emily Harvey was not only very attractive (one of the best-looking girls in Roanoke), she was also very bright and very down-to-earth. I've never been a shy person, but still, I couldn't believe how easy it was to talk with her. It seemed effortless. I've had other girlfriends since Emily, but nobody quite like her, and no one who swept me off my feet the way she did. We were really close; I shared *everything* with her. She was my best friend as well as my first love, and we're still close friends today.

That night I ended up using my brand-new driver's license to give Emily and her friends a ride home; they were a year younger and couldn't drive yet. Then I drove myself home, but I couldn't get Emily out of my mind. Meeting her had made it crystal clear: I really missed living this normal high school life.

The next morning I told my parents, "I'm not going back to Woodberry."

My dad said, "What do you mean? Yes you are!"

I said, "No, I'm not. I want to live a normal teenage life! I want to go to school here in Roanoke, drive a car, have a job, and date. I'm not going back to Woodberry."

But they insisted that I return to Woodberry for the balance of my sophomore year. We argued about it, and I pretty much decided to give in, at least for the moment. When Christmas break came to an end, I headed back to Woodberry.

I don't know if I was fully aware of it at the time, but all I'd really done was go back to school to pack my bags. When I got back to the campus in Orange, I called Emily. In fact, we talked on the phone constantly during those first few days back—and those first few days were all it took. I knew then that there was no way I was going to stay. At Christmas with my parents, I had lost the battle— but I was not going to lose the fight.

We usually buy into decisions on emotion, and it's only later that we take the time to sift through those decisions and find logical ways to rationalize them. I'd already decided that I wasn't staying at Woodberry. Now I just had to rationalize it to my parents.

I thought about calling my mom, but I knew she'd just say, "Talk to your dad." So I called up my dad at work. When he came on the line, I said, "Hi, Dad, it's Cameron. Dad, I'm not staying here, I'm leaving. I'm coming home."

I can only imagine what was going on in his mind. Probably some variation of, *Oh, dear Lord, I thought we'd settled this!*

He said, "You're *not* leaving."

I said, "I am. Dad, I want to come home. I miss you and mom. I miss my friends. I want to have a normal high school life, and it'll help me run my businesses. And I'll still get into the same college I would if I stayed here, but I'm not staying here."

I thought this was pretty compelling—especially the "I miss you and mom" part. But he was not prepared to budge.

So I did something that was probably unfair, in a way, but in another way, was as fair as could be: *I used his own sales tactics on him.*

Years ago, I learned from my dad that your goal in sales is not to convince anyone that they want what you're selling; it's to help remove any obstacles to their getting what they *already know* they want. When a customer on the showroom floor is hesitating about the car he wants to buy, the solution is not to harangue him or tell him all the reasons he ought to buy. The solution is to ask him,

"What would have to happen for you to sign the papers and drive this car off the lot today? What would it take?"

So I said, "Dad, what would it take for you to be okay with my leaving Woodberry and coming home?"

My dad is no fool; after all, he was the one I'd learned from. He didn't hesitate for an instant, and I think he probably thought he had me with his answer.

"It would take you reimbursing me for the tuition we've already paid for your year there and when the summer starts you have to get a job and not just run your own businesses. You've always made good business decisions in your life, Cameron. If you're serious about this one, all you'll need to do is write me a check for twenty-five grand."

Game, set, match.

There was no way I would call him on *that* bluff, was there?

Of course there was.

I said, "Okay, you know my dresser, up in my bedroom? There's a checkbook there. Could you grab it, and bring it with you when you come up to get me? I'll write you the check when you get here."

And I did.

On January 20, I left Woodberry Forest School for good and returned home to Roanoke.

As badly as I wanted to come home, it wasn't easy to leave Woodberry. I had forged strong ties during the year and a half I was there. I knew I would miss my new friends, and I did. They were an amazing group of guys from all over the country, many of them really brilliant, and their company and friendship were hard to leave behind. Even now, six years later, I still have friends from Woodberry whom I talk with, and for the rest of my time in high school, Emily and I would make the three-hour drive up to Orange every now and then to visit them.

Still, I didn't regret my decision then, and I've never regretted it since.

When I'm invited to speak to groups of young people, I often tell this story to illustrate a point. There have been several moments in my life when I've had to make key decisions—decisions that would totally change the path of my life. Each time, once I made and acted on that decision, I never gave a moment to wondering about whether it was the right or the wrong choice. I may think very hard about it beforehand, but once I make the decision, I never question it, never second-guess it. In fact, I never even think about it again.

The decision to shut down SurfingPrizes was one of those; the decision to leave Woodberry was another.

What will truly make you happy? It's not always easy to know the answer, but nobody else can find it for you. Listen carefully to your inner sense, and don't be afraid to act on it. You'll come out way ahead—in your work, and in your life, too.

My parents were crushed. They loved Woodberry and everyone there. I was not the only one who had forged strong ties in Orange; during my time there, my parents had made some good friends among both parents and faculty.

At the same time, while they weren't happy about my leaving, they were really happy to have me home again. I don't think my mom had realized just how much she missed me. I'll have to admit, the same was probably true for me, and after that we never had another cross word. They say that sometimes you have to go away to appreciate what you have. Maybe that was true for me.

Don't get me wrong: it's not like everything was perfect domestic harmony. I had just turned sixteen, I was smack dab in the middle of my teenage years, and as I said before, it seemed to me that everything my parents said was wrong. (Looking back, now that I'm twenty-one, I realize that only *half* of everything they said was wrong.) But we've always been close, no matter what happened to be going on at the moment, and there were no major upheavals between me and my parents after my move home from Woodberry Forest.

I dated Emily Harvey for the next year and a half, and we're still best friends today. As I write these words, in fact, she lives about a mile from where I live in Blacksburg, Virginia.

A few weeks after I came back to Roanoke for good, I was talking with Emily about that phone conversation I'd had with my dad, and I explained that in order to get him to agree to let me come home, I'd had to reimburse him the $25,000 for my Woodberry tuition.

She was floored. "How are you going to come up with that kind of money?!" she asked me.

"It's done," I said, "I paid him in one lump sum, the day he came and got me."

Her eyes went wide. "You had twenty-five grand just lying around?!"

I told Emily a little bit about what I did, and she was stunned. Up to this point, she'd had no idea that I owned businesses or had a whole other life as an entrepreneur. Even though I'd had quite a bit of publicity by this time, Emily hadn't been around for any of it, and it was not my habit to go around talking about my business life.

I generally don't talk about my businesses with my friends (except those friends I've gotten to know through business), and I don't like to talk about how much money I make or my net worth. Even in media interviews, when reporters ask me, for example, what selling price I got for a certain business, I'll give them only a general answer and not a specific number. It's too easy for these things to get out of perspective. And in terms of my friends, I don't want people to have some sort of preconceived notions about me. I'd rather they just like me for who I am.

Even through high school, there were quite a few friends of mine who were unaware of my business life. And it's not like I dressed differently or had a Rolex or a fancy car. (I'd rather put my money into investments or growing my businesses than show it off with trinkets and fancy things I don't need.) I didn't act any differently from anyone else my age. There's no way anyone would have necessarily noticed anything different about me.

It's almost as if I've lived three separate lives that have never really overlapped.

There's my life with my family. We've always been a really tight-knit group, practically all of us living within a radius of a few miles of one another and mostly within the same four blocks. I have one cousin twelve years older than I, and another two who are twins, both six years older. I was always very close with the three older boys and spent a lot of time with them. Now I also have two younger cousins, girls aged six and four.

Then there is my business life. Over the years there have been a few people like Tommy Kho whom I've grown very close to in business. (Later you'll meet a few more of them.)

And then I have my friends. And that was the best thing about being back at home: I got to spend time again with my best friends, such as Barry Wirt and Matt Bagby.

Barry and I grew up in the same neighborhood together; our dads were good friends, too. Matt and I first met during the summer before fifth grade. Matt had just moved to Roanoke from Arlington; his dad was a prominent attorney who had originally come from here. I met Matt just a few weeks before the fifth-grade school year started when he joined my soccer team, and we became fast friends.

In fact, both Matt and Barry have remained among my best friends right through to the present. Today they are both seniors at the University of Virginia in Charlottesville, where I often go to visit them. (As I write these words, Barry's coming in to visit in Blacksburg tonight, and Matt's joining us tomorrow.)

My parents were concerned that leaving Woodberry would be an academic setback, maybe even hurt my career choices. And maybe they were right; there was no way to know for sure. But I was willing to make that choice. Sometimes friends have to come first.

As it turned out, coming home proved to be a great career move in the long run, because back in Roanoke I became involved with a bricks-and-mortar business that would expand my horizons and experience enormously—more than any formal schooling could possibly have done.

When I left Woodberry and returned to Roanoke, part of the deal my dad made with me was that I would work part-time at the dealership at the end of the school year.

"You're not going to just come back here and do nothing," he had said, which really meant, "You're not going to just hole up in your room and sit on your computer; you're going to get a real summer job out in the real world."

The truth is, I didn't mind this idea at all. Even if it hadn't been part of our deal, I would have taken the job anyway, in part out of respect for my family history and legacy. My great-grandfather had started the business nearly fifty years before I was born, and both my grandfather and my father had followed in his footsteps and worked there. I certainly didn't need the $7.50 an hour I would be paid, but it seemed like an important thing to do.

I'd had summer jobs every summer since I was twelve, when I started working at my aunt and uncle's furniture store, where I helped move and deliver furniture and even did some sales. But this was my first time actually working at the dealership. I started at Magic City Ford on June 13, 2001, stripping defective tires off vehicles.

A year earlier, there had been a huge recall of Firestone tires. It was an eighteen-month ordeal in all; now, a year into the recall, there was still a wave of tire-swapping moving through the dealership. I would take the tires off the vehicles, break them down, and then drill a huge hole in the side of each one with a big power drill. I was getting my hands dirty and learning the business from the bottom up.

I worked in the service department for the second half of June and most of July, then worked in the cleanup department for another thirty days. They needed someone back there to push the others, because when no one's watching them, not much gets done.

Near the end of the summer, I found a place where I could make an even bigger contribution: Internet sales. The salesman on our staff who was responsible for managing our Internet leads wasn't thrilled with the task. I never found out exactly why, whether it was that he didn't like working on the computer or what. So I started doing it.

Some leads came in when people would directly hit our own site; others came in from people visiting the Ford Motor Company site. However it came in, I would take the lead, do all the ground-work and correspondence, then pass it on to a salesman to consummate the deal.

When September came and I started my junior year in the Roanoke school system, I kept on doing the Internet leads, working in the afternoons after school. Since it was all Internet-based, I could have started doing the work from home; in fact, sometimes I did exactly that when I was in a schedule crunch. Most days, though, I came home from school and went on down to the dealership to do the work. In February, when soccer season started back up, I would come home after practice at five-thirty or so, shower, then come in to the dealership for a few hours to catch up. I had my own little office—just a little cubicle, actually, but it was my space, and I loved going in to spend time there.

Who would have thought that this high-tech-oriented teenager would be happier spending his free time after school working in a cubicle at a Ford dealership than playing sports and hanging out with friends at an elite prep school? But that was exactly the case: I was having the time of my life.

And it wasn't just that I loved working the Internet leads; I got a charge out of coming in and seeing what was going on everywhere, just absorbing it all. It was fascinating. Pretty soon I was spending a good forty hours a week at the dealership, and I did that right through my junior and senior years as well. As Internet sales manager, I grew our Internet Sales Department to the point where it was one of the top five in the state, and we had one of the state's highest closing ratios (sales versus leads).

I loved the Internet work, but I was even more fascinated by the dealership itself, by the whole business and every aspect of it. I'd grown up in the car business and had always followed cars. My dad would often drive a different vehicle every week; I remember pleading with him as a little kid, "Dad, drive a Mustang convertible this week. It'll be cool!" (Which he did, and it was.) I grew up knowing everything there was to know about Fords—but I didn't really know the business side. I didn't know anything about selling cars or running a dealership.

There was so much I didn't know—and I wanted to know everything about it. I started bringing things home to study. In my grade school and junior high years, I used to stay up till all hours working on my own Internet companies. Now I was up late every night studying my dad's automobile company.

Leaving Woodberry was not only one of the hardest decisions I ever made, it also proved to be one of the most valuable. Had I continued there throughout my four years of high school, I would never have had the opportunity to learn the ins and outs—literally, the nuts and bolts—of how Magic City Ford worked. I would not have ended up getting the kind of comprehensive, hands-on education in business management that not even the most expensive schooling in the world can offer. And I wouldn't have discovered a calling that in time came to be a true passion. As we'll see in a later chapter, my time at Magic City Ford led eventually to one of the most profitable and long-running businesses of my career.

But even if none of that had happened, it still would have been the right decision.

Building a business is about making decisions; sometimes they're fairly easy, and occasionally they're quite tough. The tough ones are often the defining moments that determine the path you'll end up taking.

Your level of success is determined by the character of your decisions. You won't always know at the time whether you've made the best decision. In fact, often you *can't* know this at the time. But they're yours to make, and no one else's—and the conviction with which you make them and then follow through on them will go a long way toward shaping the character of your business and, for that matter, your life.

10

Adapt or Die

By the middle of 2001 the dot.coms were in full retreat, and the "Internet bubble" continued deflating well into the following year. On October 9, 2002, after a March 2000 high of over 5048.62, the NASDAQ's downward plunge finally hit bottom at 1114.11 before tentatively starting to come back up again.

A lot of people have asked me how the "Internet bubble bursting" affected me and my businesses.

My answer is always the same: "Not at all."

The truth is, it wasn't an "Internet bubble" that burst. What burst was the *online advertising* bubble and the *stock overvaluation* bubble, and this affected those who were highly invested in these over-inflated stocks and the venture capitalists who had given millions of dollars that never should have been invested in the first place.

For those who were in that unfortunate position, the bubble did indeed burst. But the Internet itself did just fine, and so did the business of doing business on the Internet. Just look at the steady stream of Internet companies that not only survived those formative years but also have gone on to become so successful that today they're household names: Amazon, eBay, Google, Netflix, Priceline, Yahoo!, Travelocity, and many, many others.

What made the difference? The soundness of the underlying business model. Too many companies premised their entire plan on the cash cow of online advertising money, and were not quick enough (or paying enough attention) to adjust when that source of revenue started drying up. Tommy, Aaron, and I were carefully watching these trends, and when we shut down SurfingPrizes (exactly six months to the day after the NASDAQ's historic high point), our decision was based in large part on our understanding that the model we were using could not long continue to thrive.

This was not unique to this time or this industry; this is a classic business error—and not just with small businesses or start-ups. Even the largest and smartest companies sometimes fail to adjust to changes in the business climate. In the early '90s, IBM thought the future of computers was in manufacturing the box itself. They failed to realize that the coming boom in desktop PCs would be in software, not hardware. They barely recovered from their mistake. (This is very similar to what was facing Sega when I was in Japan: they needed to shift their focus from hardware to software.)

When you see revenue slowing, you need to do one of two things: find ways to generate additional revenue, or immediately cut your expenses. What companies too often do, instead, is try to "grow their way" out of the crunch. But you can't grow your way out if your basic model is flawed; the only thing you'll "grow" is your losses. And that's exactly what so many dot.com companies did in those years.

At SurfingPrizes, we knew that our model was completely dependent on online advertising. As this resource began shrinking, we had little or no avenues for increasing revenue; thus our only feasible options were to find ways to cut expenses. We weighed those options and didn't like any of them. The only rational choice was to close the company.

I wasn't at all troubled by the "dot.com bust," in part because it was no surprise that the industry was due for a bit of a course correction. Another reason was that at the time, I was happy to focus more of my energy elsewhere. When I left Woodberry and returned to Roanoke at the start of 2001, I started spending more time on my social life.

I was finding that a high school social life is a lot more demanding and absorbing than a middle school social life, and I wanted to throw myself into it. I had a serious girlfriend now, and for the first time, the delicate balancing among school, business, and social life was tipping heavily in favor of my social life. I was not really on the lookout for a new business. For a while, I switched gears.

I kept in touch with Tommy, and the two of us dabbled with a number of smaller Web ideas. These businesses were more like hobbies than serious enterprises, though I continued learning new things from each of them, and they were all valuable stepping-stones to the future—something like a novelist taking time off to write a string of short stories.

Part of what we were doing during that year and a half or so was exploring the changing Internet environment and learning the new rules, even as they were in the process of inventing themselves. We didn't want to invest any major amount of time or money into any of these "short story" companies to grow them further. Sure, we could have put $10,000 or $20,000 worth of advertising into any one of them, and we probably would have generated a good deal more traffic to the site. But we never wanted to take that risk. With each one, we decided we'd rather just let it stay small, earn a little money, and keep building up our capital reserves for investing in something bigger in the future.

Even though so many dot.coms were imploding, there was still plenty of opportunity all around us. There were certainly *some* Web-based businesses that were thriving, and soon we found a way to build on one of those businesses.

Instant messaging was booming, especially among Internet-savvy teenagers (just as a few years later, text messaging via cell phones would become all the rage). This, obviously, was a market we knew well. The dominant player in the field was AOL, with its free AOL Instant Messenger service, also called AIM. (This was not long after the Time Warner AOL merger, a deal that had become an icon of the dot.coms' financial prowess. Ironically, within another few years the conglomerate would drop the "AOL" from its name and become plain "Time Warner" again.)

However, for all its popularity, AIM suffered from a limitation: it provided no way for users to expand their simple user profiles, which for many was an irritating omission. Tommy developed a site called InfiniteProfiles, which let people add pictures and other features to their AIM profiles—in fact, it let you customize and extend your profile *infinitely*.

This was a classic example of catching a market trend at just the right time to meet a huge emerging customer need, and I was intrigued. I made Tommy an offer: if he would bring InfiniteProfiles in to become part of EmazingSites (which I still had up and running), I would give him half the business. He agreed and thus became a 50 percent partner in EmazingSites, which then served as the umbrella under which a number of these little business experiments operated.

The InfiniteProfiles idea caught on and became enormously popular. People began noticing their friends' expanded profiles and wanting the same service for themselves, and before long we had about three hundred thousand registered users—without doing any advertising.

The big question we had to answer before launching InfiniteProfiles was a basic one: How would it make money? We wanted to offer the service for free, because we didn't think enough users would want to pay for it, but financing the site through the kind of online advertising we'd used to such great effect with SurfingPrizes was no longer feasible. We needed a new model.

At first we thought the solution would be to invest in quickly building a large membership base by giving free memberships to anyone who wanted them. Then, once we'd reached a membership of, say, three hundred thousand people, we would start selling premium "Gold status" memberships for $4.95 per year. (Gold status would be essentially the same service, but with ads screened out— we knew how much people hated the onslaught of ads clogging their sites.) At the $4.95 price, we figured we might get as many as 5 to 10 percent of our customers to upgrade, which would mean a revenue of $75,000 to $150,000—*if* people would pay the $4.95.

But then we came up with a better idea.

Tommy and I were always keeping up on the latest trends, exploring other successful sites, and figuring out how they were making money. We discovered an emerging type of company, one that would pay a Web site publisher for sending its members to *their* site to enter a free contest.

We contacted the company, and they said they'd love to have InfiniteProfiles as a client, and would pay us $1.25 for each user who filled out a contest form. They gave us a list of contests and even offered to change them every thirty or sixty days. We noticed that one of their contests gave away a free Land Rover—a vehicle that was quite popular with our user base (eighteen-to thirty-year-olds), and decided that would give us the highest response rate.

Now we had our new model.

We put a clickable button on our main page that said, "Enter our $50,000 Land Rover giveaway—and we'll upgrade your account to Gold status *for free* and remove all the advertisements!" We figured, offering the upgrade for free instead of for a $4.95 fee would result in not 5 or 10 percent but possibly as many as 25 percent of our people to upgrade.

Our estimates weren't bad. I don't remember the exact number, but we ended up giving upgrades to something over fifty thousand of our users—more than 15 percent—which generated a revenue stream to us of well over $60,000. Not bad for a hobby.

And that wasn't the end of it. Once the flow of upgrading members started to die down, we thought we had probably maxed out our revenue, and we sold the business on eBay—for five figures.

The contest-entering strategy we used for InfiniteProfiles had worked so well, it wasn't long before I thought about applying it again, only in a more streamlined, simplified way. I thought, "Why not create a Web site that simply promotes a contest?" Thus was born another of our Internet experiments, ChooseYourPrize.

Setting this site up cost us almost nothing—just a little bit of Tommy's programming time and some hosting off one of my servers. The contest company we used for this site was promoting an annual drawing for $35,000; they had a hundred different ways you could choose to apply the money if you won. You could win a new Lexus, a new SUV, a Disney cruise vacation, or choose among dozens of other options.

It worked smoothly. Quite a few of our members went to the site just to sign up and enter the contest, and the contest company paid us $1.25 for each entrant. At that point we could have invested some money into promoting it more widely, but decided against it, opting to sell it instead. We sold ChooseYourPrize in the spring of 2003 for a five-figure sum.

Search engines were another type of Web innovation that was doing well through these years, and we decided it would be fun to experiment with that model.

Today Google so dominates the search engine world that people use the brand name as a generic verb: "I just googled it" means "I just looked it up on the Internet." Back in 2001, though, the field was still wide open. The different search engines were getting a lot of exposure, and the public was going nuts over the power to find information.

This time, rather than developing our own version from scratch, we decided it would be cheaper and quicker to buy an existing search engine Web site and improve on it. We found and bought a search engine site called SearchOmega, which charged users on a per-click basis. Our business model was simple: we would offer SearchOmega to Webmasters as an effective way to use their advertising dollars to drive traffic to their sites.

We put links to SearchOmega on all our other sites and grew its traffic for a while, but I soon decided it wasn't worth much investment of time, energy, or development money; the context in which search engines operated was changing too rapidly.

I probably could have made a big deal out of SearchOmega and started mentioning it prominently in all my media spots, but I didn't. I had a sense that if I started promoting SearchOmega, I would be going out on a limb. There was nothing unique about it, nothing that warranted media exposure.

I've always made a very conscious choice about which companies I've promoted and which I have not. I want to make sure that whenever I'm featured in the media, I'm representing a great business concept and not just relying on my age. SearchOmega wasn't newsworthy, so I chose not to associate my name with it heavily.

This assessment turned to be right on the money. Just think about all the other search engines that were hot back then—and aren't as hot now. (Remember Lycos? AltaVista? LookSmart? Excite? Dogpile?)

We ended up selling SearchOmega to a private individual in the spring of 2002 for about triple our investment.

InfiniteProfiles was our first effort to capitalize on the Instant Messenger boom, but it was not our last.

As IM rapidly grew in popularity, the "buddy list" had become a major presence on the desktops of hundreds of thousands of Internet users. One of the ways by which people were customizing and personalizing their profiles was by representing themselves with individualized "buddy icons." In fact, there were sites making as much as $10,000 a week and more in advertising from people coming to the site to download buddy icons. I wanted to get into that business.

I found a custom-icon site called AimBuddy, bought it, and had one of my designers change the whole design of the site. In addition to making it look a lot nicer, we also automated it; when I bought it, it had required a lot of manual input by the user. We bought AimBuddy in 2002 and sold it in 2003—once again, for a significant profit.

Another branch of the Internet boom that showed no sign of slowing was the business of music downloading. In the spring of 2001, just a few months before Napster was shut down (it has recently been relaunched as a pay service), a new music download software was launched, named Kazaa. Soon we noticed that most AIM users also were using Kazaa. Once again we had found an emerging new industry that offered intriguing spin-off opportunities.

Apart from the controversy surrounding the legality of such programs, there was a secondary controversy that dogged Kazaa from the start: users complained that the software installed various forms of spyware and adware onto their computers. Aha! We had found a need just waiting to be filled.

I found a company called KazaaGator, which developed and

sold an inexpensive software program ($9.95) designed to block out all the annoying pop-up ads on Kazaa users' computers. The product worked well, but the owner (who also was the developer) wasn't making much money with it, because he didn't really know how to market it—so I bought it from him.

We marketed the product to our existing InfiniteProfiles users and other customers, and in no time the site was profitable. But the music downloading business was going through a volatile time, and it was clear that the future of free-music downloading was sketchy at best.

We sold the company and the technology in the summer of 2003.

In all my years in business, Tommy Kho has been one of my closest partners. I would trust him with just about anything, and the fun of working with Tommy was a big part of what fueled my interest in our string of high school Internet ventures.

But Tommy is two years older than I. As I was starting my junior year in high school, Tommy was starting his freshman year at UCLA. We knew we couldn't keep our partnership going forever. One by one, we had sold most of the ventures we'd brought together under the EmazingSites umbrella, and when we sold Aim-Buddy and KazaaGator in 2003, there wasn't much left. Eventually we sold the domain name, too. Like most of my former businesses, you can still find it on the Internet, but I no longer have anything to do with it and haven't kept up with what it's doing now.

Although Tommy and I went our separate ways, we still talk a few times a year, and we often check in with each other on Instant Messenger. He sits on my desktop every day, on my buddy list. But like me, he's incredibly busy pursuing all sorts of ventures of his own. After graduating from UCLA he did an internship with Google, and then returned to UC at Berkeley, where he's now working on his Ph.D.

He and I have never met face-to-face.

All this experimentation with different Web start-ups had put me in just the right creative frame of mind to recognize an intriguing opportunity when it came along. One day in late 2001, my dad asked me a question: Was there some way we could tweak our dealership's Web site to bring in a little more business? This got me thinking, which led to an idea that prompted another little Internet start-up. Little did I realize at the time that this little project would outlive all the other businesses of my high school years. In fact, it would go on to become my longest-running business ever.

Like most businesses by this time, plenty of car dealerships had Web sites, but most of them really weren't contributing that much to the business. People were just putting up Web sites because it seemed the thing to do, but there wasn't much thought given to how to leverage those sites to increase business in any significant way.

In January I told my dad my idea: What if we put a coupon on our site, and set it up so that people would have to provide us their name, e-mail, and phone number before they could print out the coupon and actually use it?

He thought it was a great idea and suggested that the coupon give customers a free oil change. But I thought we could do better. I asked him, "Do we really want to get people to come in and just get an oil change? Wouldn't we rather sell them a car?"

I knew that most customers would visit more than one dealership before actually buying a car. If we could put a printed certificate in their hands, customized with their own name and address and a cash discount on their car purchase, wouldn't they be more likely to visit us first—and thus more likely to buy from us?

I pitched him on the idea of a pop-up coupon that would give customers $100 off the purchase of *any new or used car* on the lot. He liked the idea. We pitched the concept to some other dealer friends of his, and they all liked it, too. I worked out the mechanics, and that same month we put the service on our own Web site. I called the new project AutoCertificate.com.

The idea worked just as we thought it would. Soon our pop-up coupon was generating additional sales on our lot, and I extended the concept by offering the service to other dealers at $149 a month. By midyear, the largest Ford truck dealer in the world—Prestige Ford in Garland, Texas—reported that they were redeeming close to a hundred coupons a month, and that the increase in business more than paid for the cost of the service. I asked their owner, Jerry Reynolds (who was also past chairman of the National Ford Dealer Council), if I could use his quote, along with his name and photo, in my promotion, and he agreed.

I continued developing the idea, adding other features and packaging into the site some of my own knowledge about Internet sales and Web site design and management. Before long we had more than a hundred dealerships around the country paying us monthly fees to maintain their Web sites, use one of our plug-in services, or receive our advice on how to sell over the Internet.

As with so many of my Web-based businesses, there were no real ongoing operating costs associated with AutoCertificate.com, other than the pittance it cost to host the site. After initial design costs, the site essentially ran itself—and I was grossing something like $15,000 a month.

My "little project" had turned into quite a lucrative enterprise.

By the time Tommy and I sold the last of our string of Internet experiments, AutoCertificate.com was in full swing. But it didn't stop there. Nearly two years later, an opportunity presented itself to expand the business in new ways—and what created that opportunity was another dramatic shift in the business climate.

When the government's Do Not Call registry came out in the fall of '03, thousands of businesspeople and most corporations were against it. Early estimates were that it could negatively affect American businesses to the tune of $50 billion just in its first year. (The telemarketing industry employs more than *six million* people.)

I saw it from two points of view. I don't like junk phone calls any more than I like junk mail or junk e-mail. At the same time, I could see that it was really going to hurt business in all sorts of ways. For example, let's say 20 percent of your company's revenues came from sales derived from telemarketing. You've lost that revenue in an instant. How are you going to make it up? Will you have to fire one out of five employees?

I also thought it was ironic that the regulations didn't prohibit or limit political parties or nonprofit organizations from calling names on the list. In other words, the politicians who passed these regulations didn't have to follow them themselves.

But regardless of my or anyone else's opinion, now it was law, and just as with any change in the business environment, we all needed to adapt. In fact, maybe this change could even offer new opportunities, for entrepreneurs observant enough to see them.

My friend Joe Sugarman, a master marketer and founder of BluBlocker Sunglasses, says, "The greatest success stories are created by people who recognize problems and turn them into opportunities." Could the problem posed by the new DNC laws open the door to another success?

In October 2003, my dad was approached by a company that wanted to sell him a call-list management service. They told him he needed to subscribe to their service to help him keep track of the new "Do Not Call" telemarketing list, because his salespeople would need to search each individual number before making any outgoing calls to make sure it wasn't on the list. And they would charge him only the modest price of $1,000 per month to do that.

I thought it was price gouging, plain and simple. They were trying to take advantage of the climate of fear and confusion the new regulations had created.

My dad showed me all the information and said, "Is there any way you could do all this, but cheaper?"

I said, "Absolutely."

By this time my business—I had changed its name from Auto-Certificate to Zablo—was supplying Web site services to about a hundred car dealers around the country. I put my Zablo Web guys on this, and they built it in just weeks. I went back to my dad and showed him what we had developed: a product that was better than the competition, and at one-tenth the cost. We were prepared to market this new service to our dealers for $895 per *year* (or $100 per month, for those who wanted to try it a month at a time).

With Zablo's DNC list service, you could import your FTC list into your own system as well as add new names from your own records and from new customers coming onto the showroom floor.

When you typed in a potential customer's phone number, it would display on your computer monitor in either green or red: "call them" or "don't call them."

We launched our new service that fall and became one of the first companies approved by the FTC to market a "Do Not Call" service to auto dealers. Before long we had dozens of dealers using our system.

One reason Zablo worked out so well was that, once again, I had followed the Warren Buffett investment dictum: I went with what I knew. I understood the issues that dealerships face, because I knew their business inside and out. And not just theoretically: I'd started out getting my hands dirty on the shop floor and gone on to learn as much about every facet of the business as I possibly could.

But another reason it worked was that I was paying careful attention to how business was changing.

Probably the biggest mistake that people made during the first Internet boom was to assume that the Web was so transformative, it was going to totally change the fundamentals of business. They threw ludicrously large amounts of cash into business models with seriously flawed foundations—and so did the "experts," the banks and venture capital people.

But fundamentals are fundamentals. That is the art of good business: keeping one eye firmly on the core principles, which *never* change (know your customers, don't let your expenses outrun your income, carefully calculate all risks, etc.), and the other eye on the shifting business climate, which is *always* changing.

It was those who found ways to use the new technologies to address a real market with a genuine need, premised their solution on a solid business model, and then paid careful attention to how it was performing, who survived the bust. To put it simply, they stayed in touch with reality—and they weren't afraid to adapt.

Adapt or die. It's one of the oldest business principles there is, but these days, as the pace of technological change has sped up so dramatically, it's more vital than ever before.

11

Find Great Mentors

The Internet isn't the only thing that's changing rapidly; in today's world, practically everything is changing at a faster pace than ever before, and it's only accelerating. The dictum "adapt or die" applies everywhere. A generation ago, employees could reasonably expect to stay with the same company for their entire careers. Not anymore. In the real world, people change jobs. I read recently that the average employee changes jobs seven times in a lifetime.

All this means that your *network of relationships* is more important than ever.

When you meet someone interesting—say, through an internship, or in school, or at an event—there may be no obvious way either of you can help the other . . . at least not at the moment. But who knows where they'll be, and what they'll be involved with, a few years down the road? These are all good connections to have, and it pays to stay in touch with them.

Effective connections and relationships are win-win by definition. I always expect to put more into a relationship than I take out. If everyone did this, everyone's relationships would thrive.

People open doors. That's what connections are all about. Over the years, I have collected a powerful network of contacts. Some of them have opened major doors for me, and I've done the same for them. They are all opportunities waiting to happen—opportunities for us to put our heads together and create value for others—and be paid well for doing so.

And for a successful entrepreneur, the most significant business relationships you'll ever have are those with the people who become your mentors.

My first mentors were in books. When I was twelve, I started reading biographies of the most successful entrepreneurs I could find, and the three names that always topped that list for me were Donald Trump, Bill Gates, and Michael Dell. That list, by the way, is chronological, in the order of when my admiration began. (Interestingly, the three men were born in that order, too, roughly a decade apart: June '46, October '55, and February '65, respectively.)

When I was little, I especially looked up to Donald Trump. The way he treated me and my parents during our stay at the Plaza was part of it, of course, but that wasn't all. I admired the way he thought big and the fact that he wasn't afraid to try things that would have intimidated other people.

By the time I started Cheers & Tears, Bill Gates had assumed the position of number one business hero in my mind. The first *Roanoke Times* story about me in 1996 started with this sentence:

Cameron Johnson's goal is to become the next Bill Gates.

Like Trump, Gates has taken his share of lumps in the press. That comes with the territory: when you're successful, there will always be people who try to pull themselves up by knocking you down. Lately the press on Bill Gates has been very favorable, because he has shifted his attention from running Microsoft to dedicating his billions to the cause of improving education, reducing inequities, and helping disadvantaged people throughout the world. But the passion and commitment he and his wife are now pouring into their foundation is the same passion and commitment that built a software empire out of an idea, and I've admired him for it all along.

Within a few years, I had a new hero in Michael Dell. When his book *Direct from Dell* came out in early 1999, I read it from cover to cover, and then read it again, and then again, steeping myself in the man's experiences and the lessons and principles he drew from them.

I admired Michael Dell for the way he started his business with nothing but an idea. He took that idea—a simple concept, cutting out the middleman and selling computers directly to users—and took it to the highest possible level. You'd think that most people would want to be hands on with a computer before they would be comfortable writing a check or giving their credit card number over the order line. At least, that's what nearly everyone assumed. But not Dell. He said, "Let's cut out the middleman and pass on the savings to the consumer in the form of better products and lower prices." And he was incredibly successful doing it.

Dell embodied a principle that has always been very important to me: "dream big—and start small." He started Dell Computer Corporation with a capitalization (if you can even apply that term here) of less than $1,000 and built that investment over time into a company with a market cap valued at more than $55 billion.

Another reason I admired Michael Dell was that he wasn't afraid to take risks. In 2003, Dell took the giant step of entering the home entertainment industry, producing things such as televisions and personal music players. That was an extremely risky move: the television market is one of the most overcrowded industries there is, not to mention the barrier of entry (expense of entering this market) being extremely high. But Dell didn't care. He wanted to take his "direct from Dell" model to the home entertainment industry. It hasn't been an easy launch for them, but they aren't letting up on this effort and are willing to give up short-term gain for long-term success. Dell is exceptionally well run, and despite the bumps in the road and their huge size, they're also extremely agile, which helps them stay on top. In the long run, I think the risk will pay off. And that's how we keep score: success in the long run, not gimmicks that make us rich tomorrow.

I also noticed that Dell was quick to recognize mistakes and not afraid to change course. Early on, his company got in big trouble when they had stocked way too much inventory of parts. Recognizing that mistake led to his innovative strategy of limited inventory and "just in time" supply. Another time, he came out with an amazing computer, the "Olympic," that far exceeded the capacity of anything on the market—but it turned out consumers didn't want something that powerful. Again, he immediately recognized the error, and used it to learn one of the most important lessons in Dell's history: *listen to your customers and give them what they want.*

For all my admiration of the man, I never imagined that I would have the chance to talk with him privately, person to person—let alone share a stage with him at a major public event. But when I was in my junior year in high school, that is exactly what happened.

Earlier that year, I was contacted by an organization that was putting on a symposium on technology and wanted to know if I'd be interested in speaking there. I was happy to accept their invitation—especially when I learned that they had already booked Michael Dell.

Thus Michael Dell and I were both keynote speakers at a July 2002 symposium in Austin, Texas, called the Youth International Technology Summit, sponsored by Apple, Intel, Sony, and a host of other high-tech companies. Dell was the keynote speaker for the Monday session, and I was the keynote on Wednesday.

In my talk, I related my history and shared some of my views on business, entrepreneurship, and the central role of youth in determining our future. Then it was time to take questions from the audience. Typically this is my favorite part of a public appearance. I enjoy the interaction, and it's often the time when the most learning happens. And I don't mean only on the part of the audience: I always find it an opportunity to learn something new as well. On this occasion the questions were especially excellent, and I had a great time.

But the best part of the event was getting to spend some time alone with Mr. Dell. I was, of course, in the audience when he spoke on Monday, and he was amazing. Afterward I got to spend some time alone with him and a few of his key staff. (And by the way, this is one of the things I like most about giving speeches: it's always an amazing opportunity to network and meet fascinating people.)

I knew he had to leave town right away and wouldn't be able to hear my talk later that week, so I introduced myself, told him how much I'd admired his work, and told him a little about the different businesses I'd had. He listened carefully, nodding, and saying "Yeah." He then told me a few brief things about Dell Computer Corporation.

Just two business guys, swapping stories of places they'd been and things they'd seen. Shop talk. I have to tell you, it was inspiring.

After a few minutes he gave me his business card and said, "Let's keep in touch." He introduced me to a few of his staff members and said they would attend my talk. I've stayed in contact with him through his staff ever since.

In addition to staying in touch with Michael Dell's people, after the Austin symposium I also maintained a connection with Richard Rossi, cofounder of the company that had organized the event. Richard became a mentor to me almost immediately and to this day, more than five years later, we stay in touch regularly.

Richard has introduced me to dozens of successful businesspeople, including the sharpest marketers he knows, and also invited me to join a small circle of advisers. Once a year, he brings the eight of us to Washington, D.C., to consult to his company, and we spend several days in a room, brainstorming solutions to things going on with his company. In fact, it was through this group that I met another key mentor of mine, Joe Polish.

Joe is one of the most connected people in this world. He's the king of networking. He's also considered one of the brightest marketers in the world and commands a $20,000-per-day consulting fee.

Joe Polish owns a company that goes by the unlikely name of Piranha Marketing. His slogan is "Eat Your Competition Alive," and that's just what his program teaches you to do. Among his many inventive and successful marketing and consulting creations, he also puts on an annual "boot camp" conference for carpet cleaners. Yes, you read that right: for carpet cleaners. Joe started out as a struggling carpet cleaner himself.

Like Richard, Joe has become a close friend. We do business together, we vacation together, and we talk constantly through phone and e-mail—sometimes multiple times a day. Joe has been an invaluable sounding board for many of my ideas, and he also has introduced me to some of his successful friends and business associates. I'm thankful for this relationship.

In October 2005 I was invited to be a guest speaker at one of Joe Polish's boot camps, and while I was there I shared the platform with another friend of Joe's, the famous financial adviser and author David Bach.

David is an amazing man. He has had possibly more impact on the spending and saving habits of Americans (and Canadians) than any other man alive. Known to millions through his bestselling books and his appearances on the Oprah show, David has taken the world of personal finance by storm, giving people new hope for their economic futures—and the practical means to realize those hopes. For example, David coined the term "The Latte Factor," by which he means the handful of dollars most of us spend every day on things we don't need—and which, if we instead put them into an intelligent savings plan, would in time make us all millionaires.

In one article David said, "I believe God put each one of us here to do something special. Most of us aren't doing whatever it is we were put here to do, because we're living paycheck to paycheck." I couldn't agree more. I was also fascinated to learn that like me, David was introduced to managing his own money at a very early age: his grandmother Rose inspired him to make his first stock market purchase at age seven. David and I have stayed in touch ever since the event.

Another powerful friend I've met through my network is Joe Sugarman, the multimillionaire founder of BluBlocker Sunglasses. Joe is an amazing example of how persistence pays off. Here's how Joe describes his early history: "I failed at practically everything I tried, but I never gave up. I just knew that one of these days I'd make it—if I just hung in there." He was so determined to create something hugely successful that nothing could stop him from trying idea after idea.

Back in the sixties, Joe came up with the idea of branded credit cards, and he spent thousands of dollars of his own money to produce a run of Batman credit cards. He managed to get in front of dozens of figures in banking, finance, and marketing to pitch the concept, and every single person turned him down.

While that concept was ahead of its time (and just look at branded cards today!), Joe eventually hit his stride and since then has hit home run after home run. For example, he was the first direct marketer to use toll-free 800 lines and take credit card orders over the phone, a concept that sparked an explosion of the entire mail-order catalog industry. He was awarded the prestigious Maxwell Sackheim Award in 1991 for his contributions to direct marketing.

Joe is an intensely friendly, personable guy, sometimes downright hilarious—but get him talking about marketing or copywriting and he becomes an unstoppable dynamo. Marketing is his passion, and his books—including *Advertising Secrets of the Written Word, Marketing Secrets of a Mail Order Maverick,* and *Triggers: 30 Sales Tools You Can Use to Control the Mind of Your Prospect to Motivate, Influence, and Persuade*—are considered among the definitive classics on the subject.

All these people, from my childhood heroes Trump, Gates, and Dell to my present-day friends and mentors, both those I've mentioned and many others I haven't, share certain qualities that I admire and emulate. They all have the courage and the ability to get things done. Whatever they want to achieve—whether it's to get face time with any top executive, celebrity, or politician, or to find the resources they need to bring a project from the drawing boards into reality—they will find a way.

Whatever these people put their minds to, it doesn't matter how many noes they get, they will persist until they get a yes. They have very clear objectives and never take no for an answer. They are all self-confident and powerful people who know what they want and how to get it. I am proud and honored to have them as friends— and very fortunate to have them as mentors.

In many ways I also consider my partners as my mentors. I'm always on the lookout for people who know more than I do, people who have something they can teach me. As I said before, my dad taught me how valuable it is to surround yourself with the best people; one of the benefits of doing that is that it keeps you learning. My principal business partners have gone on to study at Harvard (Aaron) and Wharton (Nat Turner—you haven't met him yet, but you will) and to work at Google (Tommy), and I've learned a lot from all three of them.

Mentors don't have to be celebrities or CEOs. You can find them everywhere if you just keep your eyes open. The world is full of unsung heroes and people who've made an enormous difference in the lives of others simply because they cared and shared a skill, some knowledge, or just their time and attention.

Two of my most important mentors were teachers I met through the Roanoke public school system.

The Roanoke high schools are no worse than many urban high schools in America—and no better. In many ways it's a pretty rough environment. Patrick Henry High School has its share of racial tension, high teenage pregnancy rates, and violence. Two different housing projects feed into the school, and so do two different gangs. There are fights in the cafeteria; bomb scares are not uncommon. (In the fall of 2001, after September 11, they were happening at least once a week.) The violence level is pretty high.

One thing that makes it possible to survive and even thrive in an environment like that is finding someone within the system who believes in you and will work to help you get what you need. In my high school years, I was fortunate to find two such mentors.

The first was Rita Bishop. My family had gotten to know Rita when I was in fifth grade. She was assistant superintendent of instruction for the Roanoke city school system, and she had recognized that I had interests the regular classes wouldn't meet. She set up a program for me with a few technically proficient high school students and one student from Virginia Tech; they came in a few times a week to work with me. Rita and my mom became good friends, and years later, when I was preparing to give my first major speech at the Virginia Business Hall of Fame, Rita helped coach me. In addition to her duties in the school system, she also was a well-respected speechwriter and a talented speaker in her own right.

When I left Woodberry and came back to Roanoke, I went to Rita to see if she could help me with a situation concerning a class credit I wanted to complete. I had started a public speaking class at Woodberry, but completed only one semester before I left. The only way I could get credit for the course was to take another semester—but there was no such class at Patrick Henry. And it wasn't just that I wanted the credit (which I did); I also really wanted to finish the course. The keynote address the previous fall had gone well, but I certainly didn't consider myself an accomplished speaker, and I knew that in the future, mastering this skill would be important to my career.

I told her about my situation and she said, "Well, I'll teach you the class myself—and I'll sign off on your getting credit for it."

And she did. I completed the course credit under her tutelage that spring, and she continued teaching afterward, too. She taught me in a one-on-one class in which she would assign me a topic, I would write the speech, and then we'd go downtown to an auditorium where I would practice giving the speech in different ways (from note cards, from a script or outline, memorized, etc.). Rita was a big part of my gaining confidence in the public spotlight, whether under the camera lights or on the speaking stage.

Her dedication to her students didn't go unrecognized, either. I am incredibly fortunate to have spent that time with Rita when I did, because she soon left the Roanoke school system and became the superintendent of schools in Lancaster, Pennsylvania.

My second mentor in the Roanoke school system was a wonderful teacher named Kimberly Williams, whose marketing classes I took—and absolutely loved—in my junior and senior years. Kim Williams also got me involved in Delta Epsilon Chi (DECA), a national marketing club for high school and college students that puts on all sorts of projects, including an opportunity to compete on a business project at the regional, state, national, and international levels.

In my junior year I competed in DECA and won at the regional level, then went on to come in first at the state level, which qualified me to travel to Salt Lake City for the national competition. In Salt Lake City, I was sure I had it nailed—but I got one question wrong on the exam. I did place in the top ten for my category, but didn't win the number one national spot. I hated not having won, but I reminded myself that I had only placed as a finalist at the Young IT Entrepreneur of the Year Award contest in Atlanta, and even so, that had turned out to be a major turning point in my life.

I entered the competition again the following year as a high school senior, and again won at both the regional and state levels and was prepared to go to Florida for the nationals—but this was the spring of 2003: the United States had just invaded Iraq, and the Roanoke City schools were not letting anyone from the school system fly.

I strongly encourage kids to participate in programs like DECA. You make lots of great contacts with people who are also going places, and it provides you with some real-life experience—something very few high school students have the opportunity to receive.

Of course, my most influential mentors I found right at home: my mom and dad.

I'm not sure which of them I take after more. I think I reflect aspects of both of them. My dad taught me pretty much everything I know about sales. He has a simple set of rules he hands out to all his salespeople. Number three of Bill's Rules is, "Everyone wants to buy from a person they like and trust. Listen; become their friend."

My dad is the nicest boss in the world to work for. He's almost impossible not to like. I'm tougher on people than he is. I can get frustrated with an employee or someone I'm working with. I'll tell my dad about it and he'll say, "Hey, it's no big deal."

Like me, my mom is a tougher manager than my dad. With her, everything's clear-cut: you either did it right or you did it wrong. I'm more like her in that way. My dad will say, "Okay, it might not be done right, but we don't have to react to it." He likes to be everyone's friend.

My abilities in sales I got from my dad, which includes the ability to listen to people, to empathize, and establish rapport with them. My nature as a manager I got from my mom, which includes both the ability to see things clearly—what's working and what isn't, what needs to be fixed and what needs to be thrown out and started over—and the willingness to call it like I see it. When you're making crucial decisions about a business, this is a very helpful trait to have.

Having those two sets of characteristics has helped make me who I am, and I'm so grateful to them both.

One more mentor I need to mention is someone who was a key figure in my life long before I started my first business—in fact, she was a key figure in my life from the time I was born.

Betty Smith was a war bride who had come over to the States from England many years before. She had three sons; my mom had gone to high school with one of them. After I was born, my mom and I both got sick. At a friend's suggestion, my mom called Mrs. Smith, and she came over to help take care of me. She was going to be there for only three months. She stayed for nine years.

Mrs. Smith—or Nana, as I called her—was wonderful. She was with me all day, Mondays through Fridays. She loved to play thinking games with me, anything that involved creativity—she was passionate about that. We also took walks every day—she was a big one for the outdoors. My mom went back to work when I was only a few months old (we both recovered our health pretty quickly), and for the next nine years, Mrs. Smith was as much a part of my life as my family. Even after I started going to school, she'd pick me up every day, and we'd spend the rest of the day together, too, straight through till dinner.

Mrs. Smith was a big part of my childhood. We were very close. Then she became ill. In February 1995, she died of pancreatic cancer. I was ten.

Losing Mrs. Smith was tough on me. It was the first real loss I'd ever experienced. My mom remembers finding me in my room, just sitting in a chair, rocking back and forth. She called my name, but I wouldn't answer. I just kept rocking and kind of staring into space. For a while I grew very introspective. She was worried about me, and talked with a family physician who also was a friend of the family. The doctor friend said, "He's probably just going through a type of shock; but he'll be okay. Just watch him and leave him alone." And he was right: I came out of it soon enough.

Still, the loss had really hurt. I'd always known that whatever was going on in my life, I could talk to her about it. Now she was gone.

Even though she passed away just as my first business was getting going, I still count Mrs. Smith as one of my most important mentors, because she really taught me to *think*. Like my parents, who weren't afraid to talk business around me or to take me on business trips, even into business meetings, Mrs. Smith treated me as an equal, as another human being worthy of respect and capable of great things.

If you can find even one person like that in your life, then you have a relationship worth more than the most expensive education money can buy.

Whether it's a high school teacher, a local businessman who takes you under his wing, or the administrator of a program you take part in, you can find mentors all around you. And you may be surprised at how available they are.

I think everyone loves being looked up to and sharing their experiences and advice with someone who shares common interests. It's one of the most satisfying ways there is to give back to the world and create value.

The lesson I learned from Donald Trump, and the care he took to respond to us in New York when I was eight years old, is one I've tried to model ever since. When people write to me or contact me, I do my best to answer them quickly, personally, and completely. It's not always easy to give free personalized advice, but I try my best—and I know dozens of other successful entrepreneurs who do the same.

Successful people love to mentor others, and if you're truly open and receptive to their interest and advice, you'll be amazed at how much you can learn from them and the doors they may help you open.

12

Seek Out New Knowledge Every Day

I've always been a big believer in education. By "education" I mean being on the constant lookout for any opportunity to learn.

Toyota talks about the concept of *kaizen*, which roughly translates as "continuous improvement." What can we do that nobody has ever thought of before? How can we do what we're already doing, only do it better than anyone ever has? It's a concept I've always believed in—and you can't have continuous improvement without continuous learning.

I think the willingness to learn something new every day is one of the most important attributes of a successful person—not just successful in business, but successful in *anything*. That's why I'm enrolled in a high-level coaching program that top entrepreneurs (including Joe Polish and some of my other friends and mentors) pay big money to join—close to the cost of a typical college tuition. Offered by master coach Dan Sullivan, the program is called Strategic Coach and meets four times a year.

Ever since I had my first business, I have always actively sought out knowledge and new ways to educate myself. I have always read books on business, along with *Forbes, Fortune,* and *BusinessWeek.* Even today, I read constantly. I go to seminars. When I'm alone in my car, I make sure there's a CD there that I can learn from.

But book learning isn't a guaranteed path to success. Plenty of people who are star performers in school run into serious obstacles when it comes to succeeding in the real business world—and some who performed poorly in school have gone on to become major business successes. Quite a few CEOs of major corporations never got college degrees. Just look at Dell, Gates, and Steve Jobs.

Don't get me wrong: I'm not *against* formal schooling. There's no question that a degree from a good college can be quite helpful, and that a degree from a business school, especially one of the top schools, can open doors that would otherwise probably be closed to you. But it's important to appreciate that a four-year degree and an MBA may not be the only route to go.

My relationship with schooling has been good generally, but not entirely untroubled. Sometimes my grades and test scores have been great, at other times not so great. Some of my teachers and I have gotten along really well. An article in the *Roanoke Times* once reported that Kim Williams had high praise for me and even invited me as a guest speaker to some of her other classes. However, the reporter went on, "Other teachers are not as impressed," and later in that same article she quoted Kim as saying that I was "bright in many ways that school does not relate to."

I couldn't have put this better myself. Honestly, I think *most* of us are bright in ways that school can't relate to.

Mark Twain once remarked, "I've never let schooling interfere with my education." As I approached the end of my senior year of high school, I was about to put that insight to the test.

To tell this part of the story right, I have to start by saying that I really hadn't planned to go to college in the first place. I didn't even start filling out applications until my friends started receiving early-admission responses.

Besides, I knew I wouldn't be going to any of the real cream-of-the-crop business schools, such as Harvard or Wharton. I had concentrated so much on my businesses that my schoolwork probably suffered for it. My grade-point average at Patrick Henry was more than 4.0 and would have placed me as one of the top students in my graduating class. However, my GPA from my Woodberry years, when I was involved with SurfingPrizes and really didn't care about college, was lower and brought my average to about a 3.3—not terrible, but not stellar, and certainly not good enough to get into a place such as Wharton (although I would later visit Wharton after all, albeit through an altogether different route).

Still, I was willing to give college a try. It's important to keep an open mind.

So finally, in December of my senior year of high school, I fired off a few applications, and Virginia Tech sent back their acceptance practically by return mail.

This was not a surprise to any of us; it had been almost a foregone conclusion that Virginia Tech was where I would go. For one thing, it was something of a family tradition: one of my cousins had gone to Tech, my mom had done a few years there, and my father's father was a Tech graduate.

What's more, a lot of my high school friends were going to Tech, and truthfully, that was probably a bigger pull for me than any other factor. (At one point I said, "If I do go to college, it will be for one reason and one reason only: to stay with my friends and network with others!")

But apart from my family history and my friends, I also had my own special connection to Virginia Tech from three years before, when I was fifteen and still at Woodberry. When I delivered that keynote speech at the Southwest Virginia Business Hall of Fame, it so happened that the inductee we were honoring was Paul Torgerson, the president of Virginia Tech.

I had met Dr. Torgerson at the event, along with the president of Radford University, Dr. Douglas Covington, and quite a few other key figures in Virginia business and education. Dr. Torgerson had said to me, "When you finish high school, you need to come to Virginia Tech and enroll in our business school."

At the time, I said, "Okay, that's great, thank you . . . although honestly, I don't really think I'm going to go to college."

But in September 2003 I packed up and drove south to Blacksburg, Virginia, about forty-five minutes down the road, to begin my freshman year at Virginia Tech's Pamplin College of Business.

*   *   *

I loved everything about college—living on campus, the great friends I made, the parties, the girls, *everything* . . .

Everything, that is, except for the classes. About them, I was not at all enthusiastic.

Still, when the administration tried to whet my interest by letting me take some advanced business classes, I was determined to give it my best shot. I *wanted* to like this experience. I wanted a challenge—and I wanted to be proven wrong and find that I really did need college.

When I started my freshman Introduction to Business class, I thought it was going to be a fun experience and, to be truthful, a fairly easy one, too. I was not surprised to find that I was fully familiar with all the concepts and terms in the textbook, and was able to share examples from my own experience on just about any concept it mentioned.

Imagine my surprise when we received our final grades for the semester . . . and I got a B.

Getting that B was a pivotal event for me. It clearly demonstrated to me something that I'd long suspected: how well you perform in school or "know" something on an academic level has little to do with how well you will actually perform the task on your own later in life. It's quite possible to ace a test and *still not grasp its concepts*. This is one of the fallacies of formal education.

The world is chock full of "business experts" who breeze through top business schools and go on to start their own businesses—only to see them fail a few short years or even months later. It's ludicrous. These students may have been experts at memorizing definitions or learning concepts. But *practicing* those concepts—leading a management team, understanding people, taking calculated risks, managing real money in real situations—these things are a whole different ball game.

And these things are generally *not* being taught in college, certainly not in high school, and, except in rare cases, not at home, either. In fact, they're not being taught *anywhere*. And that is something that ought to change. In fact, that's one of the biggest reasons why I'm writing this book. I was more fortunate than most, in that I received the best education in real-life business practices that anyone could ever receive—from my parents, by age ten. If there's one thing I always hope people will take from my story, it's this:

Parents, teach your kids about money—because chances are, nobody else will.

By the way, the reason I got a B was that I missed a single question on an exam. We were told to "List the five elements that are key to business growth and job creation that make up the business environment."

The "correct" answers, the answers I was *supposed* to list, were:

1. The economic environment, including taxes and regulation;
2. The technological environment;
3. The competitive environment;
4. The social environment;
5. The global business environment.

I'm sure you could go ask any successful entrepreneur or CEO to list for you "the five elements that are key to business growth and job creation that make up the business environment," and this would *not* be the list they'd give you. Entrepreneurs are successful at what they do because:

1. They know people and treat them well;
2. They know basic business concepts;
3. They are willing to take risks and learn from their mistakes;
4. They share a common goal with their employees;
5. They know their industry.

That other stuff is all theoretical, and it won't get you very far in the real world. Why not teach me how to manage people, learn an industry, read financial statements, or something I'll actually use?

When you're an entrepreneur running your own business, you have to know about every aspect of your business. Even when you're the CEO of a large company, with hundreds or even thousands of employees, and you might have dozens of experts in all sorts of areas, you *still* have to know about every aspect of that business. Success in business is essentially knowing what works and what doesn't—and keeping an eye on *everything*.

The most valuable education, the kind I believe is absolutely essential to success in business, can come from only one place: your own experience. More than any type of knowledge, I attribute my success to the education that came about from these three factors:

1. I am willing to work hard;
2. I follow through on my ideas;
3. I'm willing to fail.

I believe you can learn more from failure than you can from success. Failing allows you to critique your mistakes, learn from them, and correct them in the future. But this B that I got in Introduction to Business was not a mistake from which I could learn useful things; it was a measure of how far removed from reality my classes were.

As if to heighten the growing absurdity, in the midst of earning a B in Introduction to Business, I was also about to launch a new business in my spare time—one that, as you'll see in the next chapter, would prove to be the most successful business of my career to date.

As the semester came to a close, I was having serious doubts about whether I was really cut out for college. The parties were fun and I was making friendships that I sensed would last a lifetime. Maybe that is one of the real underlying values of going to college. But it didn't feel like the schooling was for me.

I had been more than willing to give it my best shot, and I did my best to just keep a low profile, fit in, and see what I could learn. But the more time I spent in my classes, the more wrong it felt. Then one day, as I took a seat in my Introduction to Business Management class, one of my good friends leaned over and said, "Hey, Cameron, did you read last night?"

As it happened, I hadn't read the assignment. I'd started to, but honestly, it was pretty boring reading. So I whispered back, "No, I didn't read it. Why?"

And she said, "Well, in the reading we did, right in our textbook, there's an article on you!"

She had to be kidding. I grabbed the book and flipped to the assigned section—and there I was, right on the page.

Back when I'd had SurfingPrizes, *BusinessWeek* had published an article on me. As a way to illustrate the principle that you could be a successful entrepreneur at any age, our college textbook had reprinted the *BusinessWeek* article, citing me as an expert young entrepreneur.

In a brief summary of their "exciting new freshmen class," Virginia Tech had pointed out that this year they had "a Nike Junior Olympic Athlete and a business star." Now everyone on campus knew who I was. So much for keeping a low profile.

During that first semester, two of my professors came up to me and said, "Cameron, exactly what *are* you doing here?" I was starting to wonder the same thing. As it turned out, what I was really doing was getting ready for my next big business venture—and an education that I would never have gotten in a classroom.

13

Use the Power of the Press

I am always thinking of ideas for future companies, but most of these ideas I file away for future reference, when I might have the free time to develop them further. That fall, I had an idea that just *could not wait*.

At this point, Zablo was running itself and I'd shut down or sold most of my other companies. I was ready for a new challenge, and I wanted to do something really big. In October 2003, after I'd been at Virginia Tech for about a month, the idea came to me—and I found it, of all places, sitting right in my wallet.

One day I noticed that I had all these gift cards in my wallet that friends and relatives had given me and that I'd never gotten around to using. A lot of them were for places where I didn't shop, and now, since I was away at school, I couldn't really spend the time to visit the stores where I could use them.

People think of a gift certificate as an easy gift to give. You don't have to pick out the right color sweater or worry about the size. You don't have to wonder whether the other person's going to like what you bought, because they're going to buy it themselves. It would feel kind of tacky to just give someone cash; giving a gift certificate has all the benefits of giving cash, yet with more perceived value.

But what do people usually do with gift cards they can't or don't want to use? They land in a drawer gathering dust, or get tucked away in the back of a wallet or pocketbook until they're cleaned out and tossed, months or even years later.

Just like the ones I noticed in my wallet.

I thought, what if you could get some value from these orphaned gift cards? Of course, you could always go onto eBay and sell them, and there were other swap-and-sell sites, too, such as Half.com, an online marketplace for books, DVDs, and movies.

But what if there were a Web site specifically dedicated to buying, selling, and trading gift certificates?

Once the idea popped into my head, I started turning it around and looking at it. Would that be feasible? How would we do it? We could charge a processing fee when the gift certificate actually sold.

Would there be enough buyers? Of course there would. People were always looking for ways to buy gift certificates at a discount. What about sellers? Again, absolutely. There were plenty of people looking to unload gift certificates at a lesser amount and take the cash or do something else with it.

I took myself as a case in point. I had a $100 gift certificate to Footlocker that I knew I was never going to use. Would I go to the trouble of selling it for less than face value? Sure I would: I'd be happy to get $80 for it. I'd certainly rather have $80 cash than a $100 gift certificate I was never going to use. That, or an $80 gift certificate for a store where I *would* be likely to shop.

Okay, so this might be a feasible model. How many customers would I be likely to find? Enough to make the investment in a new business worthwhile?

I went online and did a little research. I searched the various auction sites (eBay, Craigslist, etc.) to get a sense of how many people were selling unwanted gift cards. I soon found that there was no online marketplace devoted exclusively to gift cards—and I also found all sorts of articles on gift cards, with reams of statistics.

I was thrilled: gift certificates were a genuine trend in the marketplace. Nearly every store, restaurant, and airline was offering them. *Cleaning services* were offering them. According to the numbers I found, 70 percent of all consumers had either given or received at least one gift certificate the previous holiday season. A large percentage of store sales were now happening not before but *after* the holidays, when customers came in to redeem their gift cards. Between 2002 and 2003, the percentage of U.S. adults who had bought a gift card had doubled, from 23 percent to 46 percent.

It was a *$40 billion* industry.

All the statistics supported the idea, so I thought, let's give it a shot. I even knew what I'd call it: CertificateSwap.com. And I knew that designing this Web site was going to be a really huge task, so I thought of Nat Turner.

Nat was someone I'd developed an e-mail relationship with over the past half year. That spring Nat was named Texas's Youth Entrepreneur of the Year by Texas Christian University, and he was the featured speaker at the same event where I had spoken the year before with Michael Dell.

Nat had never spoken in public before, and he was looking for some coaching. The people putting on the event said to him, "This guy Cameron Johnson was our speaker last year. You should send him an e-mail and maybe he'll give you some pointers." So Nat e-mailed me and we went back and forth about public speaking. After his speech (which went just fine), we stayed in touch. When I started my first year at Tech, Nat was just starting his senior year in high school.

Nat is an amazing guy. In addition to being a brilliant Web designer, he did something that I could never do: he created a major business breeding and selling snakes over the Internet. His company, Ball Python Co., has sold more than $100,000 worth of snakes; one snake alone went for more than $30,000. Apparently you can just put a snake in a little cage, put the cage in a box, and mail it, and it does just fine. Nat would overnight them all over the country. He was the snake king, and his site became the number one reptile Web site in the country.

I can't even look at a snake. I think the idea's absolutely crazy. But, hey . . . maybe it's a Texas thing. And no matter how crazy it might have sounded to me, Nat had obviously done his homework, and he built a very profitable company—another example of serving a niche by starting with what you know. In any case, Nat was a brilliant Web designer, and I liked him.

As I researched the gift certificate idea, Nat kept springing to mind. Now I had the thought that maybe instead of paying someone to do the design, I could get Nat involved as a partner.

First I e-mailed him and just ran the idea by him, to see what he thought. He wrote back and said, "That's really, really good — it's a great idea! I'd love to do it with you!"

So now I had a great idea, and I had Nat as a partner. All we had to do was put it in motion.

We knew that we needed to get this up and running before Christmas, in time for the holiday season, which obviously would be the prime time for launching a gift-card-related company. It was going to be a huge job to put all the pieces together. With only weeks to go, we had to start moving immediately.

I had been completely out of the Web design business for a good three years, since my sophomore year in high school. This business is like a dog's life: one calendar year is like seven years. I e-mailed people I hadn't talked to in ages and said, "Hey, who's the best designer you know of? I've got a new project. I'm coming back!"

People e-mailed me a couple of names. One of them was a guy who lived in Russia named Ruslan Bykadorov. Ruslan sent me some samples of his work; they were amazing and both Nat and I loved them. "Okay," I e-mailed to Nat, "let's hire Ruslan to do all our front-end Web site design." With Ruslan handling the front-end look and feel of the site, I could leave it completely to Nat to take the templates Ruslan created and create all our other pages from there.

Next, I decided to hire Randy Morse, the New Hampshire Web designer who'd done all my stuff for AutoCertificate.com, to handle all the back-end, nuts-and-bolts mechanics, where all the transactions would take place.

With Nat supervising and coordinating all the site design, we had our team ready to cover the actual mechanics of the site. I would oversee the entire project, which included handling promotion and advertising—and these were going to be a critical part of this project. No matter how good the idea is, no matter how excellent its execution, the greatest Web site in the world won't do any business if there isn't any traffic coming to click on it. Having the greatest product on the planet doesn't mean a thing unless you have a way for enough customers to find out about it.

We'd done all the research; we knew the idea would work. But we also knew it would take a multimillion-dollar ad campaign to get this thing launched properly, in the time frame we had available. And that simply wasn't possible for us, because we were both already investing a good five figures each to stock our online store with inventory.

Why inventory? Because we knew that once we actually had our brand-new marketplace up and launched, it had to look like a place that people would trust to bring their business. We couldn't have Customer One on Day One looking at an empty storefront. If our potential customers came to an empty site, who would list there? Nobody.

So Nat and I had to pony up some significant cash capital to buy hundreds of gift cards from all sorts of different retailers and put them all up for sale on our site. It took tens of thousands of dollars out of our pockets to "populate the storefront." We knew we'd make back a good percentage on our investment when we sold the cards—assuming the site was a success. But still, it was a chunk of change we had to put on the line—a good example of a calculated risk. We also leveraged our own cash investment by persuading as many retailers as we could to give us gift cards on consignment (i.e., we would pay for them only after we'd sold them).

Once we were up and running, we expected that all kinds of stores would read stories about us, and contact us, wanting to join and have their gift cards represented on our site. We figured that we could even make deals with them, negotiating bulk discounts so we could sell their cards ourselves at a more substantial profit.

But all that would have to come later, once we had something to show. To launch, we knew we had to have some activity going on—or at least the *look* of activity—to generate more activity.

So with our capital tied up in inventory, how could we possibly get the traffic we needed to make this work, and with only weeks to go? There was no way we could afford to advertise.

But then, I never advertised Cheers & Tears Printing Co., either—and I got lots of customers. It worked then, and it would work now.

We would use the media.

Ever since I saw the impact of that very first article in the *Roanoke Times* when I was eleven years old, I'd always known that the media and its form of word of mouth is the most powerful form of advertising there is. The great Hollywood studios and distribution companies may spend tens of millions dollars to promote a single film, but they all know that none of those millions will ultimately get the job done. The fate of the film, whether it goes belly up or becomes the next blockbuster, is dictated solely by *buzz*—that precious word of mouth generated by the film's first weekend at the theaters. The recommendation of a friend—"must-see" or "steer clear," thumbs-up or a thumbs-down—has always been the single most powerful form of commercial promotion in the world, and it always will be.

People trust mass-media advertising less and less, but the news is still the news. Publicity is just another way of using word of mouth.

While Nat and Randy and Ruslan got insanely busy whamming together the pieces of machinery that would make the idea I'd had into reality, I set about to design the most massive PR strategy I'd ever attempted.

I knew we could get media attention. I wasn't the fifteen-year-old CEO anymore; I had just turned nineteen, and pulling the age card wasn't the automatic walk-in-the-media-park it had once been. Still, nineteen is young enough to be newsworthy if the project is major enough. What's more, there was an advantage to my advancing years: as I had grown older, my résumé had grown, too. The story was no longer, "Young Whiz Kid Starts Successful Business." Now it was, "Teenager with More than a Dozen Successful Businesses behind Him Launches His Latest and Biggest."

I knew this could work. Still, there was no way I could make it happen by myself, not on the scale we needed, not this quickly. I'd never used a PR firm before, but this was the perfect time.

I'd already researched PR firms over the years, in case I'd ever want to use this strategy, so I didn't have to waste any precious time hunting. There are hundreds of PR firms to choose from; I had looked for the ones that had experience promoting unique stories, and not just doing damage control for Fortune 500 companies. The company I chose, S&S Public Relations (www.sspr.com), had a track record of interesting product launches and had some very big names on their client list. They seemed like a perfect fit, so I called them.

They said they would charge us about $5,000 a month, so we committed $15,000 and contracted with them for three months. For the next ninety days, December 2003 through February 2004, their job was to provide us a media blitz, total exposure, all focused on our launch.

Nat and I would have to work like crazy to meet our deadline. And that was asking a lot: he was in his senior year of high school, and I had a full course load at Virginia Tech.

As the date got closer, the pressure got more and more intense. Ruslan, Randy, and Nat were all working around the clock on the site. Starting on Sunday, December 7, I didn't sleep a wink for close to forty hours: I was testing all the back-end features, the shopping cart, every process and mechanism, making sure the site was ready for the holiday traffic onslaught.

As the PR firm's efforts began to kick in, we all started to feel additional pressure from the outside world.

At the same time, I was staying in close contact with Heather Kelly, a senior VP at S&S and my contact there, so I could personally stay on top of developments. I believe you can't just hire a firm and then forget about it. A campaign like this works best when you treat it like a partnership, and as with all aspects of your business, you need to know what's going on. Professional PR is a fascinating and fast-paced game: you put out feelers for as many exposure opportunities as you can. Lots of them fall through — but lots of them come together, too. And something very big came together for us just before we were ready to launch.

Jean Chatzky from the *Today* show contacted us and let us know that she wanted to see a copy of the Web site. In addition to mentioning us on the *Today* show, she was writing a big article on us for *Time* magazine, and they urgently needed a high-resolution screen shot of the site to use as a graphic to accompany the piece.

Nat and I started hammering at Ruslan on the other side of the world, telling him, "Ruslan, we need this done!" He would e-mail back, "I know! I know!" And we'd go, "No, we really *need* it. They're asking for it at *Time* magazine!"

We reached the absolute deadline for the graphic on Friday, December 12; they positively needed to have it, in New York and in hand, by 6:00 P.M. Eastern time—which was six in the morning Ruslan's time. The pressure could hardly have been more intense. At literally the last possible hour, Ruslan came through: we managed to put it in the hands of the woman who needed it at the Manhattan offices of *Time*, just before the deadline.

And the next morning, U.S. troops from the 1st Brigade Combat team of the 4th Infantry Division caught Saddam Hussein.

This is the thing about publicity: you cannot make absolute plans. I was scheduled once to go on the *Jane Pauly Show*. I really liked Jane Pauly, and this would have been fantastic publicity for my business. What happened? Before my date came, her show was canceled.

Everyone knows that you have to back up your data; you cannot afford to have a hard disk crash and lose all your critical information. The same thing is true for promotion: you always want to have backups. You never want to be dependent on one critical link in the chain. If relying on computers has taught us one thing, it's the value and necessity of building redundancy into your systems. You never know what will crash—just as our *Time* article crashed on December 13.

Saddam got the cover, of course, with the screaming headline "WE GOT HIM!"—and our big article evaporated in the face of the big event. We got bumped to a little column in the back, headlined "Trading Gift Cards." Actually, once we learned what had happened, we didn't think we'd even be in the issue at all, but when it went on sale the following Monday and we grabbed and opened a copy, sure enough, there we were, on page 132: a one-sixth-page bulletin-style news piece by Jean Chatzky (right next to a piece three times its length on online dating).

It wasn't huge, but hey, it was *Time* magazine. And it didn't matter, anyway, because we had redundancy built into our PR, big time.

Our PR firm had done its job, and done it beautifully. Certificate Swap.com launched on December 15, 2003, right at the height of the holiday shopping season—and it was a smash success.

The instant we launched, we had media attention from around the world. With our PR firm handling all our media inquiries, I was doing half a dozen radio interviews a day. We were in *USA Today*, the *Chicago Tribune*, the *Los Angeles Times*, the *New York Post*, the *New York Times*, the *Miami Herald* . . . we were in *Time*, *Newsweek*, and every news or business publication in print. We were featured on CBS's *Early Show*, NBC's *Today* show (where Jean Chatzky reviewed us), MSNBC, and Fox News. I was doing live television interviews by satellite with news affiliates across the country. (I was set to go on *Anderson Cooper 360*, and even went through the process of a thirty-minute preinterview—but it turned out we couldn't find a satellite location that CNN could hook up with in time for the show.)

It was the biggest media blitz I'd ever been involved in. I still have a videotape we made at the time, with news clips on our site from local news channels all across the country.

Over the holidays I went to Akron, Ohio, with Matt Bagby to visit Liz Curlee, a girl I knew who lived there. While we were walking around a mall, a little camera crew came bustling up to me and asked if they could set up an interview. The CBS station in Cleveland had heard I was there and drove down to find me. How? They had read a story the previous day in the *New York Post* that mentioned I was going to be attending a Cleveland Cavs game the next night with front-row tickets—and they called my PR firm. They set up and interviewed me right then and there, as we walked through the mall.

Our first week in business, we brought a hundred thousand people to our Web site—with zero dollars in advertising. Of course, we did spend $15,000 on our PR firm, but that was a drop in the bucket compared to what that kind of exposure would have cost us if we'd tried to buy it through advertising dollars. We received what was probably the equivalent of a multimillion-dollar advertising blitz during the holiday season with prime-time exposure.

That's the power of the media, whether it's nationwide or just in your local community. We successfully launched what looked like a multimillion-dollar company, in fewer than six weeks from conception to execution, with a zero-dollar advertising budget, simply by using the media.

One of the reasons why CertificateSwap.com was such hot press was that people were hungry for good news about the future of business on the Internet. The truth was, people were hungry for good news about the future of business, period.

That June, *Entrepreneur* magazine ran a feature article called "How Tech Got Its Groove Back." The piece focused on several entrepreneurs who were helping, after the dark days of the dot.com collapse, to fuel what the story called "a tech revival." One of these entrepreneurs was me.

Of all the print pieces about me and my businesses that I'd seen, this was one of those I most appreciated. I liked it because it made a really strong point—and an accurate one—from its title right down to its details. The writer, Amanda C. Kooser, didn't just write about our accomplishment; she also wrote about *how* we were doing what we were doing, the lessons we'd learned from the era and that other entrepreneurs could learn, too. "Cameron Johnson of CertificateSwap.com may be conducting business from his dorm room, but he's helping to fuel a tech revival. Johnson has a basic suggestion: 'The best thing you can do is research. You better know who your competitors are,' he says. 'You have to know everything about everybody.'" She described how companies like ours weren't "whooping it up with indoor basketball courts" or "lavish launch parties in expansive office buildings." In fact, we operated without an office.

She quoted me as saying, "The Internet allows you to create these virtual corporations. I've got a Web designer in India, another one in the Ukraine, and one in the Netherlands. My programmer is in New Hampshire. I've got two people [who] handle customer service out of California." She noted that I had never met my partner and co-owner, Nat Turner, who lived in Texas.

There is often a preconceived notion about what makes me different or what makes my businesses successful. "Next, we're going to introduce you to a whiz kid on the computer . . ." — that's how I'm used to hearing myself introduced, and as I've said before, nothing could be further from the truth.

After Nat and I launched CertificateSwap, a story in another magazine called me "A Midas touch phenomenon." But that's not really accurate, either. It's not that everything I do turns out perfectly, or that I have any sort of magic wand or amazing lucky touch.

Being a success isn't about being a "whiz kid" or having a "Midas touch." It's not really about being special at all. It's about developing a feel for human nature and common sense, and applying that know-how with diligence.

For me, CertificateSwap.com was a confirmation of everything I'd learned to that point. Pulling it off took all the lessons I'd gleaned from all my prior experiences in business, and that, more than anything else, was why I found its success so satisfying. I knew that if I could make this business work, then I could go on to build even bigger businesses in the future.

I was starting to have serious doubts about continuing my schooling at college — but my *education* was right on track. I was doing what I loved, and more sure of my path than ever.

14

Stick to Your Guns

By March 2004, three months after our launch, CertificateSwap was getting fifteen thousand to twenty thousand hits per day. It had earned more than $70,000 in its first three months. And we had a problem.

Actually, I had *two* problems. The first was that Nat and I had not been prepared for just how fast our new company would grow and how large it would become. Our PR contract expired in February, but the publicity we'd generated had tremendous momentum, and people were still talking about us everywhere. What's more, even though the holiday season was over, people needed our service more than ever: everyone wanted to sell or trade the gift cards they'd gotten in December.

The business was not simply continuing to grow, it also was starting to swallow all our time. The way it was going, it would soon need a substantial amount of staffing and infrastructure underneath it—and that meant some serious financing.

As far as we could see, we really had three choices, and we would have to make a decision fast. We could sell our brainchild to the highest bidder and walk away with some cash. We could go find venture capital and take it to the next level ourselves. Or we could do what Tommy and I had done back in the days of Surfing-Prizes: cash in our chips and just shut it down.

One thing was for sure: we couldn't keep going the way we were, doing it on our own. Pretty soon it would start to implode under its own weight.

The other problem wasn't so much business as personal: I'd had enough of college and wanted out of Virginia Tech.

I decided to solve both problems with one plan: I would leave Virginia Tech and put my full-time attention into raising venture capital. I'd never done this before—but never having done something before had never stopped me.

One weekend, after my first semester was over and before the second semester had begun, I made the forty-five-minute drive home and sat my parents down for a talk.

"Look," I said, "I gave it a shot. It was interesting. But I've had enough. I'm not going back. I'm going to drop out of school and run CertificateSwap."

They said, "No, you're not—"

And I said, "Yes, I am! I'm serious. Look, we've been down this road before. This is an argument you know I'm going to win."

It was a repeat of our Woodberry quarrel—only this was a few years later, and I think my parents both knew I wasn't going to back down.

I said, "Mom, Dad, look at all the basketball stars and football stars who go right from high school to the NBA, or the actors and musicians who don't bother with college because their careers are already in motion. There have to be business stars, too, who don't need to go to a four-year program to learn their field. If I go through four years of college, I'll just be on a level playing field after four years—whereas now I have an *advantage*. Spending four years in school means I'll be four years *out of* the business world. Everything changes like lightning in the Internet world, and they'll all have caught up to me!"

My dad said, "A college education doesn't hurt anyone."

I said, "I agree, but it'll still be there ten years later if I still want it."

He said, "Cameron, you can lose your house, you can lose your company, you can lose your money, you can lose your wife—but you can't lose your education. It's the one thing you'll always have."

I said, "That's true, I don't disagree, but I *am* getting an education—a real-world education. Even though I'm not in the classroom every day, I'm still learning, and at a faster pace than my friends in college, because they're trying to learn about these things in the classroom, whereas I'm learning these things by actually doing them."

And then I said, "Okay, here's the deal. I will take off from school this spring and go raise $5 million in venture capital. If I'm not successful in raising the capital, I'll shut down the business and go back to school, and you'll never hear anything more about it."

I had calculated that this was about what we needed to take us to the next level, including hiring the people and investing in the ad campaign we'd need—and we would start needing to do those things fast, within a few months.

I didn't think we'd ever actually use the entire $5 million. I was pretty sure we could create a solid brand for ourselves and be so securely positioned in the public's mind that we would be in a strong positive cash flow well before we even got close to the bottom of our coffers. But access to a war chest of $5 million would buy us everything we needed to get to that point, if my projections were on target, and to cover us if my projections were way off and we grew slower than I expected.

Or, which is sometimes just as tricky, if we grew even *faster* than I expected.

This being the spring of 2004, the golden age of "Internet start-ups that can do no wrong" was well behind us; and while it was already showing strong signs of recovery, the economy had taken quite a hit since 2001. Raising $5 million for an Internet start-up would have been a piece of cake in 1999. Now, five years later, most would see it as a long shot.

Still, I was confident we could do it.

My parents gave in. What could they do? They wished me good luck and gave me their blessings.

Now the pressure was on. In the spring of 2004, I left Virginia Tech to see if I could raise $5 million in venture capital.

*　　*　　*

Venture capitalists do two things: they recruit people willing to invest a lot of money in a risky start-up, and they find a start-up to fund. Typically, they are looking for something that has a unique idea and a sound business model. These venture capitalists and their investors have so much disposable cash that they can afford to invest millions into dozens of different start-ups, even knowing that most of them will fail, because they know that the two or three that work may hit it big and earn back well more than their entire investment.

I carefully put together my package. First I prepared a solid and thorough proposal, complete with detailed projections. Then I put together a video collage of news spots and media pieces on our launch the previous December. While I could hardly claim to be objective, it all seemed pretty impressive to me.

Several years before, I had been approached by some venture capitalists, and I'd been careful to keep all their contact information organized and accessible. I started calling my list and was not entirely surprised to find that some were already broke and out of business. However, others were thriving, and pretty soon I had a few appointments.

One of the guys I called on was very interested. He was in Washington, D.C., only a few hours up the highway from Roanoke, so I went up to meet with him and sell him on our idea.

I found the firm in an impressively tall building in one of the dozens of suburbs that choke the exorbitantly priced real estate circling the D.C. Beltway. The company consisted of the person I had talked to on the phone plus two others; the three of them managed a fund of $500 million to $600 million.

I had brought along my business plan, cover letter, and promotional video. After introductions and some brief small talk, they asked me what I had for them. I asked if I could start by playing them my video.

I popped the tape into the VCR and pushed Play as they gathered around the television, wearing expectant expressions that were politely hopeful but gave away nothing.

As the news pieces began playing, I watched their expressions change. As piece after piece rolled, it was clear that they were getting pretty excited. One muttered to another, "These kids know how to get media attention!" Clearly, this was key to them—as I had thought it would be.

To be a viable investment, obviously a business proposal has to look feasible. It has to be well thought out, its projections with well-crossed *t*'s and dotted *i*'s. It needs to have a track record that shows that the concept has played out successfully in the real world, at least on a small scale.

But more than anything, these VC guys wanted to know that the business—and the people running it—could generate *buzz*. And what they were seeing on my VHS tape was some seriously great word of mouth.

My purpose was to sell the idea, and I was pretty sure that even before we got to the business plan, I'd sold it. Still, the meeting had just begun. Now we started talking over the proposal.

It was a fascinating process. They played devil's advocate— "What if you did this, and then what if that happened?"—and for every question they had, I had an answer. I had already considered and brainstormed all the potential problems they might bring up and long since solved them to my satisfaction. Every time they came up with an objection, I turned it into a positive.

VC FIRM: What if the merchants don't want to participate?

ME: Well, here's the thing: they already do. We have more than four hundred retail merchants offering their cards through our site. A member of the Fortunoff family [the Fortunoffs run a jewelry chain in New York City and throughout the Northeast] read the *USA Today* story about us. This man is one of their vice presidents. He called me and said, "Hey, what do we have to do to become a retailer on your site?"

One of my best soccer friends from Woodberry, Korbin Ming, is the son of Jenny Ming, who founded Old Navy; she and my mom are friends. I sent Jenny an e-mail and said, "Hey, I just started this company, we were just in *USA Today*. I want to buy some Old Navy gift cards, but we're going to need a discount so we can sell them on the site at a profit.

Anything we can sell is going to be additional business for you, because every time someone buys an Old Navy gift card from us they'll be buying that instead of buying a gift card from one of your competitors, like American Eagle or Abercrombie & Fitch." She wrote back and said, "I think that's a great idea. We'll sell them to you for a substantial discount, similar to what we give our employees."

We've been in contact with the gift card departments of all the big stores. Starbucks is a great example: they like to sell gift cards in bulk lots to corporations for their employees. They have a whole bulk gift card *division*.

VC FIRM: Wow. Okay, but what if the bigger merchants won't get on board?

ME: Here's the thing: they'll have to, because their competitors are all participating. If someone wants to give, say, a Best Buy gift card to their friends, they'll come to our site, and if they can't find a Best Buy card because Best Buy says they don't want to sell them on our site, then the customer's going to have to buy Circuit City cards instead. And Best Buy doesn't want that to happen. What we'll do is we'll brand ourselves with this idea: "If you want to give, sell, or trade a gift certificate—or if you want to buy one, whether secondhand or firsthand directly from the retailer—this is where you come to do it." And then Best Buy, Circuit City, and everyone else will sell their gift cards directly through our portal. They'll *have* to. And once we're the de facto online source for gift cards, we can go to Best Buy and say, "Hey, we need a million dollars' worth of your gift cards at ten percent off," and then we'll be making the spread on those—that's $100,000 in pure profit right there.

VC FIRM: What if a customer doesn't want to pay your 7.5 percent commission as a transaction fee?

ME: They're already paying twice that now on eBay. Go on to eBay and look up "gift card" and you'll bring up about thirty-five hundred results. Listing a $25 gift card will cost you $1.90. When it sells, you'll pay 5 percent of the sale price, so there's another $1.25. When you pay for it with PayPal, there's also a transaction fee of, say, 3 percent. Add the $1.90, plus the 5 percent, plus the 3 percent, and you're already up to a good 15 percent in fees. Whereas with us, you pay only a flat 7.5 percent, no hidden or added-on charges. And since we're paying only a 2 percent credit card processing fee, we're making a 5.5 percent spread.

VC FIRM: Wow . . . we didn't think of that. But couldn't eBay do the same thing?

ME: They could, but they won't, because it will be too late. What we're doing is taking a bunch of their customers and putting them on our site. At that point, the only way for eBay to get those customers back would be for them to buy us and make *us* their gift card portal. They could try to build their own gift card portal to compete with us, but we'll already have built the brand recognition. That's what we'll be doing in the next twelve to eighteen months.

VC FIRM: Wow. Okay. But what about security?

ME: The buyer pays us directly. When you buy this $25 gift card on our site, we charge your credit card the $22 you pay for the gift card. Shipping is $0.75, and the entire $0.75 is passed along to the seller, because he's got to ship it to you. We also pass along to him the $22, minus our 7.5 percent fee. Unlike eBay, we don't send our customers a bill. We simply hold on to the purchase price when it's paid. We send a notice to the seller saying, "Hey, congratulations, your gift card sold, send it to . . ." and we give him the address. But we don't give him the money until the buyer logs in a few days later and lets us know he got the card in the mail. Then funds are immediately disbursed into the seller's Certifi-cateSwap account, and he can now use those funds to buy another gift card (at which point the process starts over), or he can cash out. But you can cash out only when you get to a certain level. So we have no cash flow problem, because we're hanging on to the cash for a few days. This also means that we can guarantee delivery, because the money is not disbursed until the transaction is completed—so that also lets us protect against fraud.

VC FIRM: Ah, okay. Wow.

As you can see, I was doing most of the talking at this point.

ME: And the process is all automated, including the processing of the credit cards. We not only verify the customer's credit cards, we also check the mailing address on the credit card to further protect against fraud. It costs us an extra four or five cents for the bank to verify their address, but it's worth it, because it prevents someone from using a stolen credit card to buy all these gift cards and then be home free.

VC FIRM: How would you spend the $5 million you're asking for?

ME: We want to spend as little on advertising as possible, because that's mostly a waste. You don't spend $100,000 on advertising and get $1 million back—you spend $100,000 on advertising and get $10,000 back. That's the biggest thing that companies who take venture capital don't understand, and when they get $5 million, they think they have to spend it all. We don't. We need financing for staffing to handle the traffic, a modest amount of advertising to help build the brand— though we'll get free publicity to do most of the heavy lifting there—and further site development, as well as legal and accounting services. But we don't plan to spend more than a portion of the full $5 million. We don't want to run into a cash flow problem like all these other companies.

They ate it up. When they started getting to their feet, I knew the meeting was over.

One of them said, "We want you to know, we're interested."

And another one added, "We'll talk about it and get back to you."

Normally, those are not the words you want to hear when you're selling an idea. *We'll get back to you.* It sounds an awful lot like,

Don't call us, we'll call you—and by the way, don't hold your breath. And they had gone back to wearing those inscrutable, giving-nothing-away expressions.

But I wasn't worried. I knew that the presentation had impressed them, because even though I'd done most of the talking, I'd been paying close attention to their reactions.

I always look people in the eye when I'm talking to them—especially when I'm selling. The goal here is not to intimidate but to *connect*: I know my belief in what I'm selling comes across most effectively through direct eye contact.

I also make a point to notice their body language; if they cross their arms and lean back in their chairs, it's obvious that I'm not winning them over. During our back-and-forth over my proposal, I was getting clear signals that they were quite interested.

Of course they needed to mull it over. But there was no doubt in my mind that I'd be hearing from them again soon.

Sure enough, a few weeks later the man called and said, "Cameron, we want you to come back. We have a written offer waiting here for you."

I drove back up to D.C.

Before our meeting, the fellow who served as head of the firm took me out to lunch at a nice seafood restaurant, just the two of us. Over lunch he asked me all about the different things I'd done. He didn't discuss the details of their offer, but it was pretty clear that he and his partners were sold on the idea, and in fact, that they were quite excited about it. I could tell that whatever they had to offer, it was going to be a huge deal, certainly the biggest of my life so far.

After lunch we went back to his office for our meeting. We sat around the same table we'd sat around a few weeks earlier, when we'd played Ping-Pong with their objections and my responses.

They said, "Cameron, we're prepared to offer you $10 million; however, there are some contingencies—"

I stopped them and said, "Wait; before we get into those, why are you offering me $10 million when all I need is $5 million?"

Nat and I knew that with $5 million, we could hire ten to twenty people, including accounting, legal, and secretarial staff, as well as fund an advertising campaign and a number of other essential costs. Our PR blitz had been stunningly successful, but long-term, we needed advertising to establish and maintain our brand.

I explained all this and said, "At the end of three years, at most, we're going to be so well branded that we'll be *done*. We won't need any more venture capital. CertificateSwap.com will be a household name."

They replied, "Cameron, that's not how we work. We don't fund projects for a two- or three-year pipeline. We would be interested in giving you $10 million. From our vantage point, Cameron, $10 million is what it's going to take. You don't have to spend it all, but it will be there, in your account, available to you. You'll be in charge of how you spend it or don't spend it. You'll be in charge of who you hire and how much you pay them. But we'll dictate the salaries to you and Nat."

Aha, the salaries. According to their written proposal, Nat's would be about half of mine, because he'd still be in school. And mine would be something like $60,000 or $70,000 a year. That was less than I'd been earning in high school! I was getting uneasy with how this was sounding.

"Okay," I asked, "so what are the contingencies you mentioned?"

One, they explained, was that I would drop out of school completely and agree not to go back for a minimum of four years.

Another was that I would have to live right here, on the outskirts of D.C.

Another was that Nat and I would agree to give up seventy percent ownership in the company. Splitting the remaining 30 percent, this would leave us with 15 percent apiece.

Of course, that's standard when you take on this kind of investment. Nat and I had invested maybe $50,000; they were getting ready to invest $10 *million*. It was reasonable to expect that we'd give up majority ownership, and we expected that we would be giving up control of the company. That's one thing. But was it worth it? And what was the risk?

Agreeing to a steep pay cut, agreeing to leave behind all my friends and move to an urban neighborhood I didn't like, and then giving up majority ownership . . . I was having a hard time seeing the value here. Nat and I wouldn't be calling the shots—*they* would. And what if I didn't agree with the decisions they made?

Sure, it would be a great opportunity: I would get to fly around the country on an expense account, promoting my company . . . and in four years, if the company wasn't doing well, it would all reflect badly on me—and I would have spent four years of my life following someone else's decisions, on a salary that in Washington, D.C., one of the most expensive locations on the Eastern Seaboard, I could barely live on.

They had probably figured, "If we have this kid working for us for the next four years, we'll at least make our $10 million back. We're not going to lose. Even if we screwed it up, we'd be able to sell it for at least what we'd put into it."

I said, "My first concerns are not the four years. I hadn't planned to go back to school anyway. But I don't like being up here in D.C. I don't like driving up here, I don't like being here, and I certainly can't afford to live here on the salary you're suggesting."

They said, "We might be able to negotiate the salary a little."

A *little?* I thought. *What's "a little" going to do?* I didn't like the direction this was going. I think they saw themselves as educating me about how this kind of thing worked—and that they fully expected me to take the offer. But I didn't.

I said, "I'll have to discuss it with my partner."

I came back to Roanoke and called Nat. "Hey," I said, "I don't think this is going to work. Do we really want to give up seventy percent ownership in the company and put our names on the line, and let them use the goodwill and marketplace credibility we've built to promote their venture when we can't even call the shots? Conceivably, they could run the company into the ground, even fire us, and we'd have nothing to show for it but a damaged reputation—and all for a mediocre salary!"

Nat was getting ready to go to The Wharton School at the University of Pennsylvania, perhaps the most prestigious business school in the country. (In fact, he actually received his acceptance notice from Wharton on December 15, the day we launched CertificateSwap. An article in the *Houston Business Journal* quoted him as saying, "It was a good day." It was.)

There was never any question of Nat moving to D.C., and he'd made that clear to me from the start. It was really me they were negotiating with, me who would be the one moving to their location and being directly under the VC firm's thumb.

"It's cool with me if you want to accept this venture capital," Nat said. "I'll be okay with giving up ownership—but I'm going to Wharton."

I didn't know if the guys at the VC firm would go for that.

I called them and told them that going to Wharton was Nat's bottom line, thinking that perhaps this would crash the deal.

But they said, "We'd still be interested even if Mr. Turner were in school. But we want to see you in D.C. for the next four years. We think this is going to be a $100 million company. Cameron, you need to look past the ownership you're giving up, look past the four years of your life you're giving up, look past all the short-term issues, and see the big picture."

I knew that with all the PR we already had behind us—and with a $10 million check in hand—we would get even more PR. If we moved forward, we would be in the public spotlight in a bigger way than anything I'd ever seen before, way more than with SurfingPrizes, more than Japan, even more than with the launch we'd just been through. *Way* more.

And what if the company didn't work out? A few years from now, Cameron Johnson could be the biggest idiot on the face of the earth if the company went down the tubes.

I called Nat and told him what they'd said. He said, "Hey, it's really your call. What do you think?"

This wasn't the first time I had been presented with something that was a huge opportunity but that also had a very big risk attached. In the fall of 2000, when Tommy and Aaron and I had the chance to sell the SurfingPrizes customer database, we would have earned a massive amount of money—and possibly some big legal problems along with it. Then as now, it was a matter of weighing short-term gain against long-term consequences.

In both cases, it was no contest.

I said, "I think we need to sell the business."

Nat said, "Okay, let's do it. Let's sell it."

Nat and I had a great PR gimmick planned. Until this time (as the *Entrepreneur* article pointed out) we had never actually met in person. We thought, wouldn't it be exciting to actually meet each other *on live television* in conjunction with doing a massive launch for the next phase of the business?

But that next phase never happened. The following year, we would remember this idea and implement it, in part, when we would do a live-TV launch of our next joint business venture. But for now, the business was over.

That June Nat flew in from Texas and we did finally meet face-to-face, and we had the opportunity to reminisce together about the meteoric rise and short-lived success of our business. It was good to meet, and neither of us had any regrets about the decision to sell.

Not long after that second meeting, the VC firm e-mailed me and we had a telling dialogue.

VC FIRM: Hey, it was so great to meet you. We'd like to move forward. Let's put our attorneys in touch.

ME: Look, would you be interested in just buying the company? Instead of putting in $10 million, just buy it for a fraction of that price.

VC FIRM: To be honest with you, we're not interested in just investing $10 million in the company—we're interested in investing it in *you*. We're interested in you, the media attention you can bring to it, and having you make it work.

ME: If that's the case, I would think you'd want to offer a better salary.

VC FIRM: Well, we might be able to negotiate that some . . .

Ah. We were back to renegotiating my salary "a little."

> VC FIRM: . . . and as far as the idea of buying the business, we'd
> be open to looking at that. We'd at least reimburse your
> expenses in building it to this point.

"At least reimburse our expenses"?! We had invested maybe $50,000 into the business at this point. They were talking about buying our phenomenally successful Internet business for $50,000?! That would have been ridiculous. We knew we could get twice that on the open marketplace. And besides, if we were going to sell it, we would want to sell it to someone who would actually see its potential and do something with it.

That's exactly what we did. And it worked out really well.

We listed CertificateSwap for sale on eBay. We found that even if you don't actually sell your business on eBay, you can use an eBay listing as a market tool. We wanted to sell the company for something like $100,000, so we listed it as for sale—and set the reserve price so high that nobody would meet it (I think the amount was $500,000). We didn't really expect to get serious bids, but we knew that people would see the ad for ten days; if we listed it three times, it would be on there for a full month. Maybe people would contact us for more information or to negotiate.

And that's what happened.

In June 2004, Nat and I sold the company to an individual who worked for Moody's Investors Service, a financial firm in New York. He has run the company ever since, and as of this writing, it's doing just fine. The man who owns it is not a teenager (I think he's about thirty years old), so there's no special spin on the owner as there was when it was Nat and me. Now it's staying in the news in part because it's a great idea for a business and a good place to unload unwanted gift cards.

Last time I looked, it was still gaining momentum. Perhaps not the way it would have if we had taken the $10 million in venture capital and put some real power into it—but it's doing well, and I'm very pleased about that.

*   *   *

We could have taken that $10 million and used it to advertise nationwide, hire employees and all those things, maybe even do a Super Bowl commercial. And we probably would have done really well with it.

For a nineteen-year-old entrepreneur, being offered $10 million to grow an already successful business was an incredibly attractive proposition. It would have been so easy to take that huge pile of capital and use it to pull out the stops and create a really powerful nationwide brand. In fact, accepting this offer was probably the easy thing to do.

But the easy thing to do is not always the smart thing to do.

If the company sells for $100 million five years from now, I can't promise there won't be some part of me that will want to kick myself. But you can't miss what you never had, and I'm not worried about it. I'm glad we did what we did. We still made a hefty profit on our investment, even though we sold it for a lot less than we would have made if we'd kept it—assuming it would have performed as well as we hoped.

Which, given that someone who wasn't really running the business would have been holding the purse strings, was definitely *not* a given.

I never stay connected to a company after I sell it. I might give birth to it and develop it through its infancy, but when it grows up and moves out, it's gone, on its own. When it's over, it's over. My experience with CertificateSwap is perhaps the best example of this.

The lesson I learned from securing the $10 million and then passing on it was pretty simple: don't let short-term rewards overshadow long-term goals.

We may have let go of a $10 million opportunity. In view of how large Nat and I might have grown that business over the following years if we'd kept it, who knows? We might even have let go of a $100 million opportunity.

But I'll tell you what: the education and experiences I've had in the two years since have already been well worth it—and I've never looked back.

✻   ✻   ✻

I had told my parents that if I failed to get the venture capital, I'd go back to school. And I didn't go back on my word, because, strictly speaking, I didn't fail to secure the capital. I got the offer: I just chose not to accept it.

However, I did not return to Virginia Tech. I did a second semester online, and I still consider it an open question as to whether I might go back at some point—but for now, I was done with it.

My dad described my decision not to go back to college in one word: "devastating." Still, in the two years that have passed since I pulled out of Virginia Tech, both my parents have done almost a complete 180 and now firmly support my decision to do what I'm doing. And it's not as if I didn't have good examples before me. My mom didn't graduate from college, either: she left school to run her family's business; and her dad, being one of eleven children, never had the opportunity to go to college.

The administration at Virginia Tech thought I was only taking off a semester to work on my business. They assumed I would be back for the fall semester. But when September came and I still hadn't signed up for any courses, they realized that I was just too keenly involved in working with actual, real-life businesses to re-engage in the academic study of business theory.

They responded by doing something they had never done before: they offered me a scholarship for entrepreneurship. This was a first for the Pamplin School of Business, and I was genuinely honored by the gesture and what it meant.

But I had to turn it down. It just wouldn't have been the smartest move for me. I thanked the university and requested that they instead give the scholarship to someone who could benefit from it financially.

I said before that the biggest pull in my decision to attend Virginia Tech was that I had good friends going there. That's true, and it made enrolling a pretty easy decision. By the same token, it also made leaving an especially hard decision. But not long afterward, I found a way to have my cake and eat it, too.

✻   ✻   ✻

For close to a year, I'd been looking at the idea of buying a house. Just as I would with a business idea, I tested this idea out carefully and did tons of research. I crunched every number and researched every mortgage option. I knew the neighborhood I wanted to live in and had a great relationship with a Realtor there (in fact, I sold him his truck)—and it's a good thing I did, because he must have gotten frustrated with me. He showed me a good twenty homes before I narrowed down my choices.

It was well worth the effort, because ultimately I found the perfect house. But when I made an offer, I found myself in a bidding war with a couple who wanted it as badly as I did. When the seller accepted their offer, I authorized my Realtor to offer the buyers $20,000 to walk away from their contract—and they declined.

You'd think that I would be discouraged; but I've always believed that everything happens for a reason. Sometimes, when you don't get the result you really want, you discover later that it actually turned out better for you in the long run—and that's what happened here.

Soon after I lost that house, another house came on the market just three doors up the street. The seller turned out to be a Virginia Tech professor to whom I had sold a vehicle only a few months before. I let him name his price—and bought it at the price he named. It was a fair price, and the house was fantastic. He was happy, I was happy, and the couple who outbid me for the other house are now my neighbors.

And here's the best part. That neighborhood, the one I'd picked out as my perfect place to live? It's in Blacksburg, Virginia, not far from my old campus.

Although I left Virginia Tech, I still live nearby—and share the house with a handful of my best college friends. I found a way to have the best of both worlds.

15

Get Experience on the Ground

A few months into 2005, I was doing an interview in New York for ABC's *Money Matters*. The interviewer asked me which of my businesses had taught me the most. SurfingPrizes, I told him, because that's where I'd had to learn all sorts of things about laws and fraud and dozens of other aspects of doing big business in the real world.

Then he asked, "Out of all of them, which one has been the most fun?"

I surprised him by saying that the most fun I'd ever had in any business was what I was doing right then: working at Magic City Ford.

"Really?!" he responded, clearly surprised. "What's so exciting about selling Fords?"

"Well," I said, "having the opportunity to work every day with 140 employees is quite a high."

By this time, I wasn't just stripping tires or working Internet leads: I had become general sales manager for the entire dealership, and the majority of those 140 employees—every one of whom was older than I—reported directly to me.

He was incredulous. "What do you do when a new employee, say, or maybe an old salesman who's been on the floor for years, looks at you and says, 'My God, this guy's my boss!'?"

Of course, that would be anyone's normal reaction, and that's exactly what I told the interviewer. "It's my job," I added, "to prove to them that I can handle it, that I'm in this position for a reason. And I'm having a blast doing just that."

From the tomatoes and lemonade stands to my aunt's furniture store, I'd been involved in sales my whole life. But for the most part, I'd been focused on Internet businesses. Now I had entered the world of bricks and mortar in just about the most traditional business one could imagine, with a building full of employees to train, teach, coach, and manage. And what an amazing education it was.

I think everyone who wants to start his or her own business (especially an Internet business) ought to spend time in a traditional business environment, where you're working face-to-face with other people every day. It's easy to get carried away with technology and lose touch with the fundamentals, as so many people did at the turn of this century. That's one of the hazards of Internet businesses, and why I always encourage young entrepreneurs to get some genuine hands-on experience working on a real shop floor.

The truth is, no matter what type of business you're in, all businesses come down to understanding people. It's important to be able to read a financial statement or read the market potential for a new product. It's a hundred times more valuable to know how to read someone's *character*. Working at Magic City Ford gave me the opportunity to put to the test everything I'd learned about people.

And it also gave me the chance to work with someone who has had perhaps more influence on me than any other mentor I've had.

I first met Grover Keeney right before Christmas 2003, when he came in to talk to my dad. I was still at Virginia Tech, and my decision to leave was still a few weeks away.

My dad was in search of a new general manager. The general manager at an auto dealership runs the store; he's pretty much in charge of the whole operation. Charlie Robertson, our general manager at the time, was leaving the dealership after forty-seven years of service.

Charlie had come to work for the dealership fresh out of UVA and had worked there ever since, which means that my dad had never worked at the dealership without Charlie being there. In fact, when my dad first came on board, more than thirty years ago, Charlie was already a legend at the dealership. We all knew that Charlie would be tough to replace. But he was leaving, and my dad had to turn the reins over to someone.

Grover was one of the most experienced, competent people in the car business; he had worked at some of the largest dealerships in the country. He and my dad had known each other for years, although they had never actually worked together. Originally from this area, Grover had just decided to leave the car business and come back to Roanoke to enjoy his early retirement.

My dad had already looked at so many other candidates, and none of them seemed like they would really fill Charlie's shoes. He invited Grover to come in to talk—just to talk.

So it was that on this chilly December day, this beaming, energetic-looking man walked into the dealership, strode up to the receptionist area where all the salespeople were standing around, and said, "I have an appointment to see Bill Johnson."

Nobody else made a move or said a thing. I think that for a moment, everyone was kind of intimidated by the aura of pure relaxed confidence he exuded. Maybe they knew he was here to talk about the general manager position, and they were hoping he wouldn't fire them if he took the job. I don't know *what* was going through everyone's mind—but nobody seemed about to reply, so I walked up to him, stuck out my hand to shake, and said, "Mr. Keeney? My name's Cameron Johnson. I've heard a lot about you and I'm looking forward to you being here."

That started one of the best friendships and most rewarding business relationships I've ever had.

After Grover and my dad had talked for a bit, my dad came out and told me, "If he wants the job, it's his." He did, and it was.

Grover and I clicked immediately. That first month while I was still "on break" from Tech (I had just launched CertificateSwap.com but hadn't quite decided not to return to college), Grover would come on down to my little cubicle and hang out, just to chat and see what I had to say about whatever topic caught our interest.

From the first conversation, Grover and I could talk comfortably about anything. He never treated me like a kid, and we saw eye to eye on everything. Sometimes, when issues came up, it was as if he and I were on one team and everyone else at Magic City Ford were on another. We talked about every aspect of the car business and our dealership, but we didn't stop there; it seemed like we talked about everything in the encyclopedia.

One thing I especially like about Grover is his curiosity and his willingness to learn, even his appetite to learn. He's in pretty amazing shape, too—lifts weights, works out, a strong guy. We would cover a few miles every day, just walking back and forth over the fifteen-acre lot. That was another reason why the two of us clicked: we both have the same work habits. We'd be there till eight, nine, even ten at night; the two of us would routinely be the last two to leave the building. And we came in every Saturday.

One thing Grover and I often talked about was the used-car sales department. One day, about a month after he had started there and after I had decided to leave Virginia Tech and work on finding capital investment for CertificateSwap, this topic came up. Our used-car sales manager had just left, and I thought we had a good opportunity to make all kinds of improvements, from how the place was set up to how the sales staff could be doing things differently.

Suddenly he looked over at me and said, "Well, Cameron, do you want to do it?"

I looked back at him and saw that he meant it. "Well," I replied, "I've never done it, but I guarantee you I can."

And just like that, I was promoted to used-car manager.

It was the first time I'd ever been promoted to a position by someone else, and I have to tell you, I loved it. I'd worked summer jobs, and I'd been "promoted" to Internet sales manager—but that was really only a title for a one-man operation. This was different.

Grover took a big risk giving me that job. Yes, I'd grown up around the car business, and for a few years I'd been coming in every day and learning everything I could. But still, I was nineteen years old, and now I would be managing people twice my age and with many more years' experience on the floor. Also, he hadn't consulted with my dad—who was not happy about the idea when he first got the news.

I went to work immediately, boosting our inventory and creating a bigger selection. I ordered some reports that showed me which used models and colors were currently selling the best in our market, and stocked more of those. I went to auctions and bought really nice cars to put on the floor, knowing that nice-looking cars will always find a home.

I'm happy to say, it worked out quite well: over the next six months, our department doubled its sales. In fact, by the time we hit mid-2004, we had the best numbers in used cars that Magic City Ford had seen in its sixty-six-year history.

Some people called it our "magic season."

And because I'd proven myself and shown that I could make sales happen, Grover made a really bold move: he promoted me to general sales manager for the entire dealership.

If Grover hadn't just recently become our general manager, none of this would have happened. My dad would never have promoted me so quickly; he would have moved me gradually up through the positions, and I don't know if I would have had the patience to stay there for years on a slow track like that.

That's a lesson I learned from Grover: if you're a high performer, you're going to be noticed, especially by the high performers above you. Grover didn't even bother asking my dad about either of these promotions, because he knew my dad would probably object (which he did). And that's another lesson I learned from him: make the decisions you think you should make. Exercise your authority.

People have asked if it's been easier for me at Magic City Ford, being my dad's son. But as Grover points out, if anything, being the owner's son has been a handicap, not an advantage.

It wasn't easy when I took the job. There were salesmen who'd been in the department for more years than I'd been alive. But you can't inherit respect, and you can't demand it; you have to earn it. What made it work was that I earned their respect. Everyone had seen the kind of hours I'd put in, and the results I'd gotten running Internet sales and then used-car sales.

Managing other employees was not entirely new to me; at CertificateSwap, for example, we had about twenty part-time employees (although they were all around the world and I interacted with them only virtually). But in my capacity as general sales manager, it would now be my job to hire, fire, and run the entire sales department. I'm sure there were a lot of people watching me closely, to see how I would perform.

It worked out extremely well. In fact, by the end of 2004—a year when sales and profits were down in practically all dealerships around the nation—we had increased sales and profits by such a margin that we had our highest-profit year ever in the history of Magic City Ford.

This is not an easy thing to do. You don't make any significant money on oil changes and other such light service; the way you make real money is by selling more cars. In 2004, we sold over eight hundred more cars and trucks than we did in the previous year.

And again, this was in a down market. Ford sales were off nationwide; in almost every other dealer in Virginia, sales were lower in 2004 than in 2003. Ours went up 167 percent. Dealers were looking at our "magic season" and saying, "What the heck is Magic City Ford doing differently?"

The answer is, we were doing *everything* differently.

Running a successful dealership, like running any successful business, isn't about doing one thing perfectly; it's about doing dozens of things right, or at least well enough to make a difference. Our success at Magic City Ford was about which inventory we chose to stock, how we decided to spend our advertising dollars, how we worked deals, and how we paid close attention to the details.

But the most important thing had to do with how we dealt with each customer.

One of the most important things I've learned about selling— no matter what you're selling, whether it's a Ford Explorer, a start-up to a VC firm, or tomatoes to your neighbor—is something my father taught me: what you're really doing is helping people remove all their obstacles.

The man on the sales floor says he can't make a decision today because his wife's not here with him. The salesman may think he's just heard the man give a reason that he can't buy—but that's not the case. He's just articulated an obstacle, that's all. He hasn't told you that you can't do business today; he's told you that now it's your turn to go to work for him.

You hear this and you say, "Your wife's not here? Hey, how about we all get in and drive out there and show it to her? Where is she right now? You think she's at work?"

So you pile in and drive over to the wife's place of work, and she loves the car, and you bring her back with you to the dealership, where the happy couple does the paperwork and drives off the lot with the car they wanted.

When a customer comes onto the dealership lot, he's there for a reason. I would tell our salespeople, "The customer's not here to get a haircut—he's here to buy a car." As a salesman, your job is to find out from the customer what it will take to earn his business *today.*

At Magic City Ford, there are eighteen salesmen and three sales managers: new-car manager, used-car manager, and general sales manager. When I took over as general sales manager, we came up with a new policy: *don't let a customer leave without Cameron or another sales manager talking to him or her first.* This is an old principle and a common practice at dealerships, but we hadn't been doing it consistently, and I thought our managers were not as involved as they should be.

Sometimes a salesperson would be trying to sell a customer, and he'd come out back and tell me, "Boss, he says he's got to go home and talk to his wife; he can't do anything today."

I'd go out there, introduce myself, and say, "[Mr. Customer], I really appreciate your coming in here to talk about this today, hopefully this is the vehicle you like."

He'd say, "Yes, it is."

"All right," I'd say, "let me ask you one question before you leave: On a scale from one to ten, ten being you're ready to buy the car and take it home, one being you wouldn't take the car if I gave it to you, where would you say you are right now?"

He'll think about it for a minute and then say, "I'd be a seven."

And by the way, people almost always answer that question with a six or a seven. An eight or higher would mean their obstacle was insignificant, and if it were a five or less, they probably wouldn't be here having this conversation.

So I'd say, "Okay, that's great, let me ask you this"—and here comes the critical phrase—"*What would I have to do to make you a ten today?*"

Do you see how powerful that question is? You're asking how you can serve the customer. What *you* can do for *him*.

Sometimes the customer would say, "There's nothing you can do to make me a ten today. My wife's out of town; she'll divorce me if I buy this car." Fair enough.

But sometimes he'd say, "I really wish it had the six-disk CD changer."

In that case, I'd say, "Well, if I could give you a six-disc CD changer at no charge, or at our cost, could we do business today?"

And he'd reply, "Yeah, that's the only reason I wasn't buying it!"

Or maybe he'd say, "I didn't want to put $500 down, and your sales guy said I needed to."

No problem. I'd just say, "Well, what if we made that down payment for you; would we earn your business?" And the answer would be yeah, we would—and we did.

I was always sure to let our customers know that I wanted our salespeople to be taking good care of them. When a salesperson came to me with an obstacle, I would go onto the floor and say, "Hi, I'm Cameron Johnson, I'm the guy who works all the numbers back behind the desk. What can we do to put this together?"

"Ah, well . . ." the customer would say, "I like the car, I'm just not sure I'm ready to do this today."

And I'd say, "Okay. Well, I hope that Chris [the salesman who waited on him] has taken good care of you and answered all your questions."

"Yes, he has."

"Good. Well, let me ask you this: on a scale of one to ten . . ."

It's all about looking for your customers' needs and addressing them. When you focus on doing this, you can bring even the toughest customer around.

One day, a salesman came into my office, his face a little ashen. He looked like he'd been fighting off a pair of pit bulls. "Cameron, can you come out on the floor for a minute?"

One glance at his face and I was on my feet. "Sure. What's wrong?"

"We've got this guy in the showroom, and he says he's not ready to buy."

So we walk out onto the floor, and there's this sixty-year-old construction worker who weighs 295 pounds and looks like he could breathe fire, and he's saying, "No, I'm not gonna buy a car today at *any* price!"

I walk up to him and say, "Hi, I'm Cameron Johnson. I'm the general sales manager."

The man growls back, "Look, son, I've bought more cars than you are years old! *You* don't tell *me* how I'm gonna do it!"

An hour later, that same man is driving off our lot in his new truck, happy as could be. And the next day, when he comes back to finish some paperwork, he saunters onto the lot and accosts the first salesman he sees by saying, "Hey, where's my old buddy Cameron?" like he and I have known each other forever.

You're probably wondering, what did I do—how did I get him to buy that truck? But that's exactly the point: it isn't that I *got* him to buy a truck. He *wanted* that truck. If he didn't want to buy a vehicle, he wouldn't have come into our dealership in the first place. His only problem was that he had some barriers in the way. All I needed to do was help him move them out of the way.

The purpose here is not to put pressure on the customer, but simply to find out what we're doing wrong—and even more important, what else we can do right.

As I learned from Grover, this approach can work wonders in all kinds of situations, and not just with customers on the sales floor.

A few seasons ago, during some heavier than usual winter weather, an employee at the dealership tried to call to say he wouldn't be coming to work. He expected to get our switchboard operator, but Grover was answering the phones that day.

Startled, the man blurted out, "Mr. Keeney, I'm sorry, but my driveway is covered and they haven't gotten here to plow it. I can't make it in to work today."

Grover replied, "That's no problem. We'll come get you!"

What could the man say? He had given Grover an obstacle — and without batting an eye, Grover had removed it for him.

The man sighed and said, "Okay. Well, actually, let me give it a try . . . maybe I can get out after all." And he did.

Often the reason a customer gives at first for buying or not buying is not even close to what the truth is. They'll say, "I've got to go home and think it over," or "I've got to wait for my insurance check to come, and it doesn't come till the end of the week"—and chances are good this isn't the case at all. It's not that they're lying, it's just that they don't really know why they're hesitating.

Sometimes it's based on their assumptions. When someone comes in on a Wednesday and says, "I wrecked my car and I'm supposed to get an insurance check by Friday," I'll say, "Well, what if you just wrote us a check and we hold it till Friday—and you can take the car with you today?" And they say, "Oh, that's great!" They get a new vehicle and we make a sale—and we don't have to worry about them going to our competitors tomorrow while they're waiting for that check.

Which is exactly what they would do if we hadn't helped them remove their obstacles today.

Another big factor in our success at Magic City was a series of fairly radical decisions about how we were going to spend our advertising money. Actually, it's more a matter of how we *didn't* spend it.

One way to increase profits is to increase sales, and we certainly did that. But there's another way to increase profits, and it's just as valid: *cut expenses.*

A lot of the advertising we had been doing was extremely inef-fective. We were spending as much as $60,000 or $70,000 a month on advertising that just wasn't working. If we could cut out a good percentage of that without hurting our sales, it would automatically boost our profits. And that's what we did.

For example, we had been spending $200,000 a year on news-paper advertising. In 2004 we didn't spend a dime on the news-paper—and our sales went up.

Why? Well, ask yourself this: Where do you typically see ads for car dealers? In the newspaper, right? But do you ever really pay any attention to one of those newspaper ads? Probably not—unless it's offering insanely low prices.

And that's the thing: to get a customer to come in off a news-paper ad, you have to be offering the lowest prices *anywhere*. Because the competitor's ad is in there, too, on the same car—and if his prices are lower, that's where customers are going to go.

Now, because you need to have the lowest prices possible, you already know that if you get the sale, you're not going to make any money on it. And you're paying $10,000 or more to put the ad in there for three days, Friday through Sunday. Why would we keep doing this? To pick up three or four sales we didn't even want because we weren't making any money on them?

I talked to Grover about it and he agreed: let our competitors have those sales. We stopped the ads, left a chunk of that $10,000 in the bank, and looked for more creative and effective ways to use the rest. It didn't take long for us to come up with winning strategies.

One of the most powerful lessons I've ever learned about man-aging people is that nothing improves performance like great incen-tives. Offer people an appreciable reward for extra effort, and you'll see effort that will amaze you.

As part of our strategy, we created new sales bonuses. We'd choose a weekend where we expected lower than usual sales, and tell our sales force that we'd pay them an extra $100 for each car they sold that weekend. They picked up the pace, closed more deals, and started making more money than they'd ever made before. They did better, and we did better.

We also ran a few contests throughout the year that created tremendous incentives for our salespeople. One time, we took our newspaper ad $10,000, added another $5,000, and spent the $15,000 on a brand-new Mustang. Then we announced a thirty-day contest: whoever sold the most cars in the next thirty days would be driving that Mustang off the lot. We'd never done anything like that, and to some it sounded crazy—but we had our top three or four salespeople fighting to get that prize. With each of them pulling an extra ten sales or so, that contest generated another thirty or forty sales that month. Net result: we made back probably *triple* the cost of the new Mustang—instead of buying a newspaper ad that might have landed us at most three or four extra sales, none of which would have added a dollar to our bottom line.

That year, we gave away a plasma TV, a Ford Ranger, and all sorts of different prizes. We also had happier salespeople—and the most profitable year in the dealership's sixty-six-year history.

In many ways, managing is about making sure your team has the same goal and vision as you do. It's your job as their manager to properly explain what needs to be done and how it should be done. Of course, there are the basics, such as making sure everyone shows up on time and doesn't take extended lunch breaks. But in the larger scheme of things, those are minuscule. You might have an employee who might do little things that frustrate you, such as coming in late, but he might also be your most efficient employee.

One of the best management lessons I learned at Magic City Ford is that it's often best to overlook the little things. Instead, judge people on the job they do and the value they bring to your company. Their ability to contribute to the health and growth of the enterprise is what really matters.

Sometimes, though, those "little things" can become too big to ignore. Part of managing a business is recognizing when someone in the company is simply not pulling his weight, and being willing to take action.

The first time you consider firing someone is the exact moment when you need to openly address whatever frustrations you're having with the job he's doing. This gives him the opportunity to improve, and if he doesn't, he knows what's coming. It's amazing the difference you'll see just when people know they're being held accountable for their actions.

My dad once told me that most people who get fired are actually relieved when it happens, because they know they haven't been doing a good job, and the only real reason they're still there is that they haven't been pushed to leave their comfort zone and pursue another opportunity. Sometimes parting ways with an employer turns out to be the best thing that could happen: it can force the person to further his education, or to learn how to market himself to another potential employer, or to start his own business. Many successful entrepreneurs are "failed" employees who credit their success to being fired from their day-to-day jobs.

Still, no one likes firing anyone. I've had to fire at most a dozen people. In January 2005 I had to fire a sales manager, and that was pretty serious. While we have eighteen salesmen on the floor, there are only three sales managers; typical turnover for that position is once every ten years. This was especially hard, too, because my dad had hired this man.

Like all business decisions, even tough ones, I didn't spend a moment regretting it or second-guessing it; once it's done, it's done.

One of the best situations I can think of for the education of an entrepreneur is holding down a regular job while at the same time working on your own start-up. Working full-time at Magic City Ford didn't stop me from continuing to build Internet business. In fact, the same fall I was promoted to general sales manager at the dealership, I launched a new business on live television.

Ever since we'd started brainstorming CertificateSwap a year before, Nat Turner and I had thought it would be cool for the two of us to actually meet in person for the first time on a live TV broadcast. Not only would it be fun for us, but it also would be a great way to vividly demonstrate the power and viability of Internet businesses: "Look, these two kids created a hugely successful business together and have never even met face-to-face before this moment!"

Plus, with the live-news/reality-TV flavor of it, it would be a great way to attract a ton of publicity.

We were never able to pull it off with CertificateSwap, but the idea stayed with us. Over the spring, as Nat started preparing for his freshman year at Wharton and I was busy selling used cars, we dreamed up another business, called TrueLoot.

We had noticed that the online advertising market was starting to come back after its precipitous turn-of-the-century decline. The online world had begun to settle, and the biggest thing that had brought back online advertising was the phenomenal success of Google and their AdWord technology (the classified-ad type of listing you'll see on the right side of their search screen).

We decided to use the basic SurfingPrizes model again, only this time, instead of paying users a flat hourly rate, we would pay them in points. This made it a simpler program and more profitable as well, because not everyone would redeem their points.

TrueLoot essentially paid users to look at ads. You could earn points by watching a rotation of ads at the top of your screen, just as with SurfingPrizes. You also could earn more points by enrolling in a program where you would identify your specific interests and agree to receive a certain number of e-mail advertisements pertaining to those areas. At the bottom of each ad there was a button that would say, "I received this e-mail," so you would have to scroll through the ad to receive credit for it. When you clicked the button at the bottom, that would deposit the points in your account. This was quite valuable to our advertisers.

There was a third way to earn points: you could enroll in a program where you would receive a regular series of targeted ads on your mobile phone. This was leading-edge stuff. Estimates today are that this kind of targeting, permission-based marketing through mobile phones could become a $15 billion industry. But while we had it all programmed and ready to go in TrueLoot, we didn't actively promote it.

In mid-July, as Nat and I were putting this all together, I was suddenly contacted by Heather Kelly, my contact at my PR firm. Someone at CNBC had seen her firm's name on an article, and they contacted her to see if they could interview me on the channel's show *PowerLunch*.

I had a brainstorm. TrueLoot was just about ready to go. Why not do a live launch? Turn *PowerLunch* into "PowerLaunch"!

And on September 1, 2004, that's just what we did.

The launch went perfectly, and by the end of that fall, Nat and I had grown TrueLoot to the point where we had close to five thousand members. But Nat was now deep into his freshman year at Wharton, and I was busy with the dealership, so before the end of the year we put the business up for auction and sold it to the highest bidder for a substantial return on our investment. It was working beautifully when we sold it, and it's still running today.

I continued working at the Ford dealership for the next year and a half, until the spring of 2006, when I left to devote myself to preparing the launch of my newest business (which I'll describe in a later chapter).

Although I'd always known I wouldn't stay forever, it wasn't easy to let go. I knew I'd miss the sales floor, the constant activity, and the sheer challenge of working with all those people. I'd miss Grover, and I'd miss working with my dad. But Magic City Ford was like my graduate school, my in-the-trenches version of an MBA program in people management, and it was time to take my "degree" into the world.

16

Never Underestimate the Value of Your Customers

Ever since the days when I sat on the board of FutureKids and distributed a hundred Sega Dreamcast consoles for Isao Okawa, I've done a lot of consulting to companies of all sizes.

One thing that has always fascinated me about consulting, especially to larger companies, is that it's usually not very difficult to see where they're going wrong and what they could do to fix it. You don't need advanced business degrees to know that to be in business, your expenses have to be less than your revenue. Or to understand that to *stay* in business, you can't just keep going after new customers; you also have to take care of the customers you already have.

I know that sounds simple; it *is* simple. But often the bigger companies grow, the more they tend to lose sight of the simplest things—and the simplest things are also the most important. These days, one of those simple and extremely important things is top-quality customer service.

There's often a very fine line between success and failure. When you look at a failed company, you often can see that with a little common sense, they could have done just a few things differently and been a successful company. A lot of companies are failing for very basic reasons. And it's not just the big guys who get these things wrong; they are also huge stumbling blocks for small businesses and can make or break your success.

Not long ago, I had a few conversations with executives from one of the largest companies in the world, and it prompted me to put some of these observations on paper.

One day in June 2005 I got a call on my cell phone. The caller ID said *Unavailable*. When I answered, a voice I didn't recognize said, "Cameron?"

I said, "Yes?"

The voice said, "Cameron, this is Edsel Ford. How are you?"

Edsel Ford is a famous patriarch of the Ford family. The only son of Henry Ford II, he is named after his grandfather, who was son of the original Henry Ford. He was elected to the board of Ford in 1988 and has held various positions within the organization since. And here he was on my cell phone, calling me by my first name, as if he'd known me for years.

I said, "Well, hey, Mr. Ford, how are you?"

He told me that in a few weeks, the Fords were having a family reunion—the first they'd ever had, in fact—and he wanted to know if I would speak at the event. About thirty members of the family were getting together, some of them meeting for the first time, and they wanted me to talk to them about what it was like to be a fourth-generation Ford dealer. I was one of only a few people who fit that description.

One hot day a few weeks later, I arrived at the Phoenician Resort in Phoenix, Arizona. The Ford family had rented a major portion of the resort just for the occasion, including an entire building, a private lobby, a private pool, and more. We were there for four days, and I'll bet we never used more than a fifth of the space they had set aside.

At dinner the first night, I sat next to Edsel's sister Charlotte Ford, who owns and runs the Ford Modeling Agency in New York and who was married to the late Stavros Niarchos, a billionaire Greek shipping magnate. Charlotte is a very sweet lady and I really enjoyed her company. Her daughter Elena also was at our table; she had just been named vice president of North American Marketing for the Ford Division. It's quite a family to sit with around a dinner table.

At one point in our conversation, Elena commented to me that

she would love to have me send some of my thoughts to their product advisory board. We didn't take the idea any further than this
casual exchange, but the conversation got me thinking, and I began
considering what advice I'd give them if I were consulting for them.

About six months later, in January 2006, Ford rocked the business world by announcing that they were closing fourteen plants
and laying off up to thirty thousand workers over the next six years;
they also announced a $1.6 billion loss from their North American
operations the year before.

The following month I traveled to Orlando, Florida, to speak at
the annual convention of the National Automobile Dealers Association (NADA). This is the nation's largest convention for car dealers, with some thirty thousand people in attendance. I spoke about
the advantages of selling parts and vehicles online, and from the
group's enthusiastic response (I was told that mine was one of the
highest-rated presentations at the convention), I could see that a
huge number of dealerships still had not realized the potential of
expanding their businesses online.

I saw Elena Ford there again. She told me she'd just been talking about me to a colleague, and was still interested in what suggestions I'd make to the company. This wasn't the time or the place
to reply in detail, but I'd been thinking about it quite a bit. So far
we still have not formalized any kind of consulting relationship, and
it remains to be seen whether we ever will. But after that second
encounter with Elena Ford, I went home and began to set down
my thoughts about what I would tell them if we do.

Although I had Ford in mind when I put together these thoughts,
you can apply them just as well to any company, no matter what its
size.

1. Never Rely on Advertising

The fundamental reason why Ford's sales were off was their
poor marketing. Good marketing makes people *want* to buy your
product. Bad marketing actually *hurts* sales. Ford had good product but lousy marketing, in my opinion.

Improving their marketing doesn't necessarily mean that they should be spending *more*. One of the big lessons we learned in 2004 at Magic City Ford is that sometimes you can make more money by spending *less* and simply being more effective. If something works, do more of it—and if something isn't working, *don't keep doing it.*

I've consulted with companies who liked an ad campaign they were running even though it wasn't generating sales. They justified it to themselves by saying, "Advertising takes repetitions," and continued running the ad. I told them, "If it doesn't work, admit it—and quit wasting money." Ads don't become effective over time; either they work, or they don't.

During 2005, the same year that Ford *lost* $1.6 billion from their North American operations, they *spent* $1.5 billion on advertising in the United States. This was about a 20 percent increase over the year before—an increase of $300 *million*. They could have kept their ad budget at the same level or even cut it—and gotten far better results. How? By running only the effective ads and not the ineffective ones. And even then, Ford needs to seriously reevaluate the role of traditional advertising in their budget.

Spending on advertising is at an all-time high—and the return in advertising effectiveness is at an all-time low. Newspaper circulation rates have been down every year for the past twenty years; they've become a steadily less effective venue for advertising because nobody reads the papers anymore. People are getting their news from the twenty-four-hour news networks—or, more and more, from their computers, so TV advertising is also growing more expensive and less effective.

The same thing happened with direct mail. People are trying to personalize it with simulated handwriting and hand stamps, but those are just fads. Just as satellite radio has cut into the effectiveness of radio ads, TiVo has reduced the number of eyeballs on TV ads. It's happening *everywhere*. Ultimately, all forms of advertising become less and less effective.

2. Invest in Effective Incentives

Instead of pouring more money into expensive (and ineffective) advertising, Ford would do far better putting that money in the hands of the people who really count: their customers and sales-people.

For example, they could offer owner-loyalty incentives that would bring customers back. They could put more money into training their salespeople at the dealership level, or by motivating them with performance incentives, as we did with our Ranger contest at Magic City. During 2005, when I put these thoughts together, Ford had a national salesperson recognition program that allowed their top sales-people to earn free business cards and a $100 gift card at the end of the year. In other words, it was almost no incentive at all.

If all of Ford's salespeople improved their performance by just 10 percent—if for every ten cars a salesman sold he could instead sell eleven—then Ford Motor Company's sales would go up 10 per-cent. Impossible? Too big a task? Not at all. You can do that by spending as little as a $100 bonus per salesperson. We did it at Magic City; Ford could do it everywhere across the country. And that's a lot more effective than spending $1.5 billion on advertising.

What if, instead of increasing the advertising budget, they *cut* it by just 10 percent and diverted that 10 percent into sales training incentives? Can you imagine Ford having $150 million to spend on training their salespeople? They could give *everyone* a plasma TV for selling one more car. And I guarantee you, for a plasma TV, any-one in the world can sell one more car.

Let's take this one step further: if Ford has thirty thousand sales-people, that one extra sale per salesperson per month would mean an additional 360,000 vehicles sold per year. At the NADA conven-tion, in a special meeting for Ford franchise dealers, Ford execu-tives told us that the bottom-line reason for their drastic layoffs and closings was that total North American car sales were down by 1 million cars over five years before. That's a decline of two hundred thousand sales per year.

How would an additional 360,000 sales per year affect this picture?

3. Take Care of Your Customers

No matter what your business, the key to your future as a business is your customers—they are what keeps you going. You can survive without advertising, but you can't survive without customers. And it's a lot easier—and a lot cheaper—to keep an existing customer than it is to acquire a new customer.

According to many economic analysts, we moved from an industrial economy to an information economy during the second half of the twentieth century. But now we have left the information economy behind and moved into yet another economic dimension: a *service* economy.

Twenty years ago, information was the commodity of greatest value, just as steel, coal, timber, and other physical resources were the commodities of greatest value in the heart of the industrial era. But today we live in a *glut* of information, and much of it is just noise and not of any real value. Because of that, what's become especially valuable is people who can show us how to sift and use the best information. And what's more valuable than ever is *service*. More and more, the emerging successful businesses will be those that make *exceptional customer service* their product.

The most powerful form of advertising, and the one form that will never lose its effectiveness or become obsolete, is *word of mouth*: people who buy your products tell their friends about it. If you can get your customers to have such a great experience with you that they just have to tell others, then they'll tell *everyone*. Investing in your customers is worth more than any investment in advertising, because if you treat them well, your customers will do your advertising for you.

There's no better customer-relations policy than this: underpromise and overdeliver. That can sometimes mean the difference between a company surviving and that same company not surviving. In fact, it almost always does.

Take airlines, for instance. I fly Delta or US Airways only because I have to: they're the only carriers that serve my location with the schedule I need. If an airline such as JetBlue or Southwest provided service here in Roanoke, I'd never fly Delta or US Airways again. What would it take for these two major carriers to win back my loyalty? Simple. They'd just have to do what Southwest has done: treat their customers better.

And that difference comes from the top.

My local clothing store, Davidsons, is family-owned and -operated. Larry Davidson himself always offers me the most personalized and best service available to anyone, anywhere. The same for Fink's Jewelry, which is also family-owned and generations old: Marc Fink helps me with the best of service at his more than a dozen locations. At Magic City Ford, our employees have always seen my dad treat customers with the highest level of respect. These are three examples of the same principle: good customer service starts at the top and filters down throughout the business, to every employee in every department. Bad customer service does the same thing.

I've never met Herb Kelleher, the founder of Southwest Airlines, but I can promise you that his attitude toward his customers is a big part of what has made the airline so successful.

Whether you're a one-man operation, an entrepreneur just starting out, selling tomatoes from a wagon or services on the Internet, or the CEO of a large company with dozens or even hundreds of employees working for you, it doesn't matter: it starts with you.

I've heard both my parents say this all my life: take care of the customer and the customer will take care of you.

That was the cornerstone of Roanoke Restaurant Service, my mom's wholesale food business. It's the cornerstone of Magic City Ford, and it should be the cornerstone of Ford Motor Company— and of every other company, no matter how large or how small.

Treat your customers better than the competition does, give them your respect, and you'll earn *their* respect—and their business.

4. Create a Culture of Follow-up

I was consulting recently for a large company that relies heavily on direct mail to generate sales of a fairly high-ticket product. The CEO presented me with a problem. They needed to increase revenue from their direct-mail efforts. He wanted to know where he could find more names of qualified prospects for his mailings.

I said, "What's your response rate now?"

He said it was about 10 percent.

I said, "You don't need more names, you need a higher response rate. You just need to take that ten percent up to fifteen percent. If you get an additional five percent response rate with your existing promotion, that's better than sending out five percent more mailers, wouldn't you say? And it's also going to *save* you more money, because you're not mailing more of those expensive packages." (He uses gold foil and high-quality design on these packages; they look really good and make the recipient feel very official—and they cost him $3.00 or $4.00 apiece.)

He said, "Well . . . yeah, you're right. So how would we do that?"

I said, "How many times do you call them to make sure they got the package you mailed them?"

He said, "We don't do that at all."

I said, "Do you ever call them beforehand to let them know that they are part of an elite list who will soon be receiving a special promotional package in the mail?"

He said, "No."

"Okay," I said, "just do those two things, and you'll double your response from ten to twenty percent. By doing that, you can actually mail fewer pieces and save money, and at the same time make more money by selling a greater percentage. We don't need to get more names. We've got ninety percent of the people we're mailing to now who aren't responding. Let's go after those ninety percent and put those names to work for us."

I helped him hire a sales force and put together a call center to implement those ideas, which he's doing right now—and it's working.

Ever since I started working at Magic City Ford I've been fascinated with what distinguishes the top salespeople. In our business, the top one or two salespeople take the time to send Christmas cards or birthday cards to their customers, or even just get in touch at random to check in and say, "How are you doing?"

This is hardly unique to auto dealerships. In *any* business, your best salespeople do the best job of taking care of their customers. Whether you're a store selling jewelry or clothing, or a restaurant or a dry cleaner, the top salesperson takes care of his customers the best. That's *why* he's the top salesperson.

Ask any individual salesperson about follow-up, and he or she will tell you it's the single most important aspect of selling. But some executives and managers who run and manage companies often forget or ignore this basic truth. Too far removed from in-the-trenches experience, they lose sight of the single most important ingredient in their business: the customer.

Taking good care of your customers—not just when they're in your shop and thinking about buying, but the day after they buy, and the week after that, and the year after that—is the most important thing you can do to make your business flourish.

Follow-up is king.

Recently I spent some time doing careful research into how different businesses manage their follow-up. In the process, I came across a statistic that shocked me, although when I reflected on my own experience as a customer, it shouldn't have surprised me:

Nine out of ten companies never contact their customers after they've made a purchase.

Never. Not once. I found that absolutely amazing. It made me realize how little most businesses understand the value of their own customers.

And that gave me an idea for a new business. This would be a business that helped other people to better run *their* businesses.

It used to be that all I really wanted to do was start my own companies. Of that string of more than half a dozen "short story" enterprises I started in high school with Tommy Kho, I scarcely ran any of them for longer than a year. I was more interested in seeing if I could make each idea work than I was in maintaining it for very long. Once I'd gotten it successfully up and running and making a profit, I would grow bored and move on.

In the past few years, I stood that set of priorities on its head. I became more interested in *running* businesses than in starting them.

Managing and improving existing businesses intrigues me. There are people who have a real genius for starting companies but can't manage them worth a damn once they're going. That's not the legacy I want to leave behind. Who knows? Maybe someday I'll take a position at a big corporation that's struggling and help turn it around.

It's actually kind of ironic. So many people work for a company, slowly moving up the ladder for ten, twenty, even thirty years, then gradually come to hate the nine-to-five and wish they could leave that world and start their own business. I did the opposite: I worked for a decade in the freewheeling world of entrepreneurial start-ups, and then entered this more structured world of bricks-and-mortar management, where I was managing dozens of people and working with customers face-to-face every day—and discovered that I *love* it.

Still, I do have a passion for starting businesses—and that's why in March 2006, I finally left Magic City Ford to start my latest online enterprise.

17

Creatively Build on Your Experience

In June 2005, I sold all of Zablo's assets to a private individual in South Carolina who was in the car business. At three and a half years, from January 2002 to June 2005, this was the longest I had ever owned a single business.

The gentleman I sold to was a family man and wanted to find a way to run his own business from home. Zablo fit the bill perfectly. He has invested a lot into it and is doing well with it. I think he's really going to make it work, and I certainly wish him the best.

The package I sold included the AutoCertificate coupon and the Do Not Call service, my customer list (I didn't mind selling this, because it was all businesses, not private individuals), and the name Zablo. The one thing I held on to was the corporation itself, which I renamed Cameron Johnson, Inc. It was through that corporation that I would develop my next business venture.

Working at the dealership and putting together my recommendations to Ford Motor Company got me to thinking: Was there a way we could duplicate the kind of customer service we had developed at Magic City Ford, so that other dealers all around the country could implement it, too? Trainings and incentives clearly work, as we saw during our year of record-breaking sales in 2004. But there's a limit to how far you can go with them. As my dad says, you can *train* people to work a certain way, but you can't *force* them to.

But what if we found a way to distill the essence of the top sales-people's behavior and package that in the form of an automated system?

I looked at what we did with Zablo: essentially, we took our experiences in the dealership, looked at ways we'd found that dealerships can do business more effectively, and "bottled" those philosophies into a product.

I looked at the behavior of our top salespeople and thought, *What if we could bottle that?*

That became the concept of my new business. It would be an automated distillation of how we stay in contact with our customers, which helps us sell more service, more parts, and more cars.

It would be a bottled version of our magic season.

For me, there is a critical point where a business idea goes from being general to being specific, where it takes shape and becomes a concrete business concept.

That point generally happens when I give it a name.

Finding a good name is a key step in the birth of a business. I don't know why this is, but it is. From Cheers & Tears Printing Co. on, finding the right name for each business has been as important a step in the development of the business's life as naming a baby.

In most cases, the name has to say clearly what the business does. There are exceptions; for example, the name "Zablo" doesn't really mean anything. (It was just catchy, and I liked the sound of it.) But from MyEZMail to CertificateSwap, I have typically preferred to use business names that would immediately tell customers what that business would do for them.

Here is how I found the name for this new business:

Auto dealerships are graded by the manufacturers on their customer satisfaction rating. The scale on which this rating is measured is called the Customer Satisfaction Index, or CSI. The higher your CSI score, the greater your standing with your manufacturer and the better the benefits they offer you.

This is a very big deal for dealers, as it should be. High CSI ratings are rewarded with awards and recognition, as well as with tangible (read: financial) benefits. For example, there is the once-a-year President's Award. Our dealership is one of only 16 in the country (out of more than 4400) that have won the President's Award more than ten times. Of course, our customers don't know this. They just know that they are so happy with their experience at Magic City, they want to tell their friends.

The purpose of the new business would be to create very happy customers by applying and automating the principles of good customer service that we always sought to follow at Magic City Ford. Practically speaking, the business would help dealers achieve and maintain consistently high CSI ratings.

Hence the name: BoostCSI.com.

Typically, when you buy a car, you will never hear from that dealership again—at least not until they figure it's time for you to buy another car. Then they send you a card, which you just throw in the trash, because it feels like they're just trying to sell you something.

But what if they had kept up a relationship with you the whole time? Then you wouldn't throw their cards in the trash. You'd feel like they weren't just trying to sell you something, they were actually keeping in touch with you, looking out for you and your interests.

BoostCSI automates the process of staying in touch with the dealership's customers throughout the course of ownership and service. To keep costs extremely low, and also because it's a very flexible, highly customizable mode of communication, it does this primarily through e-mail, as well as through phone calls, postcards, and a new technology called an "audio postcard," which is basically an e-mail with an audio message attached—like a voicemail message in your e-mail.

The day after your purchase, BoostCSI sends you an e-mail saying,

> Thank you for your purchase! I know you've only owned your
> [and it plugs in the vehicle type] for one day now, but if you

have any questions now that you didn't think of before, please call me or come by.

And this is entirely branded with the dealership's name—the dealership uses BoostCSI's technology, but the messages come directly from *them*.

Once the dealer enters all this customer information into the database, it does everything from there. Of course, you can also customize how the system works. It will automatically send them notes on their birthdays, anniversaries, and certain holidays (like Fourth of July and Thanksgiving), but you also can create specific campaigns. You might have it send customers an e-mail on their birthday, say, with a discount coupon:

> Hey, it's your birthday! We're giving you a coupon for a free sundae at [fill in a local ice cream shop in town].

And when the customer goes down to, for example, the local Ben & Jerry's, Baskin-Robbins, or TCBY to redeem that coupon and eat that sundae, he or she will be thinking, "Hey, Magic City Ford paid for this sundae!"—and that's more effective than any advertising you could buy.

Or you can go into the system and find all the customers who bought, say, a 2003 Ford Explorer, and send them all a personalized e-mail:

> Hey, the brand-new 2007s are out, we've got great deals for our past customers, because we're in desperate need of preowned Explorers such as the one you're driving, so come visit us.

The result? Happier customers who will more likely tell their friends. And the next time they're ready to trade that car or buy a new car, they're going to look to you first.

One of my dad's rules of business is, "Everyone wants to buy from a person they like and trust." When customers feel that their interest is your interest, that your priority is taking care of them, they're more likely to do business with you. You rarely see this anymore, because there are hardly any truly service-oriented businesses around.

My dad taught me that the right way to do business is to build relationships in every transaction. That's the goal of BoostCSI.

Once I had the idea for this new company, it was time to do my due diligence and chase down the details. Would the economics of it work? Could I offer the service I envisioned at a price that dealers would pay? Was there any viable competition, and if so, how were they doing?

The answers were more than favorable, and the more research I did, the more excited I became.

A number of times, I've gotten an idea from seeing another service that I thought had a good idea but was way too expensive. That happened, for instance, with Zablo. But sometimes it happens the other way: first I have the idea, then I research the market and find that my competitors are highly overpriced.

That's what just happened with BoostCSI.

I found a few competitors with somewhat similar offerings, and in all cases they were a lot more expensive—in the range of $5,000 to $15,000 a month, as compared to our rates, which I had projected as being from $500 to $900 a month.

I knew I could probably have priced this new service a lot higher—say, at $2,500, which would still be only half the competition's lowest price. But then we'd have egg on our face if another competitor said, "Hey, we can give you this same service for $500 to $900." In fact, I like to price so aggressively low for exactly that reason: it helps reduce the opportunity for a competitor to see our market and take it away from us.

It's a solid, tried-and-true recipe for business success: figure out what your customer needs and wants, and then provide that in the form of a great product, at a great price, with great customer service. The only way anyone can take it away from us is to match our price and offer better service. And as long as we continually improve, they won't be able to do either.

*   *   *

Once I knew the concept would work, it was time to start assembling the pieces. At first I thought about using one of my best programmers from work I'd done in the past. But then I realized that this was too big a project to entrust to a single programmer, so I contracted with an entire company of programmers.

BoostCSI would be my first hugely scalable subscription-based service. Like all my businesses, I planned to start small. But this time I wanted to build into the system the capacity to grow large, predictably and reliably, right from the start.

Throughout this book I've emphasized the importance of doing careful research, of doing whatever it takes to make sure your business idea is supported by the realities of the marketplace and current business climate. Careful research can make the difference between a successful launch and a flop. And sometimes it can do more: it can give you an even better idea than you had in the first place.

My market research for BoostCSI had told me that I had a service that auto dealers would buy, because there was nothing like it available at anywhere near the price I was offering. But my research also told me something I hadn't anticipated: there was a much bigger market for my idea than I had imagined. If I wanted to, I could grow this business in a much bigger way than I had originally intended.

It wasn't just auto dealerships who didn't have access to the service I was envisioning. I couldn't find *any* companies, large or small, offering this type of service to *anyone*—jewelers, doctors, clothing stores, electronics outlets, restaurants, or other types of business.

It quickly occurred to me that my concept could work for *any* business, and I had virtually no competition—so I knew I wanted to make the operation fully scalable right from the get-go.

This was the most demanding programming I'd ever needed to commission. InfiniteProfiles and SurfingPrizes were both highly scalable, and both grew quite large, but they were free services. Here we'd be dealing with customers paying us every month, which meant this would have to be 100 percent reliable, with absolutely no margin of error. Any downtime could mean losing all our customers literally overnight.

The company I decided to use for BoostCSI was in India and had a team of eighty programmers who worked at an hourly rate of about $15 an hour, versus $100 an hour in the United States for someone to do the same job. They're smart, they're efficient, and they're all Microsoft-trained.

Another thing I liked about using developers in India was how well the time difference worked out for me. I could send them an e-mail every night before bed, and when I'd wake the next morning, the work would be done. This was perfect for my schedule. I could work at the dealership all day (I was still working there during the earliest months when I was designing the new business), go home in the evening, spend an hour putting together what I needed, and send them my changes, which might amount to a good eight hours' worth of programming—and everything would be done the next morning. I'm very picky, so during the day I would make time to look through everything they'd done. If they'd taken too many shortcuts, I might have them redo something or even scrap the whole thing. I wanted the work to be excellent.

Near the beginning of this book, I called the Internet "my window to the world." That has become the literal truth. I've now used developers from all around the globe—India, the Ukraine, Europe, New Hampshire, California, and everywhere in between.

Several months after we finished launching our dealer service, we rolled out EasyFollowups.com, a generic version of the same service, aimed at all types of businesses. While we targeted mainly small businesses, we also have the capacity to create custom applications for individual larger businesses, even very large businesses, such as Fortune 500 and Fortune 100 companies.

I said before that working a regular job while crafting your own start-up is a great way to get an entrepreneur's education. I'll take that a step further: working in a traditional sales and service environment is an education no entrepreneur can afford to miss. There is so much room for growth in new businesses that blend the power of the Web with the insights and hands-on experience of the traditional storefront.

Creating BoostCSI and EasyFollowups.com gave me the chance to combine all the lessons I'd learned from my online businesses together with my years at Magic City Ford. The result was a business model whose growth potential is virtually unlimited.

18

Remember What It's Really All About

No mistake about it: being an entrepreneur is hard work. As liberating as the idea of "no more boss!" might seem, it's not really accurate: when you become an entrepreneur, you still have a boss—only now the boss is *you*. This means there's nobody to blame when things are tough, no place to pass the buck. The success of the enterprise is all on your shoulders; it's up to you.

Is it worth it?

Absolutely.

More than anything else, here's what I hope you'll get from this book: being a successful entrepreneur isn't just about making money. Making good money is great; making a *good life* is even better. Money is one way to measure the health of your business. There are others, too, such as the size and growth rate of your customer base, the level of customer satisfaction and repeat business, and your reputation in the world around you. But money is certainly the primary yardstick that tells us how our business is doing.

But what about the yardsticks that tell us how our life as an entrepreneur is doing? As far as I'm concerned, these ways of measuring success are far more important. They represent the real payoff of the entrepreneurial life.

*　　*　　*

One of the biggest rewards of going into business for yourself is that it allows you—in fact, it *requires* you—to exercise your creativity. This is something I've noticed about every successful entrepreneur I've met, from Michael Dell to Joe Sugarman to my own partners: they have a passion for *creating*.

A few years ago, I had a remarkable opportunity to speak to one of the most prestigious groups of young businesspeople I could ever have imagined (actually, I'm not sure I could have imagined this), when I was invited to speak to a group of juniors and seniors at The Wharton School at the University of Pennsylvania, as part of their "Young Entrepreneur Day" event.

Wharton is arguably the best business school in the country, and these were some of the best and brightest young business minds of my generation. What could I tell them that would give them genuine value?

I chose as my topic "creativity in business."

When I arrived at Wharton, the room was packed. It was standing room only, and there were a good number of students who did in fact stand for the event. I have to confess, I was a bit in awe. It felt strange for me to be standing on that stage, talking to these people in the upper classes of one of the top business schools in the country—knowing that if I had applied to come here myself, I almost surely wouldn't have gotten in.

These are not your typical college students; they're the cream of the crop. It's also one of the most expensive business schools in the country. Donald Trump went to Wharton; his daughter Ivanka had graduated the year before.

I told them that creativity is the ability to produce things that are new, original, and unique. Mention the idea of "creativity" and people tend to think of singers, artists, writers, actors, scientists, and designers. But entrepreneurs are creative people, too, artists of their own medium who find new, original, and unique ideas and then express those ideas in the business world.

I reminded them of the extraordinary privilege they had of being in one of the top business schools in the country—and that everyone in that room had the kind of entrepreneurial creativity I was speaking about.

I cited the book *The Rise of the Creative Class*, by Carnegie Mellon University professor Richard Florida, who wrote, "Human creativity is the ultimate economic resource." Professor Florida points out that creativity must not be squandered. It is an economic force, he says, one that increases resources and productivity and improves lifestyles throughout the world. This creative capacity is intangible—it cannot be bought or sold—yet corporations will pay top dollar for individuals with this creative talent. "So don't be afraid," I concluded, "to use your innate creativity and think outside the box!"

Building your own successful business gives you the opportunity to have a tremendous impact on the world. Having the freedom to exercise unlimited creativity is a major part of that. The other side of the coin is great responsibility, and in business, that is perhaps best expressed as *ethics*.

Sound ethics must be an essential and integral part of your business strategy. We cannot let the corporate subterfuge and creative accounting practices of such companies as Enron, WorldCom, Xerox, and Anderson Consulting cloud and mislead us as investors in the future.

In a world driven by a global economy that does business in the trillions, aided by technology that develops at speeds faster than a nanosecond, ethics is more critical—not less—than ever before. Sound ethics is the cornerstone of the foundation on which all of our business relations are built. Even in the worst of times, when ethics may seem to be only a luxury of one's conscience, we must recognize it as the most important part—not the least important—of doing business.

Ethics provides a clear glimpse into the humanity that lies at the core of all business. It is the one part of the formula that cannot be duplicated by technology. Businesspeople who practice sound ethics can open closed doors, overcome seemingly insurmountable odds, and go home each night to sleep peacefully.

Creativity is the hallmark of the *skillful* entrepreneur. But creativity itself does not define the *successful* entrepreneur, because true success comes only with a profound sense of balance. Unbridled creativity without a tempering sense of ethics and social responsibility runs the same danger as any potent force run amok: of being destructive rather than productive.

Gandhi beautifully articulated this idea of balance, and of how dangerous it is when we don't achieve that sense, in something he called the "Eight Blunders of the World": wealth without work; pleasure without conscience; knowledge without character; commerce without morality; science without humanity; worship without sacrifice; politics without principles; and rights without responsibilities.

Another reward of the entrepreneurial way of life is that it can allow you to serve as an influential member of your community and have an impact on public affairs. Being a business leader can open doors to become involved in all sorts of community issues, whether on a local, regional, or even national level.

In August 2004 I was contacted by one of the managers of the Bush presidential reelection campaign, asking if I would be interested in publicly supporting their effort. They had come up with the idea of featuring a series of individual entrepreneurs on the campaign Web site as an expression of the administration's support for small business in America. They wanted to know if I would like to be one of their featured "Small Business Leaders of the Month."

I agreed.

They took my picture and posted it, along with a brief quote, on the georgewbush.com Web site as their Small Business Leader of the Month for August. (I noted that some of the other supporting business leaders on the site included Michael Dell and eBay CEO Meg Whitman, so I was clearly in good company.)

At the end of the month, I also was invited to participate in the Republican National Convention in Manhattan. This was quite a production—they did a background check, got me clearance, and had reserved passes in my name that I was supposed to pick up at the Waldorf-Astoria in New York. But I had a schedule conflict: that very same day, I was slated for my live appearance (in Washington, D.C.) on CNBC's *PowerLunch* to launch TrueLoot. I think it's safe to say that this was the biggest schedule conflict I've ever had.

As part of this program, I also participated in several conference calls with members of the Bush-Cheney campaign, including Secretary of Commerce Don Evans, Secretary of Labor Elaine Chao, and Mina Nguyen, who was then National Business Coalitions director. This was especially exciting, since there were only a handful of us on each call. In the process, I also got to know White House staffer Curtis Jablonka, who is an amazingly resourceful guy.

Whether you happen to be pro-Bush or not is not the point. The point is that it was awfully exciting to be participating in economic discussions at the presidential cabinet-member level—especially considering that I was nineteen years old, and with less than a year of undergraduate studies under my belt.

Being involved in high-profile events, such as giving speeches to prestigious audiences or participating in national political conferences, is thrilling. But for me, often the most satisfying experiences in community affairs happen far outside the public limelight.

I've always been drawn to finding ways to serve the community and help people in need. Since I was ten years old, I've made significant annual donations to my local Episcopal church, and I've always looked for other meaningful charities to support, from local groups to victims of Katrina and the Southeast Asian tsunami. When I was eleven, I received the "Arrow of Light," Cub Scouting's highest honor, for community work I did as a member of Pack 239.

As I've grown older, I've become more actively involved in efforts to help other kids lead happier and more productive lives.

A few years ago I was contacted by the office of Junior Achievement, the nationwide organization that had cosponsored both the Young IT Entrepreneur of the Year contest that brought me to the Ritz-Carlton in Atlanta *and* the Southwest Virginia Business Hall of Fame event in 2000, where I was the keynote speaker. They asked if I would be interested in teaching a class to some elementary school kids in Roanoke, and I accepted right away.

When I was in fifth grade, I had gone through a Junior Achievement program myself. What better way to give back to this program, which had done so much for me, than to share that same kind of support with other kids the same age?

That fall I started going into the Roanoke schools once a week to teach a fifth-grade class about business. I taught them what a franchise is, what a public company is, how you can buy stock in Coca-Cola, and all sorts of basic business concepts.

I was a little nervous at first. I had given speeches, but I'd never really taught a class, let alone taught one to younger kids. As we went through our introductions, I found that a lot of them knew Magic City Ford, because their parents or their friends' parents had bought cars there. They started asking me things like, "Hey, do you have any new Mustangs? Those are cool!"

We got talking about business, and I told them a little of my story. One kid raised his hand and said, "Hey, I had a lemonade stand!" Another one said, "Yeah, I had one of those, too!" And we were off and running.

Some of the questions they asked me were hilarious. One little girl asked me if I had a girlfriend. I had a blast working with those kids, and I'm still doing it today.

I soon found a way to help older kids as well, when I was invited to speak in October 2004 at the annual event for an organization called Jobs for Virginia Graduates. I gave a talk at their convention and was terribly impressed with their work. The following January they invited me to become a member of their board of directors, and I was thrilled to say yes.

Jobs for Virginia Graduates is a state chapter of Jobs for America's Graduates (JAG), an organization that operates in twenty-seven of the fifty states. JAG helps teenagers in high school who can't afford to go to college, or who are struggling in their lives and have no plans to go to college. In fact, for many of the underprivileged kids who come into the JAG programs, even graduating from high school is far from a sure thing.

We work with these kids and try to give them the kind of training they're going to need in the real world: how to manage their finances, how to balance their checkbooks, how to make good decisions, all sorts of things. It's really gratifying work—and we get results. While the public high schools in Roanoke have fairly high dropout rates, the kids who go through our program have a graduation rate of 93 *percent*. A good number of them go on to college or other higher-education programs.

What's so amazing is that with the right kind of caring and help, a substantial number of these lives can turn from potential tragedy to triumph.

I was at an event a few weeks ago that brought home to me again the value of this work. Right at the end of the event, a girl who was now a senior in high school stood and spoke to the audience:

> When I was in eighth grade, my dad died. He was stabbed to death. Two weeks later, I was raped in the bathroom of my middle school. It felt like my life was over. Then in ninth grade, I got involved with Jobs for Virginia Graduates. If I hadn't, there was no chance I would have ever finished high school. But this program helped me stay in school. Now I'm graduating—and I'm going to college.

I grew up in an environment poles apart from what a lot of these kids go through; some might say I'm in no place to understand them. But I've found that people are people, and none of us is really much different from the other. Even in my fairly privileged world, I will never forget the difference that a Kim Williams, a Rita Bishop, or a Betty Smith could make in my life.

One mentor can make all the difference—and everyone deserves to have that.

Ever since I was a kid, I have wanted to be the best businessperson I could be. While I knew I had to start small, I also had an ambition to build something huge. And while it may sound like a cliché to some, it's also true. I wanted to help make the world a better place.

Because that's what successful businesspeople do. Executives in the business world are supposed to grow companies, to grow the economy by creating new jobs and hiring people, and creating new ways of doing things that people want done.

A successful businessperson isn't necessarily the one who has the most money. It's about being happy; it's about enjoying what you do and being generous. True prosperity isn't something you take *from* the world: it's something you share *with* the world.

Part of being successful is having the ability to go home and sleep peacefully every night. That's how you know you're successful.

I know a guy in the Internet business who makes millions of dollars a year, but he does it through spam and junk e-mail. He's been sued by Microsoft and a string of other companies whose names you'd recognize. I could go out tomorrow and do all the same things he does. I know precisely how he works all his strategies. In fact, he invited me to work with him, but I said no. I could make the exact same decisions he did and make millions a year doing what he does—but that's not what I'm after.

If you comb through all the media stories on me and my businesses, going back a full decade and more than two hundred stories, you'll never find it written anywhere how much money I've actually earned. At age twelve, I mentioned that I earned $50,000 selling Beanie Babies, and ever since then, I've never disclosed my earnings. The stories always end up the same way: " . . . which he sold to a private individual for an undisclosed sum."

I don't want to give the wrong impression here: growing myself financially is important to me and always has been. But that's not how I frame these experiences. I don't say, "Here's what we did, and we made a killing," because that misses the point. And when reporters ask me, "How much money do you make?" or "How much did you sell the business for?" I never give a specific answer. For one thing, when people hear a specific number, they're going to have one of two reactions: they're going to think I'm bragging, or they're going to think "Well, that number really isn't so impressive after all." It's either going to be too high or too low.

I don't get involved in any of that. I'm not in a contest with anyone. Genuine success is its own measure.

Discovering and developing the entrepreneur within you is an exciting journey. But getting rich isn't the point of my story. That's not what I want to be known for. I'd much rather know that my success in business has in its own way made the world a better place.

19

Be the Entrepreneur You Want to Be

"So, Cameron—what's next for you?" People ask me this all the time, and I never seem to answer the question the same way twice, because I honestly never know exactly what's next.

Some people say you should have a mapped-out, written-down plan of action for your life. That may work for some people, but it's not how I operate. Different doors and opportunities are opening up all the time, and which way I go is simply a series of personal decisions that are impossible to predict until the circumstances present themselves.

I've run more than a dozen businesses in the past dozen years, and I've had a great time doing it. That's what it's all about. If you don't have fun doing what you're doing, there's no good reason to be doing it. The money doesn't make up for not having fun. I always make sure I'm having a blast. I love living in my house in Blacksburg and sharing it with three of my Virginia Tech friends. We have a great time. And I've had a ball for the past few years working at Magic City Ford.

I have certain long-term goals, and those have never changed. I want to be financially stable, free to pursue my interests, and have a happy family. But I don't have a specific life plan for achieving these things, because the future is too full of change and opportunity. It's a question of the decisions you make. Donald Trump doesn't plan out every day in every detail. He sees an opportunity, makes a decision, and does it.

I loved the line from Trump when he was going through a point when he was $900 million in debt: "I remember looking at a homeless man and thinking, 'That man is worth $900 million more than I am!'" That's one of the greatest lines I've ever read. It puts things in perspective. Trump still has plenty of debt today—and plenty of assets. He's doing what he loves, and nothing stops him. He makes decisions and rolls with them.

I believe the future is all about keeping your eyes open and seeing what's going on in front of you. What's next for me? I could talk about it or write about it—but it's really a question of *doing*.

There has never been a better time to start your own business. We're in for some amazing economic times ahead.

I hope that my story has encouraged you to start your own business. You don't have to be in love with technology and the Internet. You don't have to come from a family of entrepreneurs. You don't have to have circumstances like mine, or Michael Dell's, or Joe Sugarman's. The particulars of our stories aren't the important thing. What's important are the principles behind the stories.

And they can be learned and applied by *anyone*. Anyone, that is, who truly has a passion to do it.

The most important thing I can tell you about the success I've had is that *it's not unique*. A lot of people are starting their own businesses and doing it very successfully, whether on a global scale or based in their own community. They may not be getting national media attention, but I'll tell you what: national media attention isn't the measure of your success. The guys from Enron and WorldCom got national media attention, and I don't call them successful.

You don't have to start with a huge capital investment. Even though I came from a fairly well-to-do family, I started my first business with basically nothing.

You could say, "Yeah, but would he have done all the same things if he didn't come from the same family?" Maybe not. But at the same time, my parents didn't give me the money to start my businesses, and they didn't tell me what to do or how to do it. And they certainly didn't show me how to use a computer. In fact, in many ways they often *discouraged* me from doing the things I did. But it's where my passion was—business, making money, learning how to make things better, and doing well in the business world.

I got these skills from reading everything I could about business and from meeting and learning from successful businesspeople. I did this at a very early age, when the mind can probably still grow very quickly and learn more easily than when you're older. But you can do it at any age.

Here's the main message I'm hoping you will take away from my story: *anyone can do it.* It's never too early to start a successful business—and it's never too late, either.

I have always believed in going after the things you want in life. Because there truly are no limits to what's possible.

Follow your dreams: do what you *really* want to do. Don't start a business just because you hope to make money with it. And if you have to take a job for the money, get one that will allow you free time and energy to do what you love. Look for what's going to make you genuinely happy in life, and then do it. I have always placed fun, satisfaction, and fulfillment ahead of profit—and that has always ended up being *very* profitable.

Acknowledgments

I owe my love of entrepreneurship to my parents, Ann and Bill Johnson, the way they raised me and the things they taught me. In a way, this book is as much about them as it is about me, because so much of the success I've been able to have has come from the principles I learned from them.

I also owe my sincere thanks to:

My partners and business associates: Aaron Greenspan, Tommy Kho, Randy Morse, and Nat Turner.

My mentors and teachers over the years: Taka Tsurutani, Richard Rossi, Joe Polish, Joe Sugarman, Michael Donovan, Grover Keeney, and Rita Bishop.

My sister, Claire Johnson, for letting me sell her Beanie Babies and being a good sport; those Beanie Babies certainly went a long way.

John David Mann for his remarkable dedication to this book at every stage in the process; this project would not have been completed without his passion for perfection.

Emily Loose, our superb editor at Simon & Schuster, for her insights and guidance; and Dominick Anfuso, our editorial director at Simon & Schuster, for his vision and support.

And finally, Margret McBride, Donna DeGutis, Fay Atchison, and Anne Bomke at the Margret McBride Literary Agency for their tireless enthusiasm and dedication to the project.

There's much truth to the old expression, "You are only as good as the company you keep." I've been fortunate to keep company with the best!

Tips for Getting Started

A concise compendium of tips, guidelines, advice, and resources for planning, launching, and growing your own business

The resources I've listed below are just a small sampling from www.millionairesecrets.com/tips, where I regularly update an extensive selection of the best resources for entrepreneurs. Visit this site for information on all these topics and more, as well as columns, tips from experts, and one-on-one advice.

Whether you're starting an Internet-based business or a more traditional type of enterprise, there are more resources available today than ever before to help you every step of the way. I think starting an Internet business is an especially good idea for anyone just getting into the entrepreneurial life. With over a decade of online experience behind us, today's Internet-based business models have matured and grown far more savvy and stable, and Internet businesses typically require far less in start-up capital than conventional businesses.

Today there are also hundreds of service providers available that can help take care of all sorts of specific functions and make it even cheaper and easier to run your own business solo. My own business, EasyFollowups.com, is an example: it is an automated e-mail service that takes care of following up with your customers and giving them great customer service.

Note: All of the URLs, companies, books, and other resources mentioned below can all be found at www.millionairesecrets.com/ tips. Bookmark this site for a quick reference to all these resources.

1. Looking for Great Ideas

For brainstorming, check out Web sites that list businesses for sale. Just seeing a range of other people's business ideas can stimulate your creativity. Some may not seem that creative or interesting, but others might just spark your brain a bit.

If you are thinking about buying one of the businesses you find, remember: they are for sale because the owner no longer wants them. Be sure to find out their real reasons for selling *before* you think of buying. This also means the negotiating power is in your corner.

- www.ebay.com: Search "business for sale" and then sort by highest price. (I've sold several businesses on eBay.)
- www.bizbuysell.com: Lists businesses for sale.
- www.entrepreneur.com: Check out the "Startups" section.

For links to these and other business ideas resources, go to www .millionairesecrets.com/tips.

2. Testing Your Idea

Go online and look for similar businesses. Who's the competition? What are they charging for their service or product? Estimate how much their costs are and how much money they're making. Who are your potential customers? How big is your target market?

Are there existing companies that already offer services to your target market with whom you may be able to partner? Partnering with an already existing business and creating a revenue-sharing model can be a very good way to quickly bring your new business customers.

This kind of digging isn't difficult, with a little practice. I often start the basic research using Google to look for comparables (similar companies, products, or services). I often use Hoover's to do more detailed research, such as looking up a company's financials, although this isn't easy for private companies. Hoover's also lets you buy Dun & Bradstreet credit reports.

Alexa is another useful site. It ranks Web sites by the amount of traffic they have and shows you a list of what are currently the hottest sites, which is one way to come up with market trends. For example, hot trends right now, as I write this, are online video sites (YouTube), blogging sites (Blogger.com), and social networking sites (MySpace, Facebook, etc.).

- www.google.com
- www.hoovers.com
- www.alexa.com

Once you've done some thorough research, create a basic business outline—you can think of it as a "rough-draft business plan." Ask and answer basic financial questions about your business idea and include this information in your outline:

- What will your start-up costs be?
- What recurring monthly expenses will you have?
- What will it cost to provide the product or service?
- How much can you charge for it? If you were the customer, how much would you be willing to pay?
- How will you promote the company, and what costs will be involved?
- How quickly will you be able to build your customer base?
- What is the fewest number of customers you'll need to cover your expenses?

Once you're satisfied that your idea is sound, test it out on others. I always run new ideas by family members, friends, associates, anyone whose opinion I trust.

The Elevator Test

Even when I know I've got a strong idea, I've already done my research and know there is a strong target market, I still like to apply the elevator test. Here's how it works:

Picture yourself on an elevator, talking with someone you've never met before, and they ask about your new business. Your goal is to be able to explain it very easily—short, sweet, and to the point—and get a "wow" reaction. You have three minutes. If you can't explain it in three minutes, then maybe you're trying to do too much. If you do explain it and they don't say "Wow!," maybe you haven't got quite the right angle on your idea yet.

For links to these and other business ideas resources, go to www.millionairesecrets.com/tips.

3. Writing a Business Plan

Most businesses fail because of two things: 1) overspending, 2) lack of planning. Don't fall for this trap. Once you've decided to go with your idea, invest the time and effort for careful planning before you get started. Do this before you start, and you'll never regret it.

Follow Warren Buffett's advice: *invest in what you know.* Know your market inside and out before you enter it. Few people have ever made a dime in a market they didn't understand themselves.

A good business plan is not set in stone. It should serve as a guide, not a straightjacket. But do spend the time to make the plan solid and airtight. If there are any unanswered questions or things you're not sure about, get the answers before going further. The biggest benefit of making a business plan is the learning you go through in the process.

Bplans.com lets you search some free business plans and offers a number of calculators that can help you run projections on starting costs, breaking even, and more. They also have great links to expert advice.

- www.bplans.com: In addition to the features mentioned above, this site also offers Business Plan Pro, a good example of business plan software.

- www.millionairesecrets.com/bizplan/sba: The Small Business Administration offers a good template for a business plan.
- www.millionairesecrets.com/bizplan/amex: An excellent set of guidelines from the people at American Express.
- www.millionairesecrets.com/bizplans: Click on the "Business Plans" heading at my free resources site to see samples of abbreviated business plans I've done for past companies.

For links to these and other business plan resources, go to www.millionairesecrets.com/tips.

4. Naming and Protecting Your Business

Choosing a good name is crucial. Think from your customer's point of view: find a name that communicates your business concept in terms the customer will get. For example, instead of calling your chiropractic service Johnson & Associates, why not call it Fix My Back?

One factor that has helped my businesses grow rapidly is that when people heard the name MyEZMail, or CertificateSwap.com, they knew immediately what kind of service the business offered them.

Sometimes it's possible to brand a catchy or cool-sounding name, even one that isn't self-explanatory. But be careful. Not every Yahoo! or Google is a success story. In late 1999 a company called Flooz launched an ambitious online currency plan. They poured more than $10 million into promotion, and in a year and a half they were broke and out of business. Think about that name, *Flooz*. Doesn't it make you think of the words, "lose" and "floozy"? Or worse yet, "fleece"? It's not always easy to brand just any name; $10 million is a lot to lose.

Once you've hit on some good possibilities, search the Internet to make sure they aren't already in use. Google is your best source. Putting your search string in quotation marks will limit the search results to only that phrase. For instance, "Cameron Johnson" returns only search results where "Cameron" and "Johnson" are together. If you search my name without quotes, your results could include articles on Cameron Diaz written by reporter Joe Johnson. If your company or product/service name will be two words, make sure to search several ways and use quotations.

Domain Name

Equally important is making sure the corresponding domain name (URL) is available. Typically, your domain will be yourcompanyname.com. Your customers need to be able to find you. Search engines (Google, Yahoo!, etc.) prioritize search results; having your product's or service's domain name is very important to your search ranking—which in turn generates traffic to your site.

To make sure the domain name you want is available, use a domain registrar like Register.com. If the domain name you want is taken, you can use a look-up Web site such as www.whois.org to search for the owner, then e-mail them to see if they'd consider selling the domain name for a reasonable price, if it's not in use. If this isn't an option, then you may want to consider changing your name.

The extension ".com" was designed for businesses and is certainly the most professional domain extension (as opposed to .net, .biz, or .us, for example). When registering a new and unique domain name, I always recommend buying the .net and .org versions as well, and have those direct traffic to your site. Also, if your name is hard to spell or might be spelled different ways, buy other variations as well. If it contains numbers, get both versions with the numeral and the number spelled out (www.teafortwo.com, www.teafor2.com, www.tea4two.com, and www.tea4too.com).

- www.register.com: To search for and register domain names.
- www.whois.org: To look for existing owners of URLs you're interested in.

Trademarks

Getting a trademark for your product's or service's unique name or brand and for your company name is very important, unless you're doing business exclusively on a local basis and there's little danger of someone else using the same name. Trademarks protect your brand names from being used by other companies in the same industry, which protects your "territory" and avoids confusion for your customers.

Securing a trademark typically costs $500–$1,000, including attorney's fees. You can do this yourself by filing with the United States Patent and Trademark Office Web site. You can also search their site for existing trademarks.

- www.uspto.gov: United States Patent and Trademark Office.

Patents

If you actually create a unique, brand-new invention as part of your business, you may want to consider securing a patent. This is a more complex form of protection than a trademark. Applying patents to Internet technology is growing difficult and expensive. One reason for this is that so many patents were granted in the early days of the Internet and then later revoked or challenged (for example, Amazon's 1-Click Shopping System). A typical patent can cost you $10,000 and up.

- www.uspto.gov: United States Patent and Trademark Office.

Copyright

If you want to protect creations such as literary work, music, graphics, or recordings, it's worth it to copyright them. Copyrighting is a far less complex and costly process than trademarking: there's a $45 fee for each copyright. You can call the Library of Congress copyright office or go to their Web site (below).

- 202-707-3000 or www.loc.gov/copyright: Library of Congress, for copyright forms and instructions.

For links to these and other business name resources, go to www.millionairesecrets.com/tips.

5. Choosing a Structure

In most cases it's a good idea to set up your business as a corporation. Doing so separates your business from your personal life and finances, which is not only good for clarity's sake, but can also offer you some legal protection. For example, if your business is ever sued, the corporate structure may protect you personally from liability; or if the company should ever file bankruptcy, it's only the company doing so, and not you personally.

If you do form a corporation for your business, rather than paying yourself a regular salary, consider paying yourself a dividend several times a year instead. Dividends are currently taxed at a much lower rate than a typical salary. However, even paying yourself a salary is preferable to drawing money directly from your business as a sole proprietorship, as self-employment income is taxed at an even higher rate. Consider consulting a tax adviser to find a solution that best suits your situation.

There are two basic types of corporations: C-Corp and S-Corp. The S-Corp structure was created essentially for smaller businesses or those with no more than a few stockholders (or even one). The main distinction of an S-Corp is that unlike a C-Corp, it pays no taxes of its own, but instead passes its profits (or losses) directly on to the shareholders, who are taxed at the individual, personal level.

A C-Corp, on the other hand, is taxed itself as an entity, which is the biggest reason setting yourself up as an S-Corp is typically the better way to go for an entrepreneur.

For example, let's say your company makes a $1,000 profit. If it is a C-Corp in, say, the 30 percent bracket, this leaves your company with $700 after taxes. When you pay yourself a dividend out of that $700, that personal income is taxed again. But if your company is an S-Corp, the entire $1,000 profit is passed on to your shareholders. If you are the only shareholder, then you are taxed on the $1,000 profit just once, at the personal level.

There is a third type of business structure called a "limited liability company," or LLC, which shares many of the characteristics of an S-Corp. The differences are subtle but can be important. Do your homework (I've provided links to good articles on the subject on my resource site), and if necessary, consult a good attorney before deciding which structure you want to use.

Filing incorporation papers with your state is not a difficult process, but you want to make sure to do it correctly. At my free resource site, I've included a link for LegalZoom, a company that can help you file your corporation papers inexpensively and within forty-eight hours.

- www.millionairesecrets.com/corp: Good articles on pros and cons of different corporate structures.
- www.millionairesecrets.com/legal: Link to LegalZoom for help in filing your corporate papers.

For links to these and other business structure resources, go to www.millionairesecrets.com/tips.

6. Securing Financing

A recent survey of the Inc. 500, the fastest-growing small businesses in the United States, found that 88 percent of these successful businesses were started with the founder's personal savings as start-up capital. Sixty-nine percent also used money from family, friends, or other cofounders (i.e., partners). Total who used commercial loans: 11 percent. And total who used venture capital for start-up: 3 percent.

It's almost always best to start your business with your own capital. If you supplement this with loans from family, friends, or colleagues, make sure you draw up crystal clear loan agreements — *everything* needs to be in writing here.

Whether or not you need an attorney for this most depends on the amount involved. If you're borrowing $1,000, it's obviously not worth paying $400 in legal fees to draft a contract. In this case, you can write out the terms yourself, including the date, the two parties' names, and the terms of the agreement. (e.g., "John Bigsley loans $1,000 to Jill Sampson for her to start her own business. Jill agrees to pay back this amount with 10 percent interest within twelve months from the date of this agreement.")

If the loan amount is several thousand dollars or more, both parties should consider sharing the expense of an attorney to protect themselves.

If you do want to look for outside capital, a good place to start is the small business loans available from the Small Business Administration (SBA). For loans under $100,000, you fill out a one-page application, which they promise to process in less than forty-eight hours. The SBA houses a huge amount of resources for entrepreneurs.

- 800-827-5722 or www.sba.gov: Small Business Administration. The SBA Help Desk will connect you live with someone at SBA to help you find the government resources you want and to give you advice.

If you do decide to go the venture capital route, look for a firm that fits your needs. There has been a huge evolution in VC firms in the last few years, and they are much more specialized and specific about what areas and phases of the business they are interested in. There are VC firms that only do prestart-ups, investing in concepts and bringing them to reality. Others invest in the very early stages of the company ("stage one"), while others wait and invest once the company is successful to take it to the next level. There are also firms that invest by bringing in top talent and other resources to grow a new business rather than simply making a cash investment.

Guy Kawasaki is cofounder and director of a VC firm called Garage Technology Ventures (Garage.com). I once heard Guy in a speech give some great advice: when going for venture capital, keep any PowerPoint presentation down to ten slides, using big type. That limits how much text you can fit on the slide—which means you actually have to know your message. Guy says there's nothing worse than a group of entrepreneurs pitching him a thirty-slide presentation with three paragraphs of text on every slide. When you keep it simple, it shows them that you believe what you're saying and you know what the hell you're talking about.

- gobignetwork.com: Dubbed "the world's biggest community of startup companies," this site offers all sorts of valuable resources, including leads to investors, VC firms, and "angels."

For links to these and other financing resources, go to www .millionairesecrets.com/tips.

7. Keeping Track of Your Money

It's critically important to have a solid grasp of your cash flow. Any unsolved or unattended problems here will only become bigger problems later. Make sure you know how to track your expenses and profitability with absolute accuracy.

With Microsoft Money you can track your recurring expenses (mortgage, utilities, etc.) and also keep track of everyday expenses such as gas, food, etc. You can also create a budget for yourself and, even better, an allowance that allows for spending and saving.

Make sure not to mix your business and personal finances. Keep separate accounts and separate credit cards. Keep written records of everything. Track your bank statements, use file folders to keep everything organized. You'll want to keep a paper trail of every transaction, including your bank statements, your expenses (receipts), and detailed deposit records (income).

Get in the habit of making up-to-date financial summaries for yourself and your business at least twice a year, every quarter if you can. There are two basic statements you always want to have on hand: your *income statement*, which shows expenses versus income (sometimes called a "profit/loss statement"); and your *balance sheet*, which shows your assets weighed against your liabilities, i.e., your actual net worth.

- Money (Microsoft), QuickBooks (Intuit), and Peachtree Complete Accounting (Sage Software) are all examples of good accounting software.
- www.quickbooksonline.com: Intuit also offers a Web-based accounting system; because your information is all stored online, you can access your "books" from any computer, anywhere.

For links to these and other money resources, go to www.mil lionairesecrets.com/tips.

8. Getting Professional Help When You Need It

Being an entrepreneur doesn't mean you have to do everything yourself. There are times when you absolutely need to hire a professional. The two most common examples are: lawyer and accountant.

Most legal forms are standard, including nondisclosure agreements (NDA) and even incorporation filing papers. Some key documents, including contracts, partnership agreements, and noncompete agreements, should all be customized for your specific situation; for this, I'd almost always consult an attorney in your area.

When looking for an attorney, look for reputation. You want someone who has a solid background and impeccable reputation in your town or city. Ask around.

- www.findlaw.com: Offers online legal guides, references, and a searchable directory of attorneys organized by specialty. Remember, though, when hiring an attorney or accountant, nothing beats a good personal referral.
- Quicken Legal Business Pro, www.nolo.com: Nolo offers a good do-it-yourself package (for under $100) that will handle many minor issues. Includes texts of several valuable books, over 140 legal forms, contracts, etc., that you can edit to your needs.

For links to these and other professional resources, go to www.millionairesecrets.com/tips.

9. Creating an Excellent, Professional Web Site

There's one more professional you ought to consider hiring, in addition to lawyer and accountant: a good Web designer.

Your company's image is crucial. One of the best ways to create a powerful, professional image is through your Web site. Before you launch your business, invest the time and finances to hire a professional designer to build your company's Web site.

Hiring a Web designer is just like hiring a baby-sitter or auto mechanic: get references. Talk to past customers. Ask for past work and go visit the sites, try all the links, see how you like the look-'n'-feel. Go shopping.

Once you have a good Web site, you need to promote it. The best Web site in the world is worth nothing unless you have traffic going to it. There are services that charge a fee to get your site listed in all the search engines; this is money well spent.

- www.elance.com: Good place to find professional designers and receive bids on your custom project.
- www.coolhomepages.com: This site ranks Web site designs; it's a good place to come up with color schemes or layout ideas for your site. You can also find good designers here.
- www.htmlhelp.com: Great resource if you're looking to do it yourself.
- www.logoworks.com: Great resource for designing professional logos, which you can use on letterhead, business cards, rubber stamps, etc., as well as online. I've used them and highly recommend them.
- www.addme.com and www.submitfire.com: Good resources for getting listed on search engines.
- www.1and1.com: 1&1 Internet is a good Web hosting service.
- www.rackspace.com: Rackspace Managed Hosting is another good Web hosting service, especially if you need a dedicated server. I use both of these companies for various sites.
- www.paypal.com: PayPal (which is owned by eBay) is commonly used for bidders to pay for items they've purchased from sellers on eBay. As a business owner, PayPal also lets you use their service to accept credit cards and PayPal payments (payments from your customers' PayPal account balance) on your Web site.
- www.authorize.net: Authorize.net is a great company to use to set up a merchant account, which is required to accept credit cards directly on your site. PayPal can also do this for you, but not everyone has a PayPal account and many consumers would rather just enter their credit card info directly

on your site. Authorize.net handles the transaction (charges the customer's card) and then deducts their fee (approximately 20¢ and 2.25 percent) and deposits the difference in your checking account nightly.

For links to these and other professional Web site resources, go to www.millionairesecrets.com/tips.

10. Using Contracts

There are two rules I live by in business: 1) Always use contracts; 2) Never hire friends. The second rule is one I allow myself to bend sometimes—but not the first rule. *Always* have contracts. A contract is a written agreement that serves as protection for you and your company. When you hire a marketing company, take on a partner, hire an employee, or make any kind of agreement to join forces with another for your business, lay it all out in writing.

If you work with partners, for example, having a *buy-sell agreement* is a must. This says that one shareholder (partner) can't sell his or her stock in the company without the other shareholders' permission. This is important because without it, your partner could potentially sell his or her position in your company to anyone, potentially leaving you with a new partner you don't want.

Keep your contracts as simple as you can. Don't get bogged down in unnecessary complication. I always use a lawyer. At the same time, I don't let lawyers run my business. I don't look for their approval for everything I do.

- www.socrates.com and www.findlegalforms.com: Two good sources for premade legal forms.

For links to these and other legal resources, go to www.million airesecrets.com/tips.

11. Learning to Sell

Even if you don't think of yourself as being "in sales," every entrepreneur needs to learn and hone this craft. It's not nearly as hard as people often think: you just need to learn from the best. Here are a few of the authors I've learned from over the years; these are the true masters of the business of selling.

Note that most of these authors also sell audio programs. Buy them and keep them in your car to listen to while you drive. They will pay for themselves many times over.

- Roger Fisher and William Ury: *Getting to Yes: Negotiating Agreement Without Giving In*
- Tom Hopkins: *How to Master the Art of Selling*
- Og Mandino: *The Greatest Salesman in the World*
- Joe Sugarman: *Triggers: 30 Sales Tools You Can Use to Control the Mind of Your Prospect to Motivate, Influence and Persuade*
- Brian Tracy: *The Psychology of Selling: Increase Your Sales Faster and Easier Than You Ever Thought Possible*, and many other titles
- Zig Ziglar: *Selling 101: What Every Successful Sales Professional Needs to Know*, and many other titles

Also visit these free newsletters for all kinds of great sales tips:

- salesdog.com and briantracy.com

For links to these and other selling resources, go to www.millionairesecrets.com/tips.

12. Understanding Marketing and Advertising

People often confuse the terms "sales," "marketing," and "advertising." They are all distinct and different. Here's how my friend Joe Polish explains it: "Sales is what you do when you have someone on the phone or sitting in front of you. Marketing is every aspect of everything you do to *get* those people in front of you."

"Marketing" means everything that sends your message, including your stationery, your company's name, even the core idea of your business itself. Your pricing strategy, how you position yourself relative to your competition, the quality and uniqueness of your product or service offering, are all marketing.

Here are some of the great authors on marketing:

- Seth Godin: *Permission Marketing, Purple Cow, All Marketers Are Liars,* and other titles
- Mark Hughes: *Buzzmarketing: Get People to Talk About Your Stuff*
- Guy Kawasaki and Michele Moreno: *Rules For Revolutionaries: The Capitalist Manifesto for Creating and Marketing New Products and Services*
- Joe Polish, with Tim Paulson: *Piranha Marketing;* also the nine-CD set *Piranha Marketing: The Seven Success Multiplying Factors to Dominate Any Market You Enter*

Advertising is simply one specific aspect of marketing. The most valuable rule of advertising is this: *less is better.* There are times to spend money on advertising, but the best approach is first to exhaust all other avenues of promotion, such as publicity, customer referrals, and word of mouth. Seth Godin's book *Unleashing the Ideavirus,* for example, talks about how to use referral marketing and your own network to promote your business.

If you absolutely need to advertise to promote your business at first and start generating traffic, then make sure you target that advertising as effectively as possible. Think of your target market: What publications do they read? What radio stations do they listen to?

Once you have your customer base, focus any advertising effort you make on keeping all your customers. Ideally, you don't want your business spending advertising dollars day-in and day-out. By keeping your advertising expenses low, you can offer your customers better prices and services—which will make them more likely to tell their friends and family about your business.

- Google's AdWords and Yahoo! Search Marketing: When you enter a search on Google, look on the results page: you'll see a column on the right called "Sponsored Links." (On Yahoo!

it's called "Sponsor Results.") These are text ads that companies have bid on your search keyboard; the more they bid, the higher the ad's positioning.

- www.addme.com and www.submitfire.com: Good resources for getting your site listed on search engines. I listed these above under point 9, but mention them again here, because getting your site positioned well is an important part of promoting your business.

For links to these and other marketing and advertising resources, go to www.millionairesecrets.com/tips.

13. Providing Great Customer Service

Excellent customer service isn't a luxury: it's a necessity. This is the most critical form of marketing you have. Invest the time and resources to create a solid program in your business for making sure your customers are happy.

A great way to generate good word of mouth is to give away good value for free that people will share with their friends and colleagues. For example, if you are a CPA, lawyer, or someone else who gives advice for a living, publish some free articles in your area of expertise and distribute them to your clients and potential prospects. Create a newsletter or e-newsletter that provides real value. This is a great way to generate referrals and build reputation.

Sponsor a local organization or community event. Support something newsworthy that might generate media attention for your new business. Establish yourself as a force in your community.

Go beyond your competition. Offer something they don't—whether it's a 100 percent satisfaction guarantee, hands-on training (if you're in the service industry), free installation, whatever you can think of.

- www.EasyFollowups.com: This is my company, as described in chapter 17.
- www.liveperson.com: This service lets you add a "live customer support" feature to your Web site. Visitors to your site

can click on a little image, which opens a pop-up chat window on your (or your employee's) personal computer. Businesses of any size can take advantage of this technology—even a business of one.

- www.constantcontact.com, an automated e-mail service, and www.Intellicontact.com, another e-mail list management software, are two more examples of service providers that can help you provide great customer service.

For links to these and other customer service resources, go to www.millionairesecrets.com/tips.

14. Using the Power of PR

The key to using free publicity is that you have to have a newsworthy story. If you are simply opening a clothing store or an ice cream shop in your hometown, free media is not going to be your most effective way of getting your message out there. Reporters can see past a blatant advertising message; they look for newsworthy items. Look for whatever elements there are in your business, your personal story, or both, that are unique or intriguing.

For local press, look at other business or community-interest stories and contact the writers. Look in the "Neighbors" or "Lifestyle" sections of your paper; watch your local cable news channels and see who they feature and which reporters do the kinds of stories that might be similar to yours.

For good sample releases, go to the sites of businesses you admire and read their releases online. Also take note of the business stories in your newspaper. Their releases obviously worked and got them coverage.

What About Hiring a PR Firm?

I didn't hire an outside company to do my publicity until my eleventh business—but when I finally did make the investment, it more than paid for itself. The firm I use is S&S, at www.sspr.com.

Finding a PR firm is just like hiring a Web design firm: look at their past clients, ask about their contacts and experiences, etc. As with anyone you hire, make sure you have a written contract that spells out expectations, promises, and terms.

- www.ereleases.com: eReleases will circulate your press releases (to a range of sources you can choose) for a fee of $399. Very cost-effective—but again, for this to work you must have a newsworthy story. Their site also offers guidelines on how to write a good release.

For links to these and other PR resources, go to www.million airesecrets.com/tips.

15. Learning from the Best

Reading books about business is *sometimes* valuable; reading books written by people who've actually done it themselves is *always* valuable. Here are a few of my favorite entrepreneurs' biographies. I urge you to add to this list yourself and make it a habit to read at least one new biography a month.

- Richard Branson: *Losing My Virginity*
- Michael Dell: *Direct from Dell*
- Bill Gates: *Business @ the Speed of Thought, The Road Ahead* (revised edition)
- Donald Trump: *Trump: The Art of the Deal, Trump: How to Get Rich, Trump: Think Like a Billionaire*

I also stay as current as I can on who are the brightest minds out there on business and to read all their stuff. Here are examples of some truly great books from recent years:

- David Bach: *The Automatic Millionaire,* and other titles
- Marcus Buckingham: *First, Break All the Rules*
- Marcus Buckingham and Donald O. Clifton: *Now, Discover Your Strengths*
- Dale Carnegie: *How to Win Friends & Influence People* (a classic)
- T. Harv Eker: *Secrets of the Millionaire Mind*

- Guy Kawasaki: *The Art of the Start: The Time-Tested, Battle-Hardened Guide for Anyone Starting Anything*
- Bradford D. Smart: *Topgrading: How Leading Companies Win by Hiring, Coaching, and Keeping the Best People*

For staying on top of current trends in business, I also recommend reading *BusinessWeek, Entrepreneur,* and *Forbes.* Even if you don't read them cover to cover, it's helpful to subscribe and keep the issues around to browse in spare moments.

These days, one of the best ways to stay in touch with current trends and happenings is through blogs. Here are just a few of the most interesting and useful blogs:

- www.sethgodin.typepad.com
- http://blog.guykawasaki.com
- www.freakonomics.com/blog/
- www.blogmaverick.com

For links to these and other learning resources, go to www.millionairesecrets.com/tips.

16. Using Support Systems

There are all sorts of organizations that exist for the purpose of helping entrepreneurs get started and providing resources to help us manage and build our businesses. Here are just a few that focus on high school and college students:

- www.deca.org: Delta Epsilon Chi (DECA)
- www.fbla.org: Future Business Leaders of America (FBLA)
- www.bpa.org: Business Professionals of America
- Marketing/Business/Finance classes: Often high schools have some pretty good programs. Take any you can!

For links to these and other support resources, go to www.millionairesecrets.com/tips.

17. Managing Your Contacts Well

Networking and staying in touch with your friends and associates is so important. Whether you prefer a paper-based system or working with a PDA and computer, it's mandatory that you keep a directory of people you meet. I include a note for myself on where we met, and anything else about that person that I might want to remember later.

- www.linkedin.com
- www.myspace.com
- www.ecademy.com
- www.facebook.com
- www.zoominfo.com

For links to these and other contact and networking resources, go to www.millionairesecrets.com/tips.

18. Investing in Yourself

I think everyone needs a coach. Investing in yourself and your knowledge is the best investment of all. It's something no one can take away from you. That's why I invest tens of thousands of dollars every year in my own advancement in the areas of business, marketing, advertising, networking, etc.

Strategic Coach, run by Dan Sullivan, is the coaching organization I use. Dan's programs are high-end and expensive; however, their online store offers a ton of excellent resources that are very reasonable. There are tons of coaching organizations available, and you can find good coaching to fit any budget. On my free resources site I keep an updated compilation of the best coaching resources I've heard about.

- www.strategiccoach.com: Dan Sullivan's organization.

For links to other coaching resources, go to www.millionaire secrets.com/tips.

19. Making Your Money Work for You

The best place to invest profit is back into your business—and next in line is savings. Don't wait till you're older to start saving. Put the power of compound interest to work for you *now*.

Many entrepreneurs continue working for a company while starting their own business. If that describes you, check if your company offers you a 401(k). Many companies also offer some type of matching or profit-sharing, which is essentially free money. If you can, increase your contribution to retirement. If you're already contributing 4 percent of your income, increase it to 6 percent.

Make It Automatic

Put your savings into an interest-bearing account. INGDirect.com is an online bank that pays high interest rates. They also let you set up an Automatic Savings Plan: for example, you can set it up so that $75 is automatically deducted from checking and deposited into savings on the fifteenth of every month.

I suggest setting up an account there immediately, even if you only have $50 (there is no minimum to open and never any fees). You can then easily transfer money between your checking and savings accounts and vice versa. Try saving $50 every month, then after three or six months, double that amount. Eventually, you'll become so used to your automatic savings plan, you'll have no trouble putting 10 percent of your income into savings automatically every month.

I use INGDirect myself to save automatically. I set up my account there four days after my eighteenth birthday. Now they allow minors to set up accounts, too, as long as you have a parent on your account as well. On my MillionaireSecrets Web site, I provide you with a link that will take you to where you can set up your account automatically.

Pay Down Debt

Many experts will tell you to first pay down your debt before you start saving. My advice would be, first set up a savings account with an automatic savings plan. Once you've started saving automatically, *then* take a good portion of that savings every three or six months and apply it to whatever debt you have.

Treat Your Own Personal Finances Like a Business

Look at your monthly expenses: How can we cut costs? What if instead of paying $20 or $30 a month for premium cable channels, we invested that $360 per year in our 401(k), money-market high-yield savings, or stock portfolio?

Look at eating out, at movie rentals, at those expensive cups of designer coffee. This is what David Bach calls the Latte Factor®: money you spend every day that you really don't need to spend—money you could be putting into savings.

I'm not saying don't reward yourself. Rewarding yourself is important. I'm saying, choose your rewards carefully. There has to be a point where we say, "Enough is enough! Let's save money no matter what it takes."

- www.forbes.com and www.money.com: Both *Forbes* and *Money* have excellent "Personal Finance" sections on their Web sites.
- www.fairmark.com/rothira: Good information on Roth IRA.
- ingdirect.com: A good online bank that offers Automatic Savings Plans.

For links to these and other money resources, go to www.millionairesecrets.com/tips.

20. Learning Continuously

No list of resources is ever complete, because there are always great new books, blogs, Web sites, and organizations popping up that have unique and valuable new wisdom and insights to share. As you build your business, compile your own list of the best books, instructional CDs, blogs, and other resources. The more you know, the more you grow—and your business will only grow as much as you do. Keep learning!

Don't forget to visit my free resources site, which includes all the links featured in this guide and many, many more. Bookmark it in your browser for easy reference; you'll find yourself consulting it regularly:

www.millionairesecrets.com/tips

Index

NOTE: CJ refers to Cameron Johnson.

ABOUT THE AUTHORS

Cameron Johnson had started, run, and sold twelve successful businesses by the time he was twenty-one. His business successes have been featured in *Time, Newsweek, BusinessWeek, USA Today,* and many more, as well as on the *Today* show and *Good Morning America.* When he was fifteen he became an advisory board member of a Tokyo-based company, and his autobiography, *15-Year-Old CEO,* published in Japanese, became an instant bestseller. He has consulted to Fortune 500 companies and spoken at The Wharton School. Every one of his businesses has been a success, even in the worst days of the Internet bust. As a freshman in college, he started CertificateSwap.com, an online marketplace for gift cards, which was a runaway success, and for which he was offered $10 million in venture capital. He is now twenty-two years old and lives in Blacksburg, Virginia.

John David Mann is a business writer and editor in chief of *Networking Times.* He helped write and produce the bestseller *The Greatest Networker in the World,* published in 1992, which sold more than one million copies in eight languages.